C000246196

THE AULD ALLIANCE

An illustration from a Book of Hours painted by Jean Fouquet for Etienne Chevalier, Treasurer of France, c. 1455.

The painting, the *Adoration of the Magi*, depicts King Charles VII as one of the Three Kings paying homage to the infant Christ. Behind him are his personal bodyguard, the *Gardes de la Manche*, and in the background is a mock battle of the type staged in the fifteenth century to celebrate Twelfth Night.

By courtesy of the Musée Condé, Chantilly. Photograph: Giraudon, Paris.

THE AULD ALLIANCE

SCOTLAND AND FRANCE, THE MILITARY CONNECTION

Stephen Wood

MAINSTREAM
PUBLISHING

in conjunction with
the Mona Bismarck Foundation

For Timothy, again, who is growing
up in Scotland. In the hope that
he may eventually combine this
fortunate start in life by sharing
his father's love of France.

All rights reserved
First published in Great Britain 1989 by
MAINSTREAM PUBLISHING COMPANY (EDINBURGH) LTD
7 Albany Streeet
Edinburgh EH1 3UG

ISBN 1-85158-215-0 (cloth)

British Library Cataloguing in Publication Data

Wood, Stephen
  The auld alliance: Scotland and France: the military
  connection.
  1. France. Military relations, history with Scotland
  2. Scotland. Military relations, history with France
  I. Title
  355′.033044

  ISBN 1-85158-215-0

Typeset in Perpetua by Blackpool Typesetting Services Ltd, Blackpool, Lancashire.
Printed in Great Britain by Butler and Tanner Ltd, Frome.

Contents

Foreword

by
Lieutenant General Sir Derek Lang KCB, DSO, MC, DL

There are histories galore written about France, Scotland and England but never before, to my knowledge, has anyone attempted a concise work connecting, militarily, those three neighbouring nations through the ages. The theme of this book, as the title denotes, is the close relationship – sometimes tarnished with distrust, alas – between France and Scotland from the thirteenth century to the present day (although, as the author makes clear, there are even earlier references to Scots serving in Europe in the eighth and ninth centuries). England, sandwiched between the two countries geographically, necessarily had a great influence on Franco-Scottish links.

In *THE AULD ALLIANCE* Stephen Wood deals admirably with the complexities of the liaisons and intermarriages between the three royal houses and dynasties. He discusses the making and breaking of the many treaties and alliances between France and Scotland – nearly always made for military reasons and primarily for France's benefit – and points out the constantly changing nature of national boundaries through the centuries and the importance of Latin as a common language for the educated. He also stresses the impact that religious reforms had on soldiering – at one point Catholics barred from enlistment in Britain joined up in France whilst French Huguenots were welcomed into the forces on the other side of the channel.

Armies were raised and disbanded for specific wars in early times – they were too expensive to maintain continuously – and soldiers were largely mercenaries. Scottish regiments and individual military leaders found themselves opposing each other in battle not only in Britain but on the continent and even in the New World. Stephen Wood provides several interesting observations on this. There were three Scottish regiments in French service in the seventeenth century, while Scottish units served in the British army at the same time, and France as well as England recruited in the Scottish Highlands between the '15 and the '45. General Wolfe was Cumberland's ADC at Culloden whilst Johnstone, on the Stewart side there, was Montcalm's ADC at Quebec.

There are delightful snippets about Napoleon and about de Gaulle that I had not come across before. The fascinating story of Napoleon's Marshal Macdonald, the son of one of Bonnie Prince Charlie's loyal Hebrideans, is told fully, as are the ways that some of the great families of Scotland varied their allegiances between France and England. Highlighted is the founding at the time of Joan of Arc in 1425 of the Scottish Bodyguard of the kings of France – La Garde du Corps Ecossaise – and its disappearance in 1830. Wood also makes the point that relations between the French and the Scots in Stewart times were so close that Scots were granted naturalisation rights in France.

The more contemporary military relationships of the three nations during the nineteenth and twentieth centuries in the Crimea and in the two world wars is truthfully and boldly handled. Whilst feelings between the allies were often strained during the fighting, subsequent commemorations were generously recorded. Wood also points out that while the kilted Highlanders from Waterloo onwards have had a special appeal in France over other elements of the British army, this is a largely unfair and unjustified reflection of their achievements in battle.

This book is well-researched and provides a remarkable amount of detail over a wide span of history. The facts are lightly, wittily and honestly related, sparing the reader the inaccurate romanticisms of many authors past and present. It should certainly be read by those of military persuasion as publication is timely – 75 years after the beginning of the first world war and 50 after the start of the second. While historians will appreciate its worth, though, it deserves to reach a much wider public in Scotland, England and France, who, like the author and myself have affection for all three nations.

Introduction

Mention France or the French to any Scot, or at least any Scot educated in Scotland before the mid-1970s, and, nine times out of ten, you will get the same reaction: "Ah yes, the 'Auld Alliance'." Depending upon the interests, the knowledge, the education and the background of the said Scot, you may also be told of the variety of ways in which Scotland and France are linked. Some will tell you of French words in the Scottish dialect of English, some of the fact that most of the members of the nobility in the Lowlands are of Norman descent, some of the lilies attached to the *double-tressure* that borders the Royal Arms of Scotland. The arts will be invoked by the aesthete and mention made of architecture, of painting, of design and of the exchange of craftsmen and ideas between the two countries. The gourmet and the oenophile will discourse upon the similarities of the cooking, with difficulty, and on the Scots' taste for the wines of Bordeaux. The musician will talk of the bagpipes of Brittany. Few, except the old soldier and the military historian, will recall the military service of Scots in France and, even then, will either not realise the extent of its antiquity or may confuse the units which, at various times, composed the Scottish contingents of the armies of the Kings of France.

The function of this book, aside from showing – often for the first time – as many photographs illustrating the military connection between the two nations as is feasible, is to provide an analysis of this connection, to attempt to unravel the potential confusion presented by a similarity of the names of units and to show how France and Scotland have remained allies for nearly seven centuries. It has been an alliance that has not been without its difficult spells but even the oldest friends fall out occasionally, especially when a third party – in this case England – interferes.

The Franco-Scottish connection has been the stuff of romance: a mixture of solid and incontrovertible historical fact with a considerable *douceur* of rose-coloured or tartan-tinted mythology. Regrettably no Scottish historian has taken a long hard look at the Auld Alliance, although several individuals, some of whom can justifiably be termed historians, have glanced at it briefly while dealing with more specific matters. Perhaps the most eminent, and most recent, study in this field has been that written by Professor Gordon Donaldson in *The Auld Alliance*, a 30-page booklet published by the Saltire Society and L'Institut Français d'Ecosse in 1985. One cannot say much in 30 pages and it is to Professor Donaldson's credit that he manages to wield his broad brush with the skill for which he is justly recognised and renowned. Of greater length has been Hubert Fenwick's treatment in *The Auld Alliance*, published in England by the Roundwood Press in 1971. Mr Fenwick's overview of the relationship has reflected his nationality (Scottish), his training (in architecture), and his interest (the Stewarts), and his book is both a valuable guide and a subjective one. In more recent years, the publishers of this book have lent their support to specialised studies that do much both to publicise the civilised habits lurking beneath the supposedly dour mantle of the Scot and to illustrate, in ways that do their authors great credit, the links that exist between the kitchens and wine cellars of Scotland and France, namely *Knee-deep in Claret* by Billy Kay and Cailean Maclean (1983) and *A Caledonian Feast* by Annette Hope (1987).

The cultural awareness of both nations has been demonstrated by frequent joint exhibitions in the years since the end of the Second World War. Most recent, in Scotland, of these was *French Connections: Scotland and the Arts of France*, held in the Royal Scottish

The Great Seal of King James VI of Scotland, showing the double tressure flory counter-flory *on the shield.*
(National Museums of Scotland)

Scottish basket-hilted broadsword with talismanic blade and hilt with roped bars incorporating a fleur-de-lys, c *1715–25. Similar to types awarded as prizes at the Huntly races, Aberdeenshire, 1695–1749.*
(Major David Baxter, Baron of Earlshall; Mrs J. Smith)

Museum in Edinburgh (now the Royal Museum of Scotland, Chambers Street) in 1985. The catalogue of this exhibition, written by my distinguished colleague Mr Godfrey Evans and published by Her Majesty's Stationery Office in 1985, is a triumph of the photographer's and the art historian's skill, an indication of how assiduously Scotland's national museums have collected the aesthetic material culture of their ancient ally, and an invaluable guide to the artistic background to the alliance itself. In the bicentenary year of the French Revolution exhibitions are being staged throughout the world which themselves demonstrate the power that the event evoked and all that it still means to anyone with a broad grasp of the significance of history. The Revolution's effects in and upon Scotland were neither especially profound nor considerable yet it came as of little surprise to those intellectuals in Scotland who, in the aftermath of the American Revolution of 1775–83, were in regular correspondence with their French contemporaries. The exhibitions in Scotland, at the Record Office in Edinburgh and at the Mitchell Library in Glasgow, reflect the minimum physical effect that the Revolution had upon Scotland and the more widespread and long-term effects that war with France produced after 1793. In Paris, of course, one is spoilt for choice – as one would expect in the cultural capital of Europe – and all aspects of 1789 are investigated, illustrated, celebrated and commemorated. Among the multitude of cultural events is that staged at the Mona Bismarck Foundation in the Avenue de New York where the Auld Alliance, or *la vieille alliance*, is commemorated by an exhibition on the military connection between the two nations; this book supplements that exhibition and yet, deliberately, stands alone too.

When commemorating an event such as the French Revolution, which shocked the world of 1789 far more than the American Revolution had, one should be allowed a little iconoclasm, in keeping – perhaps – with the spirit of the times. Thus, readers hoping for an illustrated version of *Quentin Durward*, or yet another dewy-eyed biography of Mary Stuart or even a tartan-wrapped essay in the best pro-Jacobite tradition, would do well to return this book to the shelf now and browse instead under Romantic Fiction. There was little romantic about the military side of the Auld Alliance. The reality of

L'Ecossais combattant *(the fighting Scot), a lithograph of the mid-nineteenth century by Delpech after H. Vernet. Armed with a brace of wheellock pistols, a dirk and a broadsword, the figure depicted owes much to the Romantic ideal of the Highlander.*

(NMS)

soldiering, the prospect of violent death, the constant political intrigue and the persistent lack of security, of trust and of financial support all rendered the alliance a very mobile moveable feast. As for fiction, the history of Scotland and France is well enough served by the works of Scott and Dumas and no further excursions are needed into that over-perfumed field. It is time to scotch – appropriate expression – a few myths about the Auld Alliance, myths that have obscured its reality and masked not only its real importance but also the nature of its operation.

There was always a noticeable lack of equity in the alliance. After its initial ratification, it was invoked – by France – whenever it was needed (whenever France was in trouble) and ignored whenever possible on other occasions. True, France *did* send troops to Scotland to help the Scots against the English, but there were never enough of them, France's domestic needs always came first and they generally achieved little, while being frequently unpopular with their Scottish hosts. Yet, whenever France needed help against the common foe, over went contingents of Scots, spoiling for a fight and – admittedly – out for whatever they could pick up during the process; they too – despite being a necessity – were frequently unwelcome. Progenitors of the "ancient friendship" theory, a device used by politicans at all ages when the other devices of bribery, threats and coercion had failed, also often forget that neither Scotland nor France, during the period that the alliance was strongest – the late medieval and Renaissance epochs – were the same countries that they are today. Concepts of nationality and of nationalism were in their infancy and thus intercourse between what we would now call nations was very much easier and less hindered by recognised, delineated and guarded frontiers.

Because of this greater internationalism concepts of language were largely unformed, in the way that they divide nations today, and – indeed – the widespread use of Latin gave the educated and civilised a *lingua franca* in which they could communicate irrespective of where they lived. Thus, the much-vaunted retention of French words in the vocabulary of the Scots dialect of English has come to be very much overstated. There are more words in the English version of English which have French roots than there are in the Scots version. Words such as "ashet" (*assiette* – a plate) and "gigot" (*gigot* – a leg of lamb) *were* current in England; what has occurred is that they have *remained* in use in Scotland. In fact, as Annette Hope has so perspicaciously analysed, "ashet" is first noted in Scotland in 1722 and was rapidly established as a fashionable word thereafter; "gigot" has much the same history. Words owing their derivation to medieval French, and usually associated with food, do survive in use in non-Gaelic Scotland; they also survive in the rich dialects of England in a variety of corrupted forms – such was the extent of Anglo-Norman influence during the medieval period.

10

*Ornamental fountain in West Princes Street Gardens,
Edinburgh, c 1862. Designed by Klagmann, it was made in
122 pieces by A. Durenne, Sommevoire, Haute-Marne, and
placed in the Gardens, c 1869. Behind the fountain is
Edinburgh Castle and the Scottish United Services Museum.*
(NMS)

The Anglo-Norman influence permeated Britain and Ireland almost entirely. Only the
wild areas north of the Highland line and the outer western Scottish islands remained
at all untouched. Elsewhere Norman families gradually established themselves in positions of power, national and local, and Lowland Scotland was as much affected by this
as was England; no uniquely Scottish connection here. With the Anglo-Norman ascendancy came, eventually, the growth and development of heraldry and the concept of
armorial bearings, an idea unknown in its regulated formality to the Celtic and Saxon
kings in Britain. According to my distinguished colleague Charles Burnett, Ross Herald
of Arms at the Court of Lord Lyon King of Arms, the *double tressure flory, counter-flory*
does not appear as encircling the Arms of the Kings of Scotland until the thirteenth
century, by which time it is a fully-developed charge upon the shield. Mr Burnett also
believes it, with its lilies, to have a Flemish rather than a French connection, since it
is a device more common in Flemish than in French heraldry. The concept that the lilies
represented the Franco-Scottish link was, though, so well developed by the middle of
the fifteenth century that, in 1471−72, the Scottish Parliament passed an Act specifically

11

stating that this was not the case. The stylised lily flower, as a decorative feature and often as a finial, is well-known and of considerable antiquity. While appreciating the charm of the story that the lilies on the Arms of the monarchs of Scotland represent the link with France, I am afraid that it has as much chance of being true as does the story that the alliance can be traced back to the time of Charlemagne – probably less in fact.

As far as the arts, the food and wine and the music so traditionally associated with Scotland are concerned, the story is much the same. The arts of France were not uniquely appreciated in Scotland and patronised by Scots, French food and wine was often as popular in England as in Scotland and the bagpipe, in its varying forms and often associated with the type of weaving that produces tartan cloth in Scotland, is an instrument associated with pastoral communities all over the world.

What was unique and what gave the edge to all these factors now regarded as exemplifying the Auld Alliance was the alliance itself. What made it unique was its military character, since no other nation had identifiably Scottish contingents in its armies for as long as did France. Scots served in Scottish regiments in the armies of Gustavus Adolphus of Sweden in the seventeenth century and in the armies of the United Provinces of the Netherlands from the mid-sixteenth to the end of the eighteenth centuries, but only France had more than 350 years of unbroken military association with Scotland and only in France was this association exemplified by the position of two Scottish units. The first company of the King's bodyguard was Scottish in content for its first 150 years of existence and in name until its final disappearance in 1830. The first company of the gendarmerie – who were heavy cavalry and not a force of policemen – was also Scottish in content originally and subsequently in name until its disappearance just before the French Revolution. No other nations can claim this, the accurately and indisputably unique part of the Auld Alliance.

In the pages which follow, flesh will be put on the bones of what has been disarticulated and scattered here and the skeleton reassembled as a body of prose to attempt to show how a combination of political and economical interests, together with personal ambition and a great deal of luck, contrived to create and sustain the varying levels of a military alliance which existed in hard fact for nearly three centuries and contrived to remain in being, despite occasional discouragements, until the present century. The analysis and interpretation of history is by its nature a subjective business but its illustration should, in my view, contrive to be as objective as possible. As an Englishman and a civilian, writing about Scotland, France and the armed services, I ought of course to be eminently equipped to attain that most impossible of goals, true objectivity. As a resident of Scotland and a regular visitor to the next most civilised country in Europe, France, I have attempted to present a balanced view of what I perceive to be the reality of the military side of the Auld Alliance. Increasing age, growing experience, a naturally self-deprecatory nature and more than my fair share of cynicism incline me to believe that what follows is an inadequate, if colourful, account of a unique and ancient friendship between nations. I do not doubt that some of my French readers will find it prejudiced against France and that many Scots will disagree with the conclusions that I draw. While I regret this, I nonetheless feel that the story of the Auld Alliance's military side is one that deserves to be told, as it never has been before, with words and pictures that draw together the often disparate threads of what is actually the same story.

Acknowledgments

Aside from the use of sources which appear in the *Suggestions for Further Reading* section at the end of the book, I have had to call upon the help of a large number and wide variety of individuals in Scotland, France, England and the United States. I also have to record my gratitude to a number of individuals and institutions for their permission to reproduce the photographs which appear in this book. Limited space means, unfortunately, that both sets of acknowledgments have to be more compressed than the generosity of those named below deserves but to each of them I gratefully record my considerable debt for help rendered in a variety of indispensable ways.

For permission to reproduce photographs I wish to thank Her Majesty The Queen; the Dukes of Hamilton and Brandon, Buccleuch and Queensberry, Atholl and Roxburghe; Sir Donald Cameron of Lochiel KT; the Comte de Vogüe; Christopher Allen Esq; Major (retired) David Baxter, Baron of Earlshall; M. Jean-Claude Boyron; M. Georges Dickson OBE; M. E. Lamy; M. Jean-Claude Lemaire; Mrs Joyce Smith; Kenneth Snodgrass Esq; William Thorburn Esq FSA Scot.; Dr Duncan Thomson; the Commanding Officer, The Royal Scots Dragoon Guards (Carabiniers and Greys); the Trustees of the regimental museums of The Black Watch (Royal Highland Regiment), The Queen's Own Highlanders (Seaforth and Camerons), The Gordon Highlanders and The Argyll and Sutherland Highlanders (Princess Louise's); the Trustees of the National Museums of Scotland, of the National Galleries of Scotland, of the National Army Museum, of the Imperial War Museum, of the National Portrait Gallery, of the Tate Gallery and of the Victoria and Albert Museum; the Dinner Club of the 51st (Highland) Division; the Glasgow School of Art; the Historic Buildings and Monuments Division of the Scottish Development Department; the Royal Commission on the Ancient and Historical Monuments of Scotland; Marischal College Anthropological Museum; University of Aberdeen; Punch Publications Ltd; the Commonwealth War Graves Commission; the Cavalry and Guards Club; Photographie Giraudon, Paris; the Musée de l'Armée, Paris; the Bayerisches Staatsbibliothek, Munich.

For their personal and invaluable assistance I would like to thank Christopher Allen Esq; Miss Caroline Armitage; Colonel (retired) The Hon. David Arbuthnott MBE; Major (retired) David Baxter, Baron of Earlshall; M. Jean-Claude Boyron; Lieutenant-Colonel (retired) Richard Broad MC; Charles Burnett Esq; Dr David Caldwell; Alex Cameron Esq; Alastair Campbell Esq, Younger of Airds; Allan Carswell Esq; L. D. de Pinna Esq; M. Georges Dickson OBE; Monica and Guy Dunham; Miss Katrina Erskine; Lieutenant-Colonel (retired) Angus Fairrie; Helen and Martin Forrest; George Gordon Esq; Mrs Marion Harding; Captain (retired) Colin Harrison; Arnold Henderson Esq; Dr Joan Hichberger; Dr Richard Holmes; Dr Jean-Marcel Humbert; Charles Hunt Esq; Miss Vera Kaden; Mrs Susanna Kerr; M. E. Lamy; Lieutenant General (retired) Sir Derek Lang KCB DSO MC DL; M. Jean-Claude Lemaire; Professor Bruce Lenman; Sir Donald Cameron of Lochiel KT; The Rt. Hon. The Lord Lovat DSO MC TD JP DL; Ms Helen McCorry; Hector MacDonald Esq; Mrs June McDonald; Major (retired) Alan McKinnell; Dr Rosalind Marshall; M. et Mme. Georges Miraval; Dr Peter Newman; Vesey Norman Esq; A. W. Perry Esq; Mrs Edith Philip; Colonel (retired) Russell Porter; David Rankine-Hunt Esq; C. Rajakaruna Esq; Gordon Richardson Esq; Lieutenant-Colonel (retired) Alastair Rose of Earlsmiln; Ms Christina Ross; Lieutenant-Colonel (retired) Louis Sanderson OBE MC; Lieutenant-Colonel (retired) Alastair Scott Elliott; M. Bernard Sevestre; Miss Jennifer Spencer-Smith; Kenneth Smith Esq; Mrs Joyce Smith; David Smurthwaite Esq; Peter Staff Esq; Miss Nicola Thomson; William Thorburn Esq FSA Scot; The Comte de Vogüe; Major (retired) David White; Michael Willis Esq; Mrs Ruth Wilson; Lieutenant-Colonel (retired) Jock Wilson Smith OBE; Miss Clare Wright.

Stephen Wood
Edinburgh Castle
November 1989

13

Chapter One

Our Great Want and Necessity
The relationship in the Middle Ages

BURIED DEEP IN THE HISTORICAL TRADITIONS OF BOTH NATIONS IS THE CONCEPT OF an ancient alliance between Scotland and France. How ancient that alliance actually is has been a point of argument, debate, research and proclamation since well within the period under review in this chapter. There has also been considerable disagreement over exactly what form the alliance took in the years prior to 1295, when a document – which still exists in the *Archives Nationales* in Paris – was sealed between the kings of the two nations. That there were various forms of understandings between different kings of Scotland and France prior to 1295 is undoubted. It is certainly also true that, because of the nature of medieval European power-politics, these understandings had profound military underpinnings since, otherwise, there would have been little point in their existence.

The Europe of the medieval period (essentially the six centuries between the ninth and fifteenth centuries) was an area and an epoch to which few modern concepts can be applied. National boundaries meant more than they do today, in the sense that there were far more of them on the European continent and that they were constantly changing, and also less, in the sense that they were more easily crossed and that concepts of nationality, loyalty and allegiance were barely developed to maturity by the end of the period, let alone at the beginning.

In recent years, the myth of a largely static population in medieval Europe has been exploded. People did move around and although their movements tended to be limited by natural boundaries and took longer to execute than they would do today, because of the nature of travel, there is no doubt that, in terms of shared and common experiences, the population of medieval Europe was, in many ways, far more homogeneous than it is today. Educated people were linked by a common language, Latin; the Catholic Church bound society together at all levels in western Europe – although not without the occasional tremor; and the Four Horsemen of the Apocalypse stabled their mounts in most regions. Armed conflict was common, life was cheap and usually short, but those males who survived to adulthood were far more physically robust, if of lesser stature, than their modern counterparts. The feudal nature of western European society bound people to their masters and operated, with differing degrees of flexibility, from the person of the king downwards. It was, however, nowhere near as immutable as previous generations of historians, influenced by more modern concepts of legally regulated society, have implied. Famine, war, plagues and the results of agricultural incompetence all forced widespread movements of population that left deserted villages and mass graves in the landscape. The rise in population numbers that historians have tabulated as affecting most areas of western Europe from the eleventh century meant that the land had to provide for more mouths and, in the case of inherited land, had to be more parsimoniously divided. All these factors meant that there were plenty of reasons for those who could to move and few to induce people to remain where they were born.

The Great Seal of King Alexander III of Scotland.

(NMS)

Because of the *lingua franca* of Latin, the essentially ephemeral nature of national boundaries and the fact that no area of modern Europe enjoyed uninterrupted peace during the medieval period, there was never any shortage of demand for the services of professional soldiers. Maintaining a standing, or permanent, army was a very expensive business and while most rulers and magnates kept a small bodyguard and force of professional men-at-arms at their disposal, larger armies – for full-scale wars – would normally be raised and disbanded as occasions warranted. With the government of an area being indissolubly associated with the person of its ruler, the safety of that person was of paramount importance to the stability and continuity of power; therefore a ruler needed a bodyguard that was not only loyal but also disinterested. Since loyalty was a commodity which the Middle Ages tended to assess in terms of hard cash, and the granting of privileges dependent upon good behaviour towards the grantor thereof, it naturally became attractive for rulers to recruit those who had to be their most trusted followers from states outside their own.

There is a small, and by no means reliable, amount of evidence to the effect that the earliest Scots to serve in the bodyguard of a continental European ruler were those who served the Emperor Charles III, called the Fat, at the end of the ninth century. Charles, who was also King of France, was married briefly to a Scottish princess called Richarde and so the Scots said to have been in his service may have actually been in the entourage of his wife. Other sources, principally French chroniclers, indicate that Scots had served in the armies of Charlemagne during his campaign in Spain against the Moors, earlier in the century, and had aided Charles Martel, a ruler of the Franks, in his victory over the Saracens at the battle of Poitiers in 732.

Even among the mobile population of medieval Europe, the ubiquity of the Scot, and principally the Scot as soldier or trader, was remarked upon. King Louis IX of France,

Saint Louis, who died on crusade in North Africa in 1269, had taken Scottish Knights with him on his crusades of 1268 and 1249 and had a high opinion of their prowess. His biographer remarks that few parts of France were without hospitals founded for these wandering warriors. A description by Guibert de Nogent, writing of the warriors of the thirteenth century crusades, depicts the Scots men-at-arms descending from their boggy regions, barelegged, proud, undisciplined, wearing cloaks of skin, with a game-bag from one shoulder, armed in a ridiculous fashion, at least by French standards, and offering their services as faithful and devoted auxiliaries.

But Scottish soldiers in a bodyguard, assuming – probably unwisely – that that was the case at the court of Charles the Fat, and Scottish soldiers among one's armies do not make, necessarily, for a formal alliance. In any case, neither Scotland nor France existed (as other than geographical expressions) at the time of the early Carolingians (the dynasty founded by Charles Martel and brought to its height by his grandson Charlemagne), so it is inconceivable that any formal inter-national alliance – in the sense of a mutual non-aggression pact aimed defensively or aggressively at a third party – could have existed. Not until the Norman conquest of England after the battle of Hastings in 1066 is it feasible to consider alliances as such between Scotland and France. It may be, however, that those Scots who travelled for warlike purposes to the continent of Europe before the late eleventh century helped to establish among the rulers whom they served a recognition of the martial propensities of the men from the savage north of Britain. Thus, when alliances became conceivable, as Anglo-Norman England began to flex its muscles under its Angevin monarchs in the twelfth century, those seeking friends to make life difficult for the kings of England did not have far to look.

The most noted French historian of the relationship between France and Scotland, Francisque-Michel, writing in 1862, notes at least four twelfth century, 'treaties' between the two nations, without taking account of – he says – arrangements of lesser importance. Laying aside a natural tendency to raise an eyebrow at the wishful thinking and unreliable sources invoked by Francisque-Michel in making these claims (for three of the treaties involved with which he quotes a French writer of the sixteenth century, David Chambre, in his *Histoire abbregée de tous les roys de France, Angleterre et Escosse*), there is no doubt that, faced with the expansive aggression of the Angevin Empire, Scotland and France could have been expected to fall into each other's arms. Francisque-Michel's twelfth century 'treaties' were, he says, arranged between Philip I (1060–1108) and Malcolm III (1057–1093), Louis VII (1137–1180) and Malcolm IV (1153–1165), Louis VII and William (the Lion) (1165–1214) and Philip II, Augustus (1180–1223) and Alexander II (1214–49). Signing a treaty was one thing of course; keeping to it – especially if you were a king of Scotland with an aggressive and efficient neighbour – was something quite different.

Malcolm IV may have had, in any case, something of the opportunist about him since he felt able to accompany King Henry II of England in his expedition against the Count of Toulouse in 1159. Toulouse represented the remaining part of modern France, other than the French king's relatively small dominions in eastern central France, over which Henry had not managed to exercise sway and, in characteristic fashion, he set about attempting to do so with a distinct lack of subtlety. Malcolm's presence for three months at the siege gained him his knighthood at Henry's hands, a kind of seal of approval following Malcolm's earlier paying of homage to the English king, but led to a minor rebellion in Scotland among barons who used as their excuse the fact that their king had compromised Scotland's independence by fighting for the English. In fact, as A.A.M. Duncan says in Volume I of the Edinburgh History of Scotland, *The Making of the Kingdom*, it seems more likely that Malcolm was busily engaged in the game of diplomacy. A year

16

King Robert I (the Bruce) of Scotland, a sixteenth century portrait by Jamesone. (Dr Duncan Thomson)

after returning from Toulouse he married his sister to Conon, Duke of Brittany, a duchy claimed by King Henry, and two years later, in 1162, married his sister Ada to Florence, Count of Holland. While appearing, therefore, to be Henry's meek and subordinate vassal, it seems likely that Malcolm was doing his best to plough Scotland's own furrow in European politics.

There is no record of the date of William the Lion's treaty with France, but it seems likely that it was agreed in 1168, three years after his accession to the throne of his brother, Malcolm IV. William travelled to the continent, to Mont St. Michel in 1166, to pay homage to Henry II of England and to request reinstatement to Scotland of Northumberland, a parcel of land which he had inherited from his father and which Malcolm IV had deemed prudent to return to England in 1157 under typically unsubtle pressure from Henry II. Henry refused, in apparently no uncertain terms, and may have driven William – by his obstinacy over Northumberland – to seek an alliance with France. Certainly there were reports in 1168 of Scottish ambassadors in Paris negotiating for a renewal of the war between England and France that was then at the truce stage.

William paid homage to Henry's eldest son who, as was relatively normal at the period in order to guarantee an indisputed succession, had been crowned king (or king-designate) in 1170. This 'young' King Henry rose in revolt against his father in 1173 and William the Lion sided with him in return for promises of the northern English counties, leading an army, which was partly composed of Flemish mercenaries, into England. No sources indicate that the king of France sent soldiers to help William but it is possible that the Flemings were a result of an arrangement between the Count of Flanders and King Louis which provided for the former to supply soldiers on demand to the latter. At any rate, the Flemings were badly mauled in an engagement at the siege of Alnwick Castle in July 1174 and William was taken prisoner.

The failure of this first real attempt at a military alliance between Scotland and France is symptomatic of later and similar failures. William was a far from well-organised or tactically intelligent military leader. France – although giving the rebellion its blessing – did not commit itself to any noticeable extent. England was too strong at home and too dominant abroad to represent an easily crushable nut between the jaws of the relatively new alliance.

The last of Francisque-Michel's twelfth century 'treaties', that between Philip II, Augustus and Alexander II, must (if it existed) have been agreed in the thirteenth century, since Alexander did not succeed William the Lion, his father, until 1214, a year before King John of England was forced to the negotiating table at Runnymede by those of his barons who were determined to get his seal affixed to *Magna Carta*. In the autumn of 1215, by which time it had become apparent that John had no intention of honouring the Great Charter in spirit or in word, the rebel English barons invited Prince Louis of France, later King Louis VIII, to come and help himself to the English Crown. Louis duly invaded, John mustered an army to meet him, and then had second thoughts and retired to Winchester. Louis took London, received homage as king of England from Alexander of Scotland and consolidated his position. Only John's death in 1216 and the accession of a legitimate heir, the child Henry III, whose regents would comply with *Magna Carta*, prevented England being swallowed up by an increasingly expansionist France.

At the same time as inviting Louis to invade, those rebel English barons who exercised influence in the north of England had invited Alexander to do likewise. Thus, the invasion of England could be seen as a pincer movement between Scotland and France. Regrettably, it was not that simple. Alexander was on the move south in October 1215, besieging Norham Castle and attracting the attention of John. John moved swiftly north, while Louis was still in France, and burnt Berwick, Roxburgh, Dunbar and Haddington

The Great Seal of King Robert II of Scotland.

(NMS)

within ten days. Alexander moved south-west and harried Cumberland but neither attack achieved much until the French, finally, arrived in May 1216 whereupon the English barons who had renewed their allegiance to John fell over each other in their eagerness to re-pledge it to Alexander and Louis. As the English and the French squabbled about terms for a peace treaty so Scotland became increasingly ignored and all promises to restore the northern English counties forgotten by the English.

Alexander continued to raid northern England until Louis sailed for home in 1217, having concluded the Treaty of Lambeth without consulting the Scottish king. Knowing a *fait accompli* when he saw one, Alexander withdrew his armies and paid homage to King Henry III at Northampton in December 1217. There would be no further call for England's neighbours jointly to threaten her security for the next eight decades.

Not that Henry III of England was to know that, of course, at the beginning of his long reign, and neither Alexander II nor his son and successor Alexander III went out of their way to allay his fears and suspicions of encirclement. In 1239 Alexander II married, as his second wife, Marie de Coucy, daughter of Enguerrand, Lord of Coucy in France. This marriage, which took place without the permission of the English king (technically necessary since the king of Scotland was supposed to be a vassal of Henry's), together with other slightly tactless manoeuvrings over border castles and lack of frequent protestations of loyalty, meant that Henry III remained suspicious of Alexander's intentions vis-à-vis France and England.

The reign of Alexander III was marked by little of relevance to this story but by considerable internal strife. Having been a widower for four years in 1285 he married Yolande, daughter of the Comte de Dreux who, although French, acknowledged King Edward I of England as his lord. Yolande was a wife for five months, until the death of Alexander in March 1286. Regrettably the king of Scotland died without a direct male

The Great Seal of King Robert III of Scotland.

(NMS)

heir, leaving only his infant granddaughter, Margaret, the Maid of Norway, daughter of Alexander's daughter Margaret and King Erik II of Norway. Within a decade of Alexander's death, the Norwegian connection was to be resurrected.

In an age when loyalty tended to be personally – and not nationally – based, the concept of the mercenary who will fight for whoever pays most, or at least most frequently, grew up. Mercenaries were not new in the Middle Ages; the armies of ancient Egypt, of Greece and of Carthage had all employed them. Xenophon utilised the services of ten thousand mercenaries in plundering part of Persia in the fifth century BC and a century later the Gaulish, Numidian, Greek and Spanish mercenaries of Carthage tried to take over the government when their pay seemed not to be forthcoming. During the sixth century AD mercenary forces of the Emperor Justinian of Byzantium destroyed a force of Goths at the battle of Taginae, south of Ravenna and, after the battle of Hastings in 1066, many exiled Englishmen sought employment as warriors of the Byzantine empire, serving as axemen in the Varangian Guard.

But what was a mercenary? Not just a soldier fighting for pay, since all soldiers fight for some form of remuneration and even those whose primary motive is belief in a cause or loyalty to an individual or nation need to eat from time to time. J.R. Hale, in his admirable survey of war in late medieval and early modern Europe, *War and Society in Renaissance Europe 1450–1620*, makes the valid point that essential to the application of the term 'mercenary' is the criterion that the expression is rarely singular. One reads of 'bands' of mercenaries, or 'Free Companies' of mercenaries, of *condottieri*, and rarely of *condottiere*. This, of course, is also relevant, in that mercenaries are contracted (*contrarre*: Italian, to contract) soldiers who fight for employers, who hire them through agents. Their loyalty lasts as long as their employers' money and even then is perpetually in question, since what is bought can be sold. Instances are related in the Middle Ages of opposing armies of mercenaries, finding fellow-countrymen among the enemy, doing no, more than token fighting. When the money ran out so did the mercenaries. They usually lived off the land while waiting for employment. The system of employing mercenaries was advantageous to small, rich city states, such as those in medieval Italy, which did not indulge in long and expensive campaigns, were able to pay their *condottieri* to behave well and could hire and fire as required. In view of these factors, should one regard the Scottish soldiers who fought for the kings of France, or those Frenchmen who gave military service to the kings of Scotland, as mercenaries? Yes and no.

First one must define one's terms, not as regards mercenaries but as regards Scots and French. In the twentieth century the descriptive terms are well enough understood, although perhaps better by outsiders than by those who are all too aware of the internal divisions that separate Borderer from Orcadian, Breton from Burgundian. The Scots, led by Scottish knights loyal to the kings of Scotland, who served the kings of France at the behest of the kings of Scotland against the kings of England, their mutual enemies, could not be called mercenaries, despite their numbers, and neither could their French counterparts. Those Scots, however, who – for whatever reason – were not welcome in Scotland or who chose to leave for economic reasons in order to seek their fortunes among the battlefields of continental Europe, might be termed mercenaries, especially if they joined marauding bands of freebooters whose one collective skill was proficiency with arms. Between the two extremes there were, of course, numerous shades of grey – as many as in the plaid of a Border shepherd. These expatriate Scottish soldiers, roving men-at-arms or gentlemen adventurers left their native land for a variety of reasons.

As we have seen, the increase in population in the eleventh century stimulated migrations in search of land. In the pre-feudal period, before the Anglo-Norman kings of Scotland transplanted Norman concepts of land tenure and service to Scotland, that land which was inherited tended to be divided between a man's sons with the result that, inexorably and generation by generation, it and its value diminished. Finding oneself at the end of a three or more generation chain of prolific antecedents could be a miserable business and usually involved emigration. Under the later feudal system and the inheritance of land on the primogeniture basis, whereby the eldest son got the lot, being a younger sibling was also a cause for leaving home. The concept of land tenure could, of course, only apply to those of a high social status. With this status tended to be linked training with weapons and a degree, often minimal, of education. Feudalism, and the stratification of society with which it was indissolubly linked, led in the High Middle Ages to the growth and refinement of concepts of chivalry and heraldry and these foundations of the western European ruling classes combined with the power of the Church to regulate conventional society at all levels. Knight-errantry, the winning of spurs, the training in all aspects of Christian chivalry, all involved – as a matter of course – considerable amounts of travel: to tournaments, on wars, expeditions and crusades. It was therefore entirely normal that the young gentlemen of Scotland, as young Europeans, should travel widely and principally for reasons associated with combat. Especially in the late Middle Ages, few of them who wished to remain within the social orbit of their peer-group degenerated to being accurately referred to as mercenaries.

So much for the officer class. Little is known about the rank and file element of Europe's medieval mercenaries. In many cases – notably among the *condottieri* – the roving mercenary bands drew their officers from among their number and these came from relatively humble backgrounds, although often achieving great riches as a result of their trade. Scotland, and especially Highland Scotland, was a fertile recruiting ground for soldiers until after the Napoleonic Wars and the tradition of serving abroad, for any master who would pay, persisted until the French Revolution finally halted the clandestine French recruiting teams. It is not known whether the Scots who ended up in medieval mercenary bands had been recruited in Scotland, or had travelled to the continent to join up, or had travelled to the continent as part of a legitimate Franco-Scottish expedition and had then decided to move on. All these explanations are possible and none more likely than the last. Neither is it known whether Scots from beyond the Highland line formed a distinct and indentifiable group or whether they were preferred to Lowlanders, or vice versa. The development of land-wealth and agriculture in medieval Scotland, together with the increase in coastal prosperity and trade, tends to imply that little inducement for the landless to emigrate purely for economic reasons would have remained by the end of the fourteenth century. The poverty of the land in Highland Scotland and the wilder areas of the Borders, together with an entrenched tradition of warfare and the exercise of arms, suggests that it was the young men from these poorer areas who found ways to offer their services to Europe's captains of mercenaries.

Scotland's ports and trading links with the continent were well-developed by the end of the thirteenth century and it was easy for a strong young man to work his passage from Leith to Bordeaux or from Aberdeen to Scandinavia, the Low Countries or northern Germany. During the early part of the eleventh century, of course, when England was wracked by civil war between Stephen and Matilda, many Scots – and not just those from the Borders – must just have walked south in order to offer their services. After the beginning of hostilities in 1296 however, those with a capacity to bear arms and the freedom to travel in order to capitalise on their skills had to look further afield.

The death of Alexander III in 1286 left Scotland without an effective monarch. His granddaughter, the Maid of Norway, was no more than three years old and his widow, Queen Yolande, proclaimed herself to be pregnant. An ideal opportunity for a power struggle presented itself. Despite previous promises that they would never threaten the succession and always respect the lineage and rights of the Maid of Norway, the temptations of power finally became too much for Robert Bruce, Lord of Annandale, and John Balliol, both descendants of King David I and therefore cousins to the recently deceased king. A regency was formed which excluded Bruce and a short period of civil war followed between Bruce's faction and the regents or guardians of the kingdom. The situation, already politically interwoven with Scottish ambition, deceit and nationalism, was further complicated by the English King, Edward I, who remained unalterably under the impression that whoever was king in Scotland held that position directly as a vassal of the king of England. The Scots clergy resented incursions into what they regarded as their territory by the English clergy and many of the governing élite of Scotland, while welcoming Edward's offer to mediate in choosing a monarch or arranging a marriage between the Maid and his own son, Edward, resented the patronising and overbearing attitude that characterised negotiations. The marriage idea, which would eventually have united the two kingdoms, was resisted by the nationalist section of the Scottish nobility who feared a takeover bid rather than a partnership but, in any case, it came to nothing when the Maid died on her way back to Scotland from Norway in 1290.

Now Scotland really was a land without a king and the contenders for the title, who had increased to nine – including Bruce and Balliol – were forced to recognise Edward's claim to overlordship in order to get him to consider their claims. Bruce and Balliol were the principal contenders and each had roughly equivalent support from the Scots nobility; the clergy were, however, overwhelmingly on the side of Balliol. By the time the hearings opened, in late 1291, there were a further three potential kings of Scotland waiting to have their claims heard. As King Edward was himself descended from Malcolm III, he too had a claim and, as *soi-disant* feudal overlord, it might be said that his was strongest

King James I of Scotland, a sixteenth century portrait by an unknown artist.

(National Galleries of Scotland)

The cathedral of Tours.

(M. J-C. Lemaire)

if not greatest. John Balliol was eventually chosen and paid homage to Edward. The English king made it clear that Balliol reigned only with Edward's permission and only as long as he, and Scotland, behaved themselves. Between Balliol's enthronement in 1292 and the outbreak of war between England and France in 1294 Edward and the English courts repeatedly provoked Balliol and the Scottish nobility to the point where Scotland's subject status could no longer be in doubt. At the king of England's council of war in 1294 Balliol was induced to promise Scottish help against the French but returned determined to resist this final, and perhaps unthinkable, demand of Edward's.

There is some disagreement about whether the Scots or the French initiated the treaty that constituted, for the first proveable time, material evidence of a formal military defensive and offensive alliance. We know that Scottish ambassadors were sent to treat with the French king in July 1295, but were they invited or did the initiative come from Balliol or his council? As Gordon Donaldson writes in his pamphlet *The Auld Alliance* (1985), France was already at war with England by July 1295 and the treaty that was prepared in Paris on 23 October that year may have been just another in the diplomatic game of avoiding encirclement; a similar treaty was concluded between France and Norway on the previous day.

The composition of the treaty itself is similarly significant, although this may – of course – be because it was drafted in Paris and naturally reflects the fact that on this occasion the French needed the Scots, or at least what they perceived as the threat of the Scots, more than the Scots needed the French. The first part of the treaty specifies how Scotland can help France: by harrying England in the event of an English invasion of France. Only in the second part is mention made of the reciprocal aid expected of France by Scotland and it seems relatively certain, therefore, that the treaty was framed in this way as a reflection of the increasing strength of English attacks on France.

23

Irrespective, though, of the initiative in drafting the parchment that may properly be called The Auld Alliance itself, the fact remains that it was drafted for purely military reasons and invoked military responses. The exercise had little to do with cultural or linguistic links (many of these were already firmly established anyway), and yet it paid lip-service to diplomatic convention by proposing a marital link – the ultimate seal – between Edward Balliol, the king's son, and a niece of the French king. The marital link is, or may be, itself significant in reflecting Scotland's status in France's eyes since, although King Philip IV, the Fair, had a marriageable daughter, Isabella, Edward Balliol was to be fobbed off with a niece. It may have been that Philip was keeping Isabella, his ace as it were, for more important marriages and this may have been the reason that, as part of the peace treaty between England and France in 1303, Isabella married the English king's heir, the future Edward II.

The treaty was, at France's insistence, ratified by just about every and any person or body in Scotland who had a claim to being part of the government, from the prelates and nobility to the burgesses of towns, six of whom affixed their seals at Dunfermline in February 1296. The die was cast.

Since the mission to France, the actual affairs of Scotland had been in the hands of a council of twelve; composed of clerics and nobles, it put on a collectively bolder front against the coming English storm than did the Scottish king. Edward, whose actions over the previous five years had indicated the low opinion that he held of Scotland and its rulers, had his suspicions confirmed and was determined to teach a lesson. First, however, he gave John Balliol one last chance. Calling a parliament to assemble at Newcastle, he gave notice to Balliol that he and his army should attend. When, not surprisingly, they failed to appear, the English forces crossed the Tweed and bludgeoned their way into Berwick. Carlisle was held against their fellow Scots by the Bruces and their faction, who had either seen what was coming and acted accordingly or were biding their time and supporting King Edward while it was expedient to do so. The other Scottish forces never really stood a chance. Principally composed of 'the host', the feudal equivalent of a conscripted militia, Balliol's forces were ill-armed and ill-trained and the hard core of trained men-at-arms and knights were vastly outnumbered by the professional, well-equipped and well-trained English army, relatively fresh from efficiently stamping out opposition in Wales. King Edward and his army cut a swathe of destruction through Scotland, from Berwick to Elgin and back, in just twenty-one weeks between March and August 1296. The castles of Edinburgh, Stirling, Dumbarton, Roxburgh, Jedburgh and Dunbar were all taken with ease and the Scottish host was brushed aside at Dunbar at the end of April. Balliol was captured, dethroned and imprisoned in the Tower of London for two years, before being exiled to his French estates at Bailleul, in the valley of the Yaulne in Normandy.

Edward had been able to stamp out Balliol's uprising because little actual fighting was going on between England and France at the time, and what little there was effectively ceased in 1297, although relations remained strained until 1303. King Edward's initial campaign in Scotland was one of such lightning speed, and conducted so effortlessly, that France had no time to react to fulfil her side of the bargain. In any case, England was on such a war footing that she could relatively easily conduct a war on two fronts, especially when neither presented much of a challenge, and so Edward was able easily to hold France down with one foot while stamping hard on Scotland with the other. As far as Edward was concerned, the kingdom of Scotland as a separate self-governing entity had ceased to exist; the coronation stone of Scone was moved to Westminster Abbey and the Scottish king's regalia taken to the King's Jewel House in the Tower of London.

There were few Scots left who could lead the resistance to the abolition of their nation's status. Those who were not dead were prisoners or in exile, and hundreds of others had flocked to pay homage to Edward in order to escape such fates. The Bruces were still very much in evidence, expecting the crown (albeit of a vassal king) as a reward for their anti-Balliol stance during the war. Edward disappointed them and created dangerous enmity by thwarting ill-concealed ambition. The other route to the Crown was insurgency and it was this road that the Bruces followed, led by the young Robert Bruce in alliance with William Wallace, the son of a knight who became an outlaw when he failed to take the oath of allegiance to Edward. In 1297 Scotland rose under these two leaders, together with others such as James the Steward, the Earl of Carrick and Robert Wishart, Bishop of Glasgow (all of whom were suspected by contemporary chroniclers of using Wallace to further their own ambitions). This Inter-Scottish alliance was complicated by the fact that Wallace and most of the others were fighting for the dispossessed Balliol, whereas Bruce was clearly out for himself. The rising fell apart in disarray and Edward, making one of his few mistakes in believing that the internal faction-fighting prevented Scotland from being a serious threat, sailed for Flanders to have a last slap at the French. He took with him several hundred Scots prisoners who had survived the rout of the host at Dunbar and were being given a second chance by being used to fight their allies, the French, on behalf of their enemies, the English; it is easy to believe that Edward regarded them as, at best, expendable.

As Edward left England with his captive Scots foot-soldiers, so the rising flared up again in Scotland. Wallace allied with Andrew Moray, heir to vast estates in the north of Scotland and able to command huge reserves of manpower, and in the space of a month in the late summer of 1297 all the area of Scotland north of the Tay was lost to English influence. The Scots defeated an English force with great slaughter north of Stirling in September, near where the Wallace monument stands today on Abbey Craig to commemorate the event. Edward's absence on the continent until March 1298 allowed the Scottish army to take control over the whole of the country and to invade northern England; it also effectively prevented the French from sending aid. Upon his return Edward led an army into Scotland and avenged the battle of Stirling Bridge by savaging Wallace's forces at Falkirk in July.

The campaign prior to Falkirk, as well as the battle itself, demonstrated aspects of medieval European warfare that were to characterise the Scots' method of waging war and the battles of the Hundred Years War. In the preceding campaign, both during the Scots' occupation of northern England and in the retreat ahead of Edward's advancing forces, a 'scorched earth' policy had been practiced. While undoubtedly effective, it made the soldiers few friends and was to be commented on almost with disbelief by later French commentators who witnessed it in action. From the viewpoint of the battle itself, although it is easy to over-emphasise the powers of the concept of chivalry and its attendant and supposed glories and nobility, the fact remains that the medieval period was one in which battles tended to be fought in a set pattern and, at least by the knights, according to certain rules of behaviour. Even by Wallace's time although the Scots were famed as spearmen and axemen (their Norse ancestry showing through), they were not noted for the quality of their cavalry (the knights) or their archers. At Falkirk, the Scots spearmen were grouped into four *schiltrons*, or massed block-like formations, and were supposed to be protected by the cavalry and the archers. Many of the cavalry chose to make discretion the better part of valour and the Scots spearmen and archers became easy targets for the English cavalry and Welsh archers, who overwhelmed them with terrific slaughter.

There are no records of any Frenchmen fighting with the Scots at Falkirk in 1298 but there were certainly several knights from France at the siege and capture of the castle of Caerlaverock in 1300. These, however, were Bretons, Gascons, Normans and knights from Lorraine, all of whom were fighting for King Edward against the Scots, and thus serving as a reminder that the king of France did not have jurisdiction, at the beginning of the fourteenth century, over all the area which we now think of as France. Gascony, in particular, was virtually an English fief and Gascons were to be found in English armies throughout the Hundred Years War.

Although, apparently, France sent no troops to help Wallace, she interceded with Edward to effect a truce and made as a condition for peace between England and France a specification that any peace treaty was to include all three nations. Edward, who had clearly hoped to have a free hand in Scotland, did his best to resist this but rumblings from across the Channel and veiled threats of a Franco-Scottish invasion caused him to extend the truce when it became due for renewal in 1301. Such a situation was acceptable as long as the king of France stood firm and no one rocked the boat. Unfortunately, French forces were badly defeated by England's Flemish allies at Courtrai in 1302 and, at the end of the same year, John Balliol wrote to King Philip of France absolving him of the need to consider Scottish interests in negotiating with England. A week after this inexplicable communication, a force of Scots trounced an English army at the battle of Roslin.

It was to be a short-lived triumph. His hands free of the threat of French interference, with the Franco-Scottish alliance dead if not yet buried, Edward campaigned in Scotland again throughout 1303 and until the spring of 1304. Only Stirling Castle held out against him and that fell in July 1304. Some Scottish nobles capitulated, others went into exile in France, but Wallace was captured and executed with all the bloody ceremony meted out in 1305 to those whom the state perceived to be traitors. Kind Edward died in 1307.

By the time that the Hammer of the Scots had conceded his throne to his son, Edward II, Scotland was in revolt again, this time under the undisputed, but not consistently successful, leadership of Robert Bruce. Matters certainly picked up for Scotland after the death of Edward I, since his son lacked the forcefulness and single-minded determination to crush Scotland that had so characterised the last years of Edward I, almost to the point of obsession.

By the end of 1309, after the years of consistently successful campaigning in what was, essentially, a civil war, only about a third of Scotland lay outside Bruce's immediate control. At a parliament in 1309, held in St. Andrews, a document was drafted which answered a friendly letter from the king of France. Although in no way seeking to renew the alliance formally, the letter had made clear France's continuing interest in maintaining contact, king to king as it were, especially in the event of renewed war between England and France. Bruce's position as King of Scots had now been recognised by a major European monarch and the road to Scotland's independence was now far more secure. Flanders, Norway and the north German ports were all on friendly terms with Scotland too and their ships continually ran the English blockade to keep Scotland supplied with war materiel. By 1314 almost all of Scotland was in Bruce's hands and he had been able to launch successful, and profitable, raids into northern England. Like his father had done, Edward II used Gascons extensively in guarding the castles of the Border region, that of Roxburgh – which fell after a night attack at the end of February 1314 – being commanded by Guillemin de Fenes, a Gascon knight.

From surviving accounts, it seems likely that the only French soldiers who might have been at the battle of Bannockburn in 1314 would have been on the side of the English. Edward is known to have bought the services of several hundred French mercenaries (French in the sense that they came from within the boundaries of the country we now call France) for his campaign in Scotland and so some may have been at the English defeat which marked the mid-point of the Scottish wars of Independence.

The remaining twelve years, before Scottish independence from England was finally recognised, were ones of continued success for Scottish arms. Periods of war alternated with truces, as the England of Edward II found Scotland too resurgent and too powerful to subdue. The seal, literally, was set upon Bruce's ambitions for his kingdom by the renewal of the Franco-Scottish alliance in 1326. At Corbeil a treaty was enacted between Bruce's representatives – three clerics, Thomas Randolph, Earl of Moray and Lord of Annandale and Man, and Robert de Keith, marischal of Scotland – and the French king, Charles IV. The treaty was, again, as reflective of the different status of Scotland and France (in French eyes) as had been the one of 1295. Scotland had to undertake, in the event of war between England and France, to make war upon England to the utmost of its power. In return the French king would do his best as a loyal ally to aid Scotland in the event of an English attack. While it may not have been the most equitable of treaties, the fact that it was concluded at all reflects not only the worsening international situation but also the fact that Scotland was acceptable once again as a useful ally of France. On this occasion, too, it appears that approaches to contract this new alliance were made by Scotland.

While England was riven by civil war, involving the imprisonment of Edward II and the government by Queen Isabella and her lover, Mortimer, neither Scotland nor France had much to fear. Certainly Scotland was triumphant in its independence, formally recognised by England in 1328. In 1329 Robert Bruce died, to be succeeded by his five-year-old son, David II. In 1330, however, Edward III staged a *coup d'état* in England and took over the reigns of government from his mother and her paramour; the grandson of the Hammer of the Scots was now in the saddle in England.

For the next seven years, until the outbreak of the Hundred Years War in 1337, Edward III continually attempted to affect the balance of power in Scotland. David and his infant bride fled to France in 1334 as Edward attempted to seat Edward Balliol, a son of the too-easily deposed John Balliol, on his father's throne. Fortunes swung towards Balliol and back again, sometimes David's supporters winning a battle or taking a castle, sometimes the Balliol faction – principally Anglo-Scots of recent Norman lineage whom Bruce had dispossessed – being triumphant. The prospect of French aid, which never actually materialised in other than diplomatic terms, kept the Bruce supporters in the field against the might of Edward III and Edward Balliol. Even the English might was dispersed, however, since the coast of England had to be protected against French raids. Prospects of an invasion became serious in 1336 when a fleet of French Mediterranean galleys, moved from Marseilles where they had been assembled for a crusade, materialised in the northern French ports. Edward's attack on France in 1338 greatly relieved the pressure on Scotland and also enabled the Scots supporting David II, still in exile in France, to redouble their pressure on the French king for, as it were, a second front in Britain. David's Court at Château Gaillard seems to have put up the money for a raid on Southampton by French galleys in October 1338 and certainly, it is said, paid a French pirate to blockade the Tay estuary in order to starve out the English garrison at Perth.

Accounts of the Hundred Years War have usually been written from the viewpoints of the two principal protagonists: England and France. English accounts have seen the conflict as revolving primarily around the great victories of Crécy, Poitiers and Agincourt; French accounts are often incomplete without lengthy treatment of Joan of Arc. Scotland generally remained on the periphery of the actual long drawn-out conflict but was continuously involved nonetheless as France's most strategically situated ally. Scotland principally assisted France, on land, in two ways: by always making the Border area insecure (and therefore tying up numbers of English troops), and by sending expeditionary forces to France to fight the English. The fighting potential of Scotland and the Scots was such that, despite having a king in exile, the threat that it presented to England on its northern border meant that neither Edward nor any of his successors was able to release enough men from a home defence role in order to secure final victory in France. Thus, although regularly beaten, France was never entirely conquered and, indeed, gained more in the long run than did England from the conflict.

The first part, until 1347, all went England's way. The battle of Crécy was won, Calais fell to Edward and the Scots were defeated at the battle of Neville's Cross in 1346. David II had returned from France in 1341 to try to co-ordinate Scots opposition to England in order to relieve pressure on France, especially during the protracted siege of Calais. A series of raids into northern England followed over the next five years, the English Parliament of 1344 receiving a report to the effect that the king of France had only to let the Scots know that a little pillage would be in order for it to occur. At the beginning of the Crécy campaign in July 1346, no sooner had Edward landed in Normandy than a formidable Scots force raided Cumbria; Edward's victory at Crécy may have made the Scots wonder whether they had been a little hasty in attacking him while his back was turned. A month after the siege of Calais began, David II led a Scottish army into England and got as far as Durham before being stopped and soundly beaten at Neville's Cross on 17 October 1346. The Scots' king was taken prisoner and confined in the Tower, the siege of Calais continued uninterrupted and it fell in August 1347.

The intervention of the Black Death, an epidemic of bubonic plague, in 1348 effectively put the war into a state of suspended animation while untold numbers of people died throughout Europe. At first, the Scots were jubilant about the effect that the plague had upon the fighting potential of England and, indeed, had gathered a strong raiding force in Ettrick Forest to take advantage of England's discomfiture when the plague struck Scotland in 1349. The plague and its aftermath, together with England's dominant position in France and David's captivity, made for an effective truce but, by the mid-1350s, events were shaping up for a renewal of the conflict. In 1355 King John II of France sent the Sire de Garencières and fifty men-at-arms to Scotland, together with ten thousand marks in cash to persuade the government of Scotland to re-open hostilities with England. Garencières and his men, together with the Earls of Angus and March and their forces, surprised and captured Berwick, laying siege to its castle, in November 1355. Garencières' forces returned home and Edward returned from a foray in the environs of Calais and expelled the Scots in the following January.

The beginning of the new campaign on the continent, the Poitiers campaign, was characterised by an increase in the organised pillaging expeditions which scythed through the French countryside, burning and looting in a frenzy of destruction aimed at wearing down the French will to resist. The last of these prior to the battle of Poitiers in September 1356 was a three-pronged affair, one prong being led by Edward, the Black Prince, who scorched his way north and east from Bordeaux. In the French army that met him at Poitiers were two Scottish knights, Robert Gordon – who was killed there – and William Douglas, later Earl of Douglas, who escaped after the battle knowing, as the chronicler Froissart says, that his English enemies would not have ransomed him. King John of France was taken at Poitiers and joined King David of Scotland in the Tower; both their countries were governed by regents and England was triumphant. In 1357 David was ransomed for one hundred thousand marks (£66,000) and returned to Scotland to try and find the money, which was payable over a ten-year period.

In 1359 France reluctantly offered to pay half the ransom in the following year, on condition that Scotland attacked England again. Edward's successful campaign of 1359–60 prevented this from happening and, at the Treaty of Bretigny in 1360, the

French were forced – on paper at least – to foreswear the Franco-Scottish alliance. Neither of the old allies took that provision seriously and it has to be doubted whether Edward actually thought that it would work. The Treaty of Bretigny was, in fact, no more than a truce; fighting continued in France between the forces of the king and those – largely composed of mercenaries rendered temporarily unemployed at Bretigny – of his ambitious noblemen. Many of these mercenaries and freebooters were Scots, a great many were known to be English.

By the end of the 1360s England and France had drifted into outright war again; French envoys came to Scotland to seek promises of assistance, the gloriously named Archibald the Grim was sent by King David to France to discuss a formal renewal of the treaty. David died in 1371 and was succeeded by Robert the Steward as King Robert II, the first of the Stewart dynasty of Scottish kings which was to enjoy such a special relationship with the kings of France. One of Robert's first acts was to agree a further treaty of alliance with France, which was ratified at Vincennes in June 1371, three months after Robert's coronation.

Hostilities over the next twenty-five years were characterised not by spectacular English victories but rather by a gradual wearing down, by France, of English possessions on the continent. Edward and his son, the Black Prince, both died in the late 1370s and the schism which split the Church between a Pope in Rome and one at Avignon polarised the conflict into a semi-religious one – perhaps the most destructive kind. Scotland and France both supported the claims of the Avignon pope, Clement VII – who was pro-French; England adhered to Pope Urban VI – who was anti-French.

Despite ratifying a mutually defensive treaty with France, Robert II had little intention of conducting a full-scale war with England on France's behalf until the fourteen-year truce of 1369 expired in the early 1380s. This did not mean, of course, that covert operations could not replace overt ones, and many Scottish soldiers fought the English in France. At sea, too, ships crewed by Scotsmen and paid for by Scottish merchants harried the English coast. Robert's nobles conducted raids into northern England and counter-raids penetrated into Border Scotland. A cold war in the Borders region persisted, with occasional flashes of incandescence, until the truce expired in 1384.

During the previous year, Robert had agreed to an arrangement with France that French troops would be supplied to Scotland in the event of an Anglo-Scottish war. An advance party of thirty or so knights, together with attendants and men-at-arms, landed in Scotland early in 1384, joined forces with some Border lords and raided England again. They were followed by a French expeditionary force, led by Admiral Jean de Vienne, which landed in Leith and Dunbar in the spring of 1385. De Vienne's force was the largest body of French troops ever seen in Scotland: seventy-five knights and knights-banneret, and over one thousand men-at-arms. They came well-provided with French gold too, and rapidly set about establishing their presence in Northumberland. The chivalric ideals of the French troops contrasted with the pragmatism of the Scots: chivalry demanded a glorious pitched battle in which honours could be won; reality indicated that the tried-and-trusted scorched earth policy was best in the face of an English advance. As the English army advanced, so the Franco-Scottish forces retreated before it, burning crops and driving off people and cattle. Although the English reached and captured Edinburgh, starvation soon forced a return home and the French did likewise, disappointed in their hope of knightly glory. Despite the alliance, and mutual enmity towards England, it is clear that, in Scotland at least, Scots and French soldiers did not co-operate and that the Scots government had a decidedly ambivalent view of their allies' activity in Scotland. De Vienne had to remain in Scotland once his troops had embarked for home while representations and claims were made by Scots against the king of France for damages and expenses occasioned by the French troops. It was not a happy experience and, notwithstanding the continuation of the alliance, the friendship of the two nations (especially when it concerned the habits of one nation's soldiers in the other's country) was to be characterised by frequent expressions of resentment and even hostility. Such, perhaps, is the nature of diplomatic friendships.

The war continued until a truce between France and England of 1396. In Scotland it remained a matter of cross-border raids, one of which – in 1388 – culminated in the Scots being victorious at the battle of Otterburn (known as that of Chevy Chase in England). Following the death of Robert II in 1390, the alliance with France was renewed in 1391 but this was simply the form on the accession of a new monarch and did not lead to renewed warfare since an Anglo-French truce was in operation.

The last half of the Hundred Years War was the part in which Scotland was most extensively, and significantly, involved in the fighting on the continent. From the expiry of the truce in 1396 to the eventual end of hostilities in 1453, Scotland, in a sense, institutionalised the alliance in a way that had long-term significance for the military history of France and cemented personal links between the two countries. The ending of the truce in 1396 meant that cross-Border and cross-Channel raids could continue legitimately (they had never really ceased) and the war was intensified between England and Scotland, the English defeat at Otterburn being avenged at Homildon Hill in 1402. Henry IV of England had internal political troubles which prevented him from active warfare against either Scotland or France, but the involvement of Scotland in his power struggles with the Percies of Northumberland – who sought French help against the English king – meant that no chance of either peace or a truce existed. Robert III of Scotland had a power struggle of his own and attempted to send his son James, later James I of Scotland, into safety in France to preserve the succession but James's ship was waylaid and the young prince confined to the Tower of London. The shock killed Robert and so, once again, a king of Scotland was a prisoner in the hands of the English.

All three nations passed the best part of the next decade undergoing different degrees of civil war. In France King Charles IV suffered from intermittent bouts of mental illness. In England King Henry IV was unable to maintain control of his overmighty subjects who were, without necessarily knowing it, setting a precedent for the internecine strife later to be called the Wars of the Roses, and in Scotland the continued absence of the king – although not resulting in a truce with the English – had not contributed to a settled state of affairs. All three kingdoms lacked strong helmsmen and each took advantage of their enemies' disarray, without becoming embroiled in open, protracted or serious warfare. The situation changed rapidly once Henry V became king of England in 1413.

France's problems were compounded, in a way that was to dog that nation until the Revolution, by rivalries between the different Royal houses and their princely representatives. The ducal houses of Orléans and Burgundy had become traditional enemies and blood-feuds had developed by the first decade of the fifteenth century, during which period the Earl of Crawford, admiral of Scotland, took service with the Duke of Orléans and the Earl of Mar service with the Duke of Burgundy. The duchy of Burgundy was, of course, far more in terms of area and influence than just a French province and it wielded considerable power on the continent, the Duke controlling large areas of the Low Countries, from which a lucrative trade with Scotland was carried on.

Henry's victory at Agincourt in 1415, and the virtual annihilation of the French nobility which resulted, was accompanied in the Borders by the Scots breaking a truce and invading England once more. This invasion, and the others which followed upon Henry's next campaign in France in 1417, seem to have caused the English king little real annoyance and certainly do not seem to have improved France's position. The

30

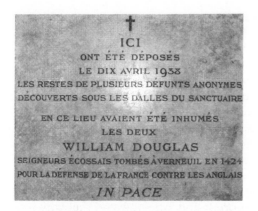

A memorial tablet in Tours cathedral recording the interment of the remains of the Douglasses who fell at the battle of Verneuil in 1424.

(M. J-C. Lemaire)

Sir John Stewart of Darnley, first seigneur of Aubigny-sur-Nère, a sixteenth century portrait.

(The Comte de Voguë; M. J-C. Lemaire)

turning point, for all three nations, came in 1419.

The government of France had finally disintegrated. The Burgundians occupied Paris and proclaimed Queen Isabeau regent; the Dauphin – later Charles VII – escaped to Bourges where the Armagnacs proclaimed *him* regent. Isabeau and the Burgundians were perceived as being pro-English and so, when the Dauphin sent the Comte de Vendôme to Albany, regent of Scotland, to beg for his assistance "in our great want and necessity" by sending an expeditionary force to be accompanied by John Stewart of Darnley, the three Estates of the Scottish parliament readily complied. Their agreement may have been a result of the Dauphin offering to fund the expedition but, whatever the motives, it was assembled, set off and landed at La Rochelle in October 1419. Commanding the force was John Stewart, Earl of Buchan. Archibald Douglas, *soi-disant* Earl of Wigtown, accompanied him, along with Stewart of Darnley – for whom the Dauphin had specifically asked. Stewart of Darnley was Constable of the Scottish army and a veteran of several campaigns against the English.

The three nobles took with them six thousand men-at-arms, all of whom were transported to La Rochelle in forty Castilian ships. It was the first time that so considerable a force of Scottish troops had served in France and, because most French people's experience of Scottish soldiers had hitherto been of those in the bands of wandering mercenaries known as "routiers", they were not uniformly welcomed, some of their detractors dismissing them as "wine guzzlers and eaters of mutton – *sacs à vin et mangeurs de mouton*". Some of the resentment or hostility expressed in this phrase may reflect more on the original ownership of the wine guzzled or the mutton eaten than on the Scots' gastronomic preferences, but the Dauphin hurled the taunt back at the taunters after the Scottish force – reinforced in late 1420 – destroyed an English army at the battle of Baugé in March 1421. The Duke of Clarence, heir presumptive to Henry V, was killed at Baugé and Lord Buchan made Constable of France as a reward. Stewart of Darnley received the lands of Concressault and later those of Aubigny-sur-Nère in Berry.

Henry V had attempted to cut the ground from under the feet of the Dauphin's Scots by securing the allegiance of King James I, who was still his prisoner, thus making the Scots allied with the Dauphin traitors. When the town of Melun capitulated to the English in November 1420, the Scottish officers of its garrison were hanged as traitors, as an example to their countrymen who continued to aid Henry's enemies. As a result of the Dauphin's proclaimed illegitimacy (his mother, Queen Isabeau, had agreed to be named an adultress), it was the infant son of Henry V and Catherine of Valois, the Dauphin's sister, who was proclaimed King of France and England upon the deaths of Henry and Charles VI in 1421.

Initial Scottish successes in France were not maintained after Baugé and the combined forces of the Dauphin and his Scots allies were defeated by the English at Cravant in 1423 and Verneuil in 1424. Earlier in the year of Verneuil James I had returned to Scotland with an English Queen after eighteen years of captivity, and secured a truce in the Anglo-Scottish conflict. This truce specifically excluded those Scots still in the service of France.

By the end of 1424 Stewart of Darnley was the only one remaining of the three veterans who had led Scots troops to France five years earlier. He had lost an eye at the battle of Cravant but had been paroled. The Earls of Buchan and of Wigtown had both been killed at Verneuil. Stewart had gone on a pilgrimage to Jerusalem after being captured at Cravant and returned to France in 1426 to begin campaigning in Brittany. In 1428 he led a mixed force to relieve the siege of Orléans but he and his brother William were both killed at the battle of 'the Herrings' near Rouvray St. Denis in 1429. The battle was fought in an attempt to stop a convoy of provisions from reaching the English besiegers at Orléans; most of the provisions were barrels of salted herrings and this gave the battle its name.

In 1428 James I of Scotland had concluded a new alliance with Charles VII of France, an alliance which specified a marriage treaty between James' daughter Margaret and the Dauphin, Louis, and the provision of six thousand Scots for the French service. Although the marriage took place in 1436, the promised soldiers were never sent.

By the time of the royal marriage, however, a force of Scottish soldiers had been in the French service for eleven years. Regrettably, no document exists which establishes beyond any doubt the date at which the French king, Charles VII, chose to establish a Scottish company of his Bodyguard. The earliest references to it which indicate that a Scottish company existed in the Royal Bodyguard, as opposed to outside it, date from 1425. It is possible, therefore, that the establishment of what became the Scots Bodyguard, from whose ranks were drawn the *Gardes de la Manche*, was in commemoration of the Scottish losses at the battle of Verneuil in 1424. Because there were other companies of Scottish soldiers in the service of France from the 1420s onwards contemporary references often confuse the Guard and Scotsmen serving in these other companies. Historians have not been able to clarify the position and no documents exist which specifically differentiate between the Scots Bodyguard and the other Scots in the French service until later in the fifteenth century.

Whether or not the Scots Bodyguard was founded as a result of the defeat at Verneuil, that disaster brought upon the scene in France one of the most remarkable phenomena of an age rich in such occurrences. Joan of Arc remains for many people a symbol of French nationalism and her effect upon the English is best summarised by a consideration of the manner of her death: burnt at the stake, the sentence of heretics and witches. She came into contact with many Scots during her brief span on the stage of the war, one of whom – whose name is translated as James Power or Hames Poulvoir or Polwart – is said to have painted her personal standard. She certainly led Scottish troops at the relief of Orléans and at the battles of Jargeau and Patay in 1429, and the Bodyguard would have been with the king, as she was, at his coronation in Rheims later that year. Scots, probably of the Bodyguard, fought alongside the king as Senlis in August 1429 and a force of Scots, probably not of the Bodyguard and commanded by a knight called Sir Hugh Kennedy, fought with Joan and defeated an English force outside Lagny-sur-Marne in April 1430. An unnamed Scotsman, after returning to Scotland following Joan's execution, continued the chronicler Fordun's manuscript *Scotichronicon* when a monk in Dunfermline Abbey and recorded how he had seen and accompanied "the marvellous Maid" in her attempt to bring about the recovery of France.

Between the execution of Joan of Arc and the truce of 1444 the French cause was largely triumphant and the King's Scots Bodyguard accompanied him on all his campaigns, in Spain as well as in France. A French chronicler, describing the King's state entry into Paris in November 1437 numbers his Scots Bodyguard at 120 men. Eight years later, in 1445, the French army was finally organised into a permanent and regimented force (although the regiments were called companies, were smaller than might later be expected and were commanded by officers of the rank of captain). The organisation of the senior Scottish contingents of the French army dates from this regimentation of 1445. In his *Histoire de la Cavalerie* (1874) General Susane quotes an account book of the Royal Household which mentions the *gens d'armes et de trait* – men-at-arms and archers (literally men "of arrows") – who had been the responsibility of Sir John Stewart of Darnley since 1422 and who had served in unbroken association from then until the organisation of 1445. This company, from 1445, became known as *Les Gendarmes Ecossais* and, later, the 1st company of the Gendarmes. *Gen d'arme* was a word used in the medieval period to denote a mounted gentleman, or knight, in complete armour – the ancestor of the heavy cavalry.

Each of the companies formed, or at least reorganised, in 1445 consisted of 100 'lances'. A 'lance' was actually composed of six men: the *gen d'arme* himself (known as a *maître*), his page, his valet (or *coutilier*) and three mounted archers (or *clients*). A condition of being eligible for service in one of the new *Compagnies d'Ordonnance* reorganised in 1445 was that every man must be of noble birth. The *gen d'arme* was armed as a knight, with lance and sword and his page would have carried his other weapons. The *coutilier* was dressed in a brigandine or jack (a quilted doublet reinforced with small metal plates) and armed with a short sword, or *coutille*, and a short halberd, or *guisarme*. The archers carried crossbows and lances or maces; their role was that of light-armed cavalry. As pay the *gen d'arme* received 120 livres a year, the *coutilier* 60, the page 36 and each of the archers 48 livres a year.

33

The reorganisation of the *Compagnies d'Ordonnance* in 1445 also regulated the Scots Bodyguard which became the First, or Scottish, Company of the King's Bodyguard or *Compagnie Ecossaise de la garde du corps du Roi*. The *Gardes de la Manche*, 24 in number, were selected from among the 1st Company of the Guard. Their commander, called *premier homme d'armes de France* (the first gentleman at arms of France), was also selected from among the 1st Company and brought the number of the personal bodyguard up to 25. Their title *Gardes de la Manche* (guards of the sleeve), reflected their close position to the king's person at all times. Although their numbers varied from time to time, the figure of 120 is quoted by chroniclers describing the Scots Bodyguard in attendance upon Charles VII at his state entry to Rouen in November 1449; the description is also among the first of their appearance and mentions their wearing of the king's personal livery colours of red, white and green:

> "... archers and crossbowmen (sic), about 120 more gorgeously clad than the rest. They wore jackets without sleeves, red, white and green, covered with gold embroidery, with plumes in their helmets of the same colours, and their swords and legharness richly mounted in silver."

This uniform can be seen in the two paintings by Jean Fouquet, the *Adoration des Mages* (Musée Condé, Chantilly) (see frontispiece) and the *Lit de Justice de Vendôme* (Staatsbibliothek, München).

The Scots in the service of France continued to distinguish themselves against the English invaders after the truce of 1444 had ended in 1445 and by 1453 – and the end of this chapter – the Hundred Years War was effectively over. Only Calais remained in English hands and the days of its possession were numbered. As was said earlier, France ultimately did better out of the war than England; Scotland's position remained largely unaltered. The military alliance between France and Scotland had, however, taken on a new shape in the last three decades of the war and had also adopted a permanence, in the shape of the Bodyguard and the Gendarmes Ecossais, that was to remain once the alliance of the diplomats had foundered.

*A seventeenth century engraving from a tapestry depicting
the entry of King Charles VII into Reims for his coronation
in 1429. The King is preceded by Joan of Arc and in the
foreground at right of centre and at extreme left are four
dismounted archers of his bodyguard.*

(NMS)

Chapter Two

The Stuart Connection 1453–1688

THE 235 YEARS BETWEEN THE ENDING OF THE HUNDRED YEARS WAR AND THE ENFORCED exile of King James VII of Scotland and II of England saw the Franco-Scottish alliance develop rapidly from its promising active beginnings in the first half of the fifteenth century. It received something of a jolt in the middle of the sixteenth century when the extension of the Reformation to Scotland rendered its official religion Protestant, but the relationship was sufficiently well-developed by that time, and manifested itself so strongly in personal links, that it contrived to continue in a variety of ways – many of which reflected its profound military nature. A factor common to these two centuries was the presence on the throne of Scotland of members of the Stewart dynasty.

It will be relevant at this point to digress slightly in order to explain why the spelling of Stewart has been adopted thus far. The name derives from that of Walter the Steward, who was appointed to the position of High Steward of Scotland by King David I. The title, and position, became hereditary and by the time of the sixth High Steward of Scotland the family's surname had become Stewart, spelt thus. This Walter Stewart, then the eponymous High Steward of Scotland, married Marjory, daughter of Robert (the Bruce) and their son, the founder of the dynasty, was born in 1316, becoming king of Scotland in 1371. From that point until the reign of Mary, Queen of Scots, in the mid-sixteenth century, the spelling *Stewart* was used, not only to denote the Scottish dynastic surname but also that of cadet branches of the family. It seems likely that, by the time Mary arrived in France in 1548, the French branches of the family had adopted a spelling that more accurately suited French pronunciation (from the point of view of spelling the word as it sounded), namely *Stuart*. Mary adopted this spelling and when her son became king of Great Britain in 1603 this spelling was retained. It remained the spelling of the royal dynastic surname, and, to be pedantically correct, of only the royal dynastic surname (and its direct offshoots), until the death of the last of its representatives, Cardinal York in 1807. To avoid confusion, and because all the Stewarts, or Stuarts, referred to in this chapter were more French than Scots – including, it might be said, Mary herself – the French spelling will be used unless very inappropriate.

The marital alliance of Margaret, daughter of James I, to the Dauphin Louis in 1436 had been followed in 1437 by the murder of the Scottish king at the hands of the members of his baronial opposition who sought the throne for the Earl of Atholl. James II was six years old at the time and so a regency had to be established. His first regent was Archibald, Earl of Douglas (and also Duke of Touraine and Count of Longueville), who remained regent until his death in 1439. In 1448 the Franco-Scottish alliance was renewed at Tours and, in the following year, James II married Mary of Guelders, the niece of the Duke of Burgundy. Although Guelders was a Netherlandish duchy, Burgundian influence there was paramount and the marriage treaty bound Scotland and Burgundy to perpetual friendship. Seven years earlier, in 1442, one of James's sisters, Isabella, had married the Duke of Brittany and so, by midway through the fifteenth century, Scotland and France were sewn together in a triple alliance aimed specifically at a divided and overstretched England.

A nineteenth century depiction of a gentleman of the Scottish company of the Bodyguard of King Louis XI, c 1463, drawn by Major H. de Grandmaison.

(NMS)

A nineteenth century depiction, using fifteenth century sources, of a gentleman of the Scottish company of the Bodyguard of King Charles VIII, c 1498, drawn by Major H. de Grandmaison.

(NMS)

Scotland experienced three periods of civil war between 1450 and 1455 as the young king sought to establish his authority over the Douglasses, but by 1455 their power had been broken and that of King James II established. He was not to enjoy it for long since, in August 1460, when attending the firing of a salvo by his artillery at the siege of Roxburgh Castle, he was struck by a fragment from a bombard which exploded and he died shortly afterwards. His heir James III, was eight years old. In the following year, King Charles VII of France, the great friend to Scotland who had put his personal Scottish Bodyguard on a permanent footing and established the Scottish companies of the Bodyguard and Gendarmerie, also died, to be succeeded by Louis XI.

Under Louis (who died in 1483) and his successor Charles VIII (who died in 1498), France at last became united into a country recognisable today. In 1481 the provinces of Anjou and Provence devolved upon Louis by reason of the death of their last male ruler. In the following year Picardy and Burgundy joined the French crown after the Treaty of Arras, and in 1491 Charles VIII invaded Brittany and married the daughter of its last duke, who had died in 1488 leaving her the duchy. The alliance between the two countries was renewed after the succession of James III and Louis XI and again by James III with Charles VIII in 1484.

On this last occasion, in March 1484, the ambassador chosen to represent the new king of France at the Scottish court was Béraud Stuart, the grandson of John Stewart of Darnley, Concressault and Aubigny-sur-Nère and captain of the French king's Scottish Bodyguard. Béraud (or Bernard) Stuart had sold the Concressault estates in 1480 to a fellow countryman, a Franco-Scot called Alexander de Monypeny, and the family was settled at the chateau of La Verrerie in Aubigny. When James III was assassinated in 1488 he was succeeded by James IV and Béraud Stuart headed another embassy to Scotland to reconfirm the alliance. Between the two trips to Scotland, Stuart had led a company of French troops, many of whom were Scots, to assist Henry Tudor gain the throne of England at the battle of Bosworth in 1485. The victory of the Lancastrians over the Yorkists suited Scotland's book too, since the kings of Scotland during the Wars of the Roses in England had chiefly been allied to the Lancastrian cause. Franco-Scottish help in gaining the English crown prejudiced Henry VII of England strongly in favour of both nations and that, allied to his own natural parsimony and distaste for expensive wars, resulted in a period of relative peace between England and the allies. Notwithstanding the peaceful attitude of England, which did not outlast Henry VII, the Franco-Scottish alliance was most usually renewed whenever there was a change of sovereign in either country. Until the final abrogation of the formal alliance in the middle of the sixteenth century the treaty was renewed in 1512, in 1517, in 1543 and in 1547.

The ending of the wars between France and England meant that France no longer had need of large quantities of Scottish troops to come to her aid. Although that side of the alliance was to be invoked until the mid-sixteenth century by both partners, and continued for a good two centuries after that, its invocation was intermittent rather than prolonged or continuous. Because of the existence, however, not only of the Scottish element of the French king's Bodyguard and the Scottish company of the Gendarmes but also of many Scottish nobles in France, most of whom had received grants of land from the kings, the military nature of the alliance continued and manifested itself increasingly in these and other Scots making France their home. Principal among these, in terms of their status and also their close personal regard by successive French kings, were to be the Stuarts, once Stewarts of Darnley but, by the late fifteenth century, Stuarts of Aubigny-sur-Nère.

In the previous chapter, the career in France of John Stewart of Darnley – founder of the Aubigny line – was briefly mentioned. The military career of his grandson, Béraud Stuart is of equal interest and, because of its relevance and significance to the history of France, a brief biographical excursion will be attempted. His birth, in about 1450, coincides neatly with the beginning of this chapter and the ending of the Hundred Years War. He was the son of the original John Stewart's youngest son, John, the second seigneur of Aubigny. Béraud is first listed among the men-at-arms of the Scottish company of the Gendarmerie in 1469. Among his 95 comrades, ten have the surname Cunningham (spelt Conygham) – one of whom was the Captain, Robert de Conygham – and there are three Ramsays (Ramezay) and two Abercorns (Abrecorme). Almost all of the men-at-arms bore Scottish surnames, most of which are comprehensible to a modern eye. By 1483 Béraud had become Captain of the Scottish Company of the Gendarmerie, in succession to Robert Cunningham's son, John, and in 1493 he again

An illustration from Béraud Stuart's book on the art of war, c 1503.   (NMS)

succeeded John as Captain of the Scots Bodyguard, being succeeded in that post on his death in 1508 by his son-in-law's brother, John Stuart of Oizon. The relationship between the two distinct Scottish corps of the king's household does seem to have been that it was normal – at least in the latter period of the sixteenth century – for the Captain of the Scottish Company of the Gendarmerie ultimately to succeed to the command of the Scots Bodyguard. It certainly seems to have been almost a "family" appointment for a while, since John Stuart of Oizon was succeeded in 1512 by his brother, Robert Stuart of Aubigny.

As well as proving an effective ambassador in Scotland for the French kings, Béraud Stuart was one of their most trusted and successful senior soldiers too. He was made commander of the French army that invaded Calabria in 1493, and, in the following year, was the architect of a victory over the Spanish occupiers of southern Italy at Seminara, following which he was made a Knight of the Order of St. Michael by King Charles VIII. Béraud Stuart remained in command of the French army of occupation in Naples until his health became so bad, and the condition of his soldiers so neglected as a result of intermittent pay, that he was forced to withdraw to France.

The death of Charles VIII in 1498 left the crown to Louis XII who renewed the war, and Béraud Stuart's involvement in it, in 1499. Lombardy and Genoa fell rapidly to the French forces who, with their light, mobile and effective bronze siege artillery, repre-sented the period's equivalent to what the twentieth century has learnt to call *blitzkrieg*. Stuart was ordered into the kingdom of Naples again and defeated Spanish forces at Terra Nuova, only to be defeated, near Seminara, in April 1503. Most contemporary observers of the French forces in the early years of the wars in Italy, when they are not marvelling at the latest French artillery technology, enthuse about the appearance, stature and fighting qualities of the Scottish Company of the King's Bodyguard and the fact that, drawn from them, were the 25 men of the *Gardes de la Manche* who never left the king's side in battle; such demonstrable loyalty seems to have been remarkable. Béraud Stuart returned to Aubigny after the defeat of 1503 and, in semi-retirement, wrote a treatise on the art and conduct of war: *Ung livret et traicté pour entendre quel ordre et train ung prince ou chef de guerre doibt tenir pour conquester ung pays ou passer ou traverser le pays des ennemys, composé par Messire Bérault Stuart (Un livre et traité pour entendre quel ordre et train un prince ou chef de guerre doit tenir pour conquérir un pays ou passer ou traverser le pays des ennemies, composé par Monsieur Béraud Stuart); A book and treatise to understand what measures a prince or commander must take to conquer a country or pass through or cross the country of his enemies, composed by Sir Béraud Stuart.*

The marriage in 1503 of James IV of Scotland, at the age of thirty, to Margaret Tudor, daughter of Henry VII of England, at the age of thirteen, together with a "treaty of perpetual peace" between the two nations signed in the previous year, had made King Louis of France concerned for the continuity of the Franco-Scottish alliance. Accord-ingly, in 1506, he sent Béraud Stuart for a third time to the land of his ancestors in order to have his fears allayed and the alliance confirmed. Terms having been agreed, and – by all accounts – tournaments and other festivities undertaken, Béraud went back to France to seek advice, returning once again to Scotland to ratify the treaty in 1508. He died, before reaching the Scottish king, in the house of Sir John Forrester in the village of Corstorphine to the west of Edinburgh. He is said to have been buried either in Cor-storphine church or in the church of the Blackfriars in Edinburgh, but the former has no monument to this effect and the latter disappeared under the buildings of the Cowgate during and after the Reformation of the mid-sixteenth century.

The death of Henry VII brought Henry VIII to the throne of England. Although Henry VIII confirmed the Anglo-Scottish peace treaty in 1509, shortly after his accession, and

The carved decoration above the gateway to the palace of Linlithgow, c 1536. Commissioned by King James V, it demonstrates the extent of his alliances by showing the insignia of the Orders of Chivalry to which he had been admitted. Left to right: the Garter (England), the Thistle (Scotland), the Golden Fleece (Spain), the St Michael (France).
(Author)

made a peace treaty with France in 1510, it is clear that the former was regarded by the young English king as little more than a convenience and the latter nothing more than a trick. James IV ratified a new treaty with France in July 1512, three months after the birth of his first legitimate son, the future James V. For the next four years, until the birth of Mary Tudor to Henry and Catherine of Aragon in 1516, Margaret, the queen of Scotland, was heir presumptive to the English throne. The existence of her son, king of Scotland after the death of his father at the battle of Flodden in 1513, both rankled with Henry and threatened the succession of the English crown. In addition, Henry had become inveigled into an anti-French alliance with his father-in-law, Ferdinand of Aragon, and with Venice. In 1512 England attacked France and in June 1513 a major English expeditionary force landed in France and laid siege to Thérouanne in Artois. Frantic appeals from France for a Scottish invasion of England were met, initially, by prevarication as arguments ensued about which course – peace or war – was the wise one to adopt.

The invasion of England and the battle of Flodden was the result of the dithering. The Scottish bishop of Moray, Andrew Forman, had been sent both to Rome and to Paris by James IV in order to obtain guarantees and promises vis-à-vis James's claim to the English throne and France's aid in the event of an English attack. He had encountered hostility in Rome and equivocation in Paris but seems to have been promised the archbishopric of Bourges – which he subsequently received – if he would persuade his royal master to invade England. The Scots fleet sailed for France in July 1513, a month after the siege of Thérouanne had begun, and had a slap at the English stronghold of Carrickfergus in Ulster on the way. In August the first raid into England was sent, and at the end of the month the fullscale invasion force crossed the border and besieged Norham Castle, which was captured after six days. Brought to battle by the English commander, Lord Surrey, at Flodden on 9 September, the Scots initially occupied – uncharacteristically, it was remarked at the time – a fortified and defensible position. This may have been the result of advice from the king's French advisers who were with the Scots at Flodden, some of whom would have had experience of new methods of warfare in Italy, or might even have read Béraud Stuart's book. Jean de la Motte, ambassador to Scotland from the French king, was among the fallen. Outflanked by Surrey, the Scots left their positions and began with an artillery duel, of which the English cannoneers got the best since the Scots' foreign artillery experts had gone to France with the force of 3,000 soldiers sent with the fleet. Accurate English artillery broke up and demoralised the packed Scottish *schiltrons* of pikemen, and the Highland companies, led by Lords Lennox and Argyll, shattered the strength of the mass by breaking away and attempting flank attacks. Wind and rain made organised archery useless and so the battle was essentially one of English bill and halberd against Scots spear and sword; the pole-arms told eventually. Two senior clerics, eight Scottish earls, the king and a high propor-tion of the 20,000 Scots who had been at the battle were slain; quarter was not granted and only those who fled survived. The new king of Scotland, James V, was seventeen months old when he succeeded to the throne.

The Scottish force sent to France appears not to have been used and the war rather stagnated. Lord Arran, who had commanded the troops, returned to Scotland in November 1513 – as much to be involved in the wrangle over who should be regent for the infant king as anything else – and no mention can be found of their involvement in the battle of the Spurs in 1513.

One cannot be sure how long the news of the catastrophe of Flodden took to reach the French court and so one cannot, equally, be certain whether the next significant step in the progress of the alliance was as a direct result of the defeat or not. Interpreters of the actions of King Louis XII disagree about his motives and his influences but there is no doubt that, in his *Concession de lettres de naturalité pour les Ecossais résidant en France*, Louis absolved all Scots resident in France from having to obtain naturalisation before they could make wills or otherwise dispose of their property as they wished. This was an important consideration and certainly made Scots feel welcome in France; it may also have encouraged even more Scottish soldiers to settle since they now, automatically, had the same rights as native-born Frenchmen. It is probably no accident that this action was, apparently, urged upon the king of France by Robert Stuart of Aubigny, Captain of the Scots Bodyguard, and Andrew Forman, newly-installed archbishop of Bourges, since one was a major power and landowner in France and the other had just become so. Whatever the motives, the *Concession* was sealed in Amiens at an unknown date in September 1513. In its preamble, the king mentions specifically not only the long tradi-tion of military aid that Scotland had given, most especially in the previous century, but also that his ancestor Charles VII had recognised this by the establishment of the Scots Bodyguards and the Scots company of the Gendarmes. Specific mention is also made of the *Gardes de la Manche* as being closest to the royal person and most entrusted with the king's safety.

Letters of naturalisation had been issued before, of course, but only to specific individuals, not in the mass or to one nationality. Records survive in the Archives Nationales which are grants of naturalisation to Scots; those quoted here refer specifically to members of the Scots Bodyguard: Vastre Artus *(natif du pays d'Ecosse), garde du corps du roi* – Tours 1457, John Nesbet and Thomas Aigne *(natifs du pays d'Ecosse), archers de la garde du corps du roi* – Chinon 1462. Artus and Aigne may not be immedi-ately recognisable as Scottish names and so are probably a scribe's corruption of their actual names. The earliest letter of naturalisation still in existence was issued to Robert Petillot (Patillo, Patullo?), described as Squire of the King's Stable, at Tours in March 1453. A Robert Patillo is recorded as having been the first supposed commander of the Scottish Company of the Bodyguard, in the 1420s, and so his appointment to the stables and granting of naturalisation may well, if it is the same man, have recognised his services to the king; he had come a long way from his native Dundee. If it is the same man who

Blackness Castle, on the Firth of Forth, from the east,
showing later fortifications but also sixteenth and seventeenth
century gun-ports at the lower level of the walls. Blackness
was garrisoned by French troops in the 1550s.
(Historic Buildings and Monuments, SDD)

commanded Scots said to have been in the service of the French royal household in the 1420s, his naturalisation in 1453 only confirmed his earlier nickname of *le petiti roi de Gascogne* (the little king of Gascony), a nickname coined to reflect his depredations there in the name of Charles VII.

By the accession of Francis I to the throne of France in 1515 (an event celebrated in part by the new king creating Robert Stuart of Aubigny a Marshal of France), the organisation of the Scots Company of the Bodyguard seems to have been established. Two further companies had been raised in 1473 and 1475, and the fourth and last company was to be raised by Francis I in 1545. All the other three companies were French in composition. The muster rolls of the Scots company of the Bodyguard, reproduced so diligently by Father William Forbes-Leith S.J. in his *The Scots Men-at-Arms and Life-Guards in France* (1882), show that, by the 1470s, the breakdown between, roughly, 25 *Gardes de la Manche* (described as *Archiers du Corps*) and the remainder of the Scots Bodyguard (described as *Archiers de la Garde*) at, roughly, 75 was being diligently observed. The Captain of the Scots Bodyguard seems always to have been attended by two men-at-arms and, in 1531, the ranks of *Lieutenant* and *Enseigne* first appear, that of *Lieutenant* going to the senior of the men-at-arms attendant upon the Captain and that of *Enseigne* going to the *Archier du Corps* at the top of the list. From 1531 until 1542, when he died, Robert Stuart of Aubigny was attended by two other Stuarts, John the elder and John the younger, the elder John being his *Lieutenant*. The elder John Stuart gave up the lieutenancy in 1551 and the Stuart monopoly became a Montgomery one as Gabriel and François de Montgomery became men-at-arms to Jacques de Montgomery, who had succeeded Robert Stuart of Aubigny in 1543. Although as we saw in the previous chapter, the title of *premier homme d'armes* was given to the commander of the *Gardes de la Manche*, this title first appears (in Forbes-Leith's transcription of the Body-guard's muster rolls) in 1559 and is given to Jacques de Montgomery, seigneur de Cor-buzon, the junior of the two *hommes d'armes* attendant upon the Captain. He retained this title until leaving the Bodyguard in 1564 but the title persisted, if intermittently recorded, for his successors.

The late 1550s and early 1560s were difficult years for the Scots Company of the Body-guard and ones in which it underwent a fundamental change. In June 1559, Gabriel de

Montgomery, Lieutenant of the Scots Bodyguard and son of the Captain, Jacques de Montgomery, accidentally killed the French king, Henry II, in a tournament. He went into voluntary exile from the court, retaining his rank in the Bodyguard, until 1561, in which year he finally fled to England and became a Protestant. The accident, followed by his change of allegiance, combined with the early death of Henry II's successor Francis II and the subsequent return to Scotland of Francis's queen, Mary, Queen of Scots, to weaken relations between France and Scotland. This resulted in the Scottish Company of the Bodyguard inexorably, but fairly slowly, becoming more French and less Scottish in composition. Although Franco-Scottish names continue to appear in the muster rolls after the 1560s, the Captains after 1562 are uniformly French. The title of the Company continued, though, to remind observers of its original links until its final dissolution in 1830.

In 1515, however, all this was in the future and the future looked bright to the new king of France, Francis I. A contemporary and rival of both Henry VIII of England and Charles I of Spain (soon to become Charles V, Emperor of the Holy Roman Empire), Francis had all of Henry's lust for glory, none of Charles's pragmatic good sense and a love of splendour and grandeur that was not to be exceeded by any king of France until Louis XIV. Early on he stamped his personality on the uniform of the Scots Body-guard by arraying them in white, his personal livery colour, charged with a crowned gold salamander, his personal badge. A mere eight months after his accession Francis I renewed the campaign in Italy against the combined forces of the Empire and Spain. The French army, commanded by the Chevalier Bayard and by Robert Stuart of Aubigny, trounced their enemies at Marignano in September, the Scots Bodyguard being involved at the engagement but not, it appears, the 1st Company of the *Gens d'Armes*. The victory at Marignano was celebrated, by order of the regent, with bonfires in Edinburgh.

By the time of these joyous conflagrations, Scotland had been without a king, except in infancy, for two years. The position of regent to the infant King James V had been offered to his great-uncle, John, Duke of Albany, who had spent most of his life in France and who had served as a soldier there. Scotland was still spoiling for a fight with England after Flodden and had to be held back, diplomatically, by Francis in order not to wreck the truce that was being negotiated following the English victory at the battle of the Spurs. Peace finally came, albeit temporarily, in 1514 and Francis I renewed the peace treaty with England after his accession. Albany arrived in Scotland in 1515, but without the troops which the Scots had been expecting to accompany him. The drafted treaty of Rouen of 1517, which was not ratified by Scotland until 1521, since it involved organis-ing a marriage for James V which took some time to arrange, provided the next best thing to a renewal of the alliance. Albany remained in France from 1517 until he returned in 1521 with a clear remit from his king to seek active Scots help against England, which was felt by Francis I to be about to break the peace between them.

The renewal of the war between England and France was more manifest in Scottish terms by Border conflicts, which concentrated the power of England against Scotland, than by Scots harrying England's back door while the bulk of English forces were commit-ted on the continent. Not surprisingly, therefore, there was a marked reluctance within the government of Scotland to take an active part in the conflict on France's behalf, despite the presence in Scotland of about 4,000 French troops brought by Albany in 1523 to stiffen Scottish resolve. These French troops, aided by a rather reluctant Scottish 'host', laid siege to Wark Castle at the end of that year but were beaten off and, faced with a sustained lack of Scottish interest in perpetuating a serious campaign, Albany and the surviving French soldiers left for France in 1524. In the following year, Francis I was soundly beaten and taken prisoner by the forces of the Empire at Pavia, where both

The island of Inchkeith from the north-west, showing
Edinburgh in the background. Inchkeith was garrisoned by
French troops in the 1550s and 1560s, their fortifications
occupying the area now occupied by the lighthouse.
(Royal Commission on the Ancient and Historical
Monuments of Scotland)

the Scots Bodyguard and Scots *Gens d'Armes* were heavily engaged and suffered considerable losses. England and France agreed a peace treaty in 1527.

Albany's position as regent had been usurped almost as soon as he left Scotland for France in 1524 by the sixth Earl of Angus, who had married James V's mother. James took the government into his own hands in 1528 and, for almost the next decade, set about securing for himself and for Scotland an alliance with France that would enable Scotland once more to be a force in European politics. His position and aims were aided by the action of Henry VIII of England in supporting (for his own dynastic ambitions initially) the Reformation; this action put England, at least in theory, beyond the pale in a still principally Catholic Europe. It is possible, however, to overstate and overestimate the significance of the question of religion when surveying the prospective alliances which had all the important European rulers jockeying for position in the 1530s. It remained a convenient excuse, and protestations of adherence to the old faith were always useful if one wanted something out of the Pope, but adherence to the new Protestant religion, especially if it manifested itself in the type of ambivalent Anglo-Catholicism practised by Henry VIII, proved far less of an impediment to alliances than might be supposed. James, a bachelor with a growing brood of illegitimate offspring, let it be known that he was in the market for an alliance or two, preferably sealed by a suitably remunerative marriage, and waited to be wooed.

An idea of the style of the wooing is well demonstrated by the decoration of the gateway of the Palace of Linlithgow, which was carved in 1536. Even in the sixteenth century the concept of bribing people with decorations was well advanced, and successively, James received the Order of the Golden Fleece from the Emperor Charles V (1532), the Order of the Garter from Henry VIII (1534) and the Order of St. Michael from Francis I (also 1534). Charles V also offered ordnance and ammunition, which arrived, and a choice of Danish princesses, who did not. Charles V gradually moved closer to England, with the result that Scotland and France managed to work out an arrangment, and James married Madeleine, daughter of Francis I, in 1537. She died after only six months in Scotland and was rapidly succeeded in James's affections by Mary of Guise, who became Queen of Scotland in 1539.

What the marriage to Madeleine of France had begun, that to Mary of Guise continued. James had spent on a lavish scale, in imitation of all that he admired in France, since coming into his own in 1528 and the money acquired in the dowries of his two wives enabled him to maintain his standard of living. Mary of Guise encouraged and supported him and may well have provided the inspiration and impetus to maintain the links, in terms of armaments, which had begun in the early sixteenth century and which James V continued. French armourers had been imported and followed their trade; manufacturers of artillery from France were also encouraged and a flourishing cannon foundry was established in Edinburgh. James's energy and ambition, together with Mary of Guise's shrewd support and the powerful French connection that she represented, made him seem quite rapidly to become a power to be reckoned with in Europe.

However, Scotland was increasingly divided internally over its reaction to the reformed church south of the Border and becoming gradually more resentful of the growing taxation necessary in order to keep the king's court in a manner to which it had become accustomed. Powerful cliques among the nobility could see certain advantages to the sequestration of church property, as practised by Henry VIII, and grew gradually closer to England while beginning seriously to question the continuing validity of the French alliance. Mary of Guise did her best to soften what resentment there was of her powerful position at court, and much of the clergy, aware that the continuance of Catholicism in Scotland depended to a great extent not only upon royal stability, but also upon maintaining the alliance with France, supported her against the more secularly inclined noble factions. Part of the problem, which had always dogged Franco-Scottish relations, was that the Scots nobles, who largely constituted the government, had fairly consistently resented the fact that the alliance always seemed to work to France's advantage and rarely to that of Scotland. The resentment was, of course, especially marked among those of the nobility whose personal ambitions had not been accompanied by preferential treatment either in Scotland or France.

46

A nineteenth century depiction, from a contemporary engraving, of two gentlemen of the Scottish company of the Bodyguard of King Charles IX 1561, drawn by Major H. de Grandmaison.

(NMS)

The internal divisions within both church and state in Scotland were revealed during the renewal of war between England and Scotland in 1542. The war was more of an anti-English crusade precipitated by the Church and the king than a national movement, and the lack of commitment of sections of the nobility, together with the resultant dilatoriness of the Scots army's commanders, made the Scottish defeat at Solway Moss in 1542 almost predictable. James's surviving child, Mary, was only six days old when she succeeded her father who died – largely, it is said, of disappointment at the failure of his grand design against England – on 14 December 1542. Once again, Scotland was a land without a king and once again she required a regent.

Because of the divided nature of the power-base in Scotland, although the (relatively) pro-French and Catholic 'party' held sway, the infant Queen of Scots became a pawn: Henry VIII of England was determined that she should marry his son Edward and so bind Scotland into a Tudor alliance. The Earl of Arran, who had had secret dealings with Henry, was proclaimed governor of Scotland in January 1543 and he headed a council of regency for the queen which included Cardinal David Beaton and Mary of Guise – both of whom regarded Arran as a heretic. Henry succeeded in concluding the treaty of Greenwich in 1543 with Arran, which undertook to marry Mary to Prince Edward in due course. The council split over this decision, which was principally contrived by Lord Arran, and, supported by Francis I of France, moved the queen to Stirling Castle and had her crowned at the age of nine months in the chapel there. Arran, whose personal ambitions vis-à-vis

A pikeman of European infantry, c 1608, engraved by Jacob de Gheyn. His pike would have been about six metres long at this date, later shortened to about four metres. This is one of the stances adopted when the pikemen were placed in formation to repel cavalry.

(NMS)

England conflicted with his marital ones vis-à-vis Mary of Guise, promptly changed both sides and religions and shortly after the young queen celebrated her first birthday the Greenwich treaty had been overthrown and the alliance with France renewed.

It would be understating the case to say that this change of plan annoyed the English king and he soon began negotiations with disaffected Scots nobles to overturn the regency of Mary and Arran. Chief among the pro-English Scots nobility was Matthew, Earl of Lennox, brother to John Stuart of Aubigny, Captain of the *Gens d'Armes Ecossais*. Lennox's defection to England in 1544 gained him the hand of Henry VIII's niece, Lady Margaret Douglas, and his brother a stay in the Bastille until the death of Francis I in 1547. The son of Lennox's marriage became Lord Darnley, second husband of Mary, Queen of Scots, and father of King James VI of Scotland and I of England.

As civil war progressed in Scotland so each side received help from their foreign supporters. A small French fleet had brought supplies and artillery into Dumbarton in 1543 but these had been taken over by Lennox, who used them to raid Glasgow and Paisley before leaving for England in 1544. The English king, seeing his support slipping away by the regeneration of the anti-English forces in Scotland, launched several raids into Scotland, across the Border and on the coast, in 1544 and 1545. In the latter year a force of 3,000 infantry and 500 horses, led by Jacques de Montgomery, Seigneur de Lorges and Captain of the Scots Bodyguard, landed in Scotland to try and relieve the pressure exerted by the raiding English. Cardinal Beaton, apart from Mary of Guise probably the most pro-French of the council, was murdered by members of the pro-English faction in 1546 in St. Andrews Castle, which was promptly put into a state of siege. The siege of St. Andrews lasted until mid-1547 when it fell to a French assault, after which most of the beseiged garrison – including the Protestant preacher John Knox – were sent to the French galleys. The fall of St. Andrews was followed by a major English invasion, resulting in the battle of Pinkie in September 1547, and English forces followed up their victory there by garrisoning strongpoints throughout south-east Scotland.

Mary the young queen was moved around the country from stronghold to stronghold as the civil war raged, in order to keep her out of English hands. After Pinkie the situation appeared desperate and a further French expedition was mounted, commanded by André de Montalembert, Sieur d'Essé and comprising some 6,000 soldiers. The new king of France, Henry II, who had succeeded his father in 1547, sent the French royal galley to collect Mary while his soldiers set about trying to expel the English invaders. France opened a second front against England by attacking Boulogne in 1549 and this, combined with increasing Franco-Scots pressure in Scotland, gradually wore down the English for-tifications. Mary of Guise left for France in 1550 and in her year's absence the French envoy in Scotland, D'Oysel, gradually exerted an influence which, backed up by French soldiers, strengthened her party's cause. French troops garrisoned the castles of Inchkeith, Blackness, Dunbar and Broughty and seem to have been as unpopular as ever with the Scots, perhaps because they were soldiers rather than because they were French.

The succession of the Catholic Mary Tudor in England in July 1553 removed much of the English threat to Scotland since, although Mary naturally inclined to Spain rather than to France, her faith made her more of an ally than an enemy. Mary of Guise became sole regent, displacing Arran, whose compliance had been secured by the French dukedom of Chatelherault, in 1554, and until the accession of Elizabeth I of England in 1558, despite the growing rumblings of the religious reformers in Scotland and con-tinued resentment against French influence, the kingdom was relatively quiet.

Although France enjoyed a period of comparative peace, internally, during the early 1550s, her external policy, under Henry II, was broadly to continue the trial of strength with the Emperor Charles V that Francis I had begun. Both the Scots Bodyguard and the first company of the Gendarmerie were involved, the latter having been reorganised in the 1530s by having the archers formerly attendant upon each *gen d'arme* removed and formed into separate corps of mounted, light-armed troops, known as *chevaux-légers*, or light cavalry. It appears that the light horse troops retained some connection with their original Companies of the Gendarmerie since Father Forbes-Leith records a Captain Achisson of the "Scots Light Cavalry" commanding one of the breaches at the siege of St. Quentin in Picardy by Charles V in 1557. John Stuart of Aubigny, reinstated as Captain of the Scots Company of the Gendarmerie in 1547, led 35 men-at-arms and 57 archers under the Duke of Guise to capture Calais, the last English outpost in France, in early 1558.

In November 1558 Mary Tudor died, placing her Protestant half-sister Elizabeth I on the throne of England. Six months later Henry II was killed in a tournament, and his son Francis II rose to the throne of France. This united the crowns of France and Scotland as Francis had married Mary, Queen of Scots, in April 1558. The marriage settlement, although never really in doubt since Mary had fled to France, involved a great many con-cessions to France and thus resembled most of the former alliances between the two nations. Scotland granted rights of naturalisation to resident French people – just as had been granted four decades earlier by Louis XII to Scots resident in France. Secret clauses were added, which did not remain secret for long, to which only those Scots in the government who were favourable to the alliance were privy. These included the ceding of Scotland to France, should Mary die without heirs; that Scotland should be considered a province of France until the outstanding debts incurred for its defence against England by French troops should be paid off; and that Mary would not be a party to any move by the Scots government to renounce any of these secret clauses once they leaked out.

Francis II of France and I of Scotland was young, underdeveloped physically and intellectually, and uninterested in the business of government. The Queen Mother, Catherine de Medici, effectively held the reins of government and led a powerful Catholic faction which had far greater success in holding back the reforming Protestant tide in France than Mary of Guise was having in Scotland, which she was attempting to govern in her daughter's absence. The accession of Francis II did, at last, put Franco-Scottish joint policy on a firm basis and, a month or so after his accession, 2,000 further professional French soldiers landed in Scotland, approximately doubling the number already there.

In early 1560, therefore, England and its new queen had good cause for concern. In the eyes of Catholics, who represented the governments of Scotland and France, Elizabeth was both illegitimate and a heretic. In those same eyes, Mary, Queen of Scots, was also the rightful queen of England, by the right of her descent from her Tudor grand-mother; Elizabeth's heresy made her a justifiable target for deposition. The cause of Pro-testantism had not advanced effectively in Scotland throughout 1559, French garrisons held firm in the forts of Leith and Inchkeith and Mary of Guise was relatively impertur-bable as long as a sea route to France, for supplies and soldiers, remained open. But Mary of Guise died in June 1560 and the Queen of Scots ceased to be queen of France when Francis II died six months later. Representatives from England and France had agreed peace terms, involving the disembarkation from Scotland of both countries' armies, three weeks after Mary of Guise's death and Mary, the Catholic queen, returned to a Scotland which was inexorably becoming wholly Protestant in August 1561. The apotheosis of the Franco-Scottish alliance, which had lasted from the marriage in April 1558 to the death of Francis II in December 1560 and which had looked so promising – at least from the French point of view – fell apart rapidly.

The internal collapse of France undoubtedly contributed since, engrossed in suicidal wars of religion, France had little to do with outside matters until the 1590s. The gradual success of the Counter-Reformation Catholic forces in France against the Protestant minority involved barbarities, like the massacre of St. Bartholomew's Day in 1572 – in which about 2,000 Protestants were murdered by the Paris mob – which steadily strengthened the Protestant cause in Scotland by appearing to demonstrate what Catholics were capable of. The effect of the wars of religion on the Scottish troops in France seems to have been most noticeable in the way that the two Companies gradually became emptied of Protestants and filled by exiled Scottish or other Catholics. The French service, as a military bolt-hole for exiled Scots who were also Catholic in faith, became established as such as the two nations began to move apart politically and diplomatically. The French army largely disintegrated in the face of civil conflict and individual units sought their own allegiances. The Bodyguard remained in being and, once purged of Calvinists, seems to have remained loyal to the successive monarchs, but the 1st Company of the Gendarmerie had a hard time, threatened with disbandment in the 1560s and seriously diminished in numbers. John Stuart of Aubigny, its Captain, died in 1567 and Mary, Queen of Scots, appears to have succeeded in persuading her brother-in-law, King Charles IX of France, to grant the title of Captain of the 1st Company of the Gendarmerie to her son, Prince James, later James VI and I, and to all subsequent Stuart princes. Prince James was a year old at the time.

The 1st Company went into a sort of suspended animation until it was reorganised in 1600 and in the following year Prince Henry, son of James VI and I, became its titular Captain in succession to his father, whose position had been no more than nominal yet had still maintained the Franco-Scottish military link. Prince Henry was seven in 1601 and held the titular and honorary position of Captain until his death in 1612. Henry's brother Charles, later King Charles I, inherited the position in 1612 and held it until his succession to the British throne in 1625 but, at least in 1612, executive control of

A nineteenth century depiction, from a contemporary engraving, of two gentlemen of the Scottish company of the Bodyguard of King Louis XIII, 1610, drawn by Major H. de Grandmaison.

(NMS)

A nineteenth century depiction, from contemporary sources, of a gentleman of the Scottish company of the Bodyguard of King Henry IV, c 1608, drawn by Major H. de Grandmaison.

(NMS)

the Company was exercised for him, as it may have been for Henry, by Ludovic, Duke of Lennox and Earl of Darnley, who was also Great Chamberlain and Admiral of Scotland. Lennox died in 1624 and was succeeded by George, Lord Gordon, Earl of Enzie, and subsequently second Marquess of Huntly. He held the position until 1648 when it reverted to a prince of the house of Stuart, James Duke of York – later James VII and II. James retained the Captaincy until 1665 and was the last Scot to be Captain of the 1st Company of the Gendarmerie.

The convulsions that shook France during the wars of religion were finally suppressed, after the murder of Henry III of France in 1589, by his successor the Protestant Henry IV, King of Navarre. Henry IV, besides his Scots Bodyguard, took 6,000 Scots auxiliaries into his service on his accession to help him assault and capture Paris. The Scots were offered to the French king by James VI of Scotland who, while being relatively tolerant of religious differences, preferred to see a Protestant on the throne of France rather than a Catholic. The Scots, the advance party of whom were commanded by Sir James Colville of Easter Wemyss, attracted comment in a curiously familiar way on their arrival, the comment being directed at the comparatively anachronistic nature of their dress and arms. It was noted, however, that they were accompanied by the sound of bagpipes and hautbois. His Scots auxiliaries helped secure the throne of France for Henry IV and, although he had become a Catholic in order to be crowned, he renewed the naturalisation of Scots resident in France in 1599.

Neither Henry IV nor either of his two predecessors had been able to do anything to assist Mary, Queen of Scots, whose life after her return from France in 1561 and eventual fate became more bound up with growing hostilities between England and Spain than with the old ally where she had spent her formative years. After being the centre of civil war in Scotland for six years she abdicated in 1567 in favour of her infant son, James VI, who was to become – in 1603 – the first Stuart king of Great Britain. Mary was executed in England in 1587 and, while her abdication finally extinguished the formality of the Auld Alliance, her family's connection with France was to endure and would be periodically resurrected for two centuries after her death.

Five years prior to the marriage of the Dauphin Francis and Mary, in 1553, French military records indicate that what was probably mercenary activity was not dead. Records exist of a small regiment, part of the army of Picardy in that year, commanded by an officer called Glaney (almost certainly Irish) and comprising four Scottish and two English ensigns. This probably indicates a maximum of three companies of infantrymen, two Scottish and one English. After the peace of Cateau-Cambresis in 1559 the two Scottish companies were incorporated as footsoldiers "for the service of the king's guard", not necessarily the Scots Bodyguard. In 1561 they were added to the strength of the *régiment de Richelieu*. In 1589, another regiment, known as Dowyn's Scots (*Dowyn écossais*) was raised, in May; it was disbanded in the same year.

It is clear that James VI and I and Henry IV had a close relationship (despite Henry's description of James as the Wisest Fool in Christendom), and one which both considered to be exemplified by the continuity of the military link represented by the Scots Bodyguard and the Scottish Company of the Gendarmerie. There were other links too, since Scots merchants trading with France had also had their privileges renewed, in March 1599, three months prior to the renewal of the naturalisation already mentioned. After the death of Henry IV in 1610 and the succession of Louis XIII, matters began, barely perceptibly, to change. Louis did not renew the letters of naturalisation or the trading privileges, although an Act exists, dated 1612, which indicates that individual requests for naturalisation would still be sympathetically considered.

Resentments at the alliance had never been exclusively or peculiarly those expressed in Scotland against the French and, after the death of Henry IV, opportunities seem to have been taken to attack some of the privileges which the Scots Bodyguard apparently regarded as uniquely theirs. The Captain of the Scottish Company of the Bodyguard, Philibert, Marquis de Nerestang, had been appointed in February 1611, less than a year after the death of Henry IV, and (it was reported by Sir Ralph Winwood to the British Ambassador in Brussels) was felt by certain of the Scots Bodyguard to be exercising and transferring privileges believed by them to be exclusively Scots in nature rather than to do with the entire Bodyguard, which was reported as being two-thirds French. Regrettably, the nature of the grievances has not been reported but the Scots in the 1st Company of the Bodyguard were clearly getting nowhere in having them redressed by the young King Louis XIII or his mother and regent, Marie de Medici, and so they petitioned King James to try and get matters dealt with. This did not work either, probably because James declined to become personally involved but preferred to delegate the matter to ministers who were only able to reach their French opposite numbers, who were not sympathetic. De Nerestang relinquished the Company in 1612 to Charles d'Estourmel, Seigneur de Blainville, and so matters may have improved. Shortly before

George Gordon, 2nd Marquess of Huntly, by Van Dyck. He wears a waist sash covered with fleur-de-lys and served as commander of the 1st company of the gens d'armes from 1624 until 1648.

(The Duke of Buccleuch and Queensberry)

his death in 1625, James was in contact with Louis about putting the 1st Company of the Gendarmerie on an active footing and no more is recorded of problems with the Scots Bodyguard after that date, so the privilege question may have been resolved.

The resentment by natives of privileged foreigners is understandable. To understand what was actually resented – and jealously guarded by the Scots Bodyguard, and especially by the *Gardes de la Manche* – we should consider the enumeration of those privileges while remembering that actual comprehension of their importance is, naturally, closely bound up with the etiquette of one of the most formal courts of Europe. In *Memoirs concerning The ancient Alliance between The French and Scots, and the Privileges of the Scots in France* (Edinburgh 1751) the actual privileges and duties of the *Gardes de la Manche* are specified. French court life being what it was, it is unlikely that much had changed between 1611 and 1751 – if anything, it had become more complicated and formal.

'The ancient rights and prerogatives of the Scottish life-guards were very honourable. Here follows the description which those same Scots guards give of the functions and prerogatives of their company, and especially of the 24 first guards; to whom the first Gendarme of France being added, they make up the number of 25, commonly called Gardes 'de Manche', (sic) *sleeve-guards*, who were all Scots by nation.

Two of them assisting at mass, sermon, vespers, and ordinary meals; on high holidays at the ceremony of the royal touch, and by the election of knights of the king's order, at the reception of extraordinary ambassadors, and public entries of cities, there must be six of their number next to the king's person, three on each side of his majesty; and the body of the king must be carried by these only, wheresoever ceremony requires, and his effigy must be attended by them. They have the keeping of the keys of the king's lodging at night, the keeping of the choir of the church, the keeping of the boats when the king passes the rivers, the honour of bearing the white silk fringe in their arms, which is the coronal colour of France; the keys of all the cities where the king makes his entry given to their captain in waiting, or out of waiting. He has the privilege in waiting, or out of waiting, at ceremonies, such as coronations, marriages, funerals of the kings, baptisms and marriages of their children, to take duty upon him; the coronation robe belongs to him; and this company, by the death or change of a captain, never changes its rank, as do the three others.'

As can be appreciated, this was quite a recipe for resentment, especially in an age when the Divine Right of Kings and Absolute Monarchy were largely unquestioned concepts, especially in France. Such closeness to the monarch would, detractors could believe, give the guard power over him in the granting of favours and in the making or breaking of reputations, of families and of fortunes. Under the circumstances, it may be regarded as strange that outbreaks of jealousy were not more common; perhaps they were not because they would have been unjustified.

In 1625 James VI of Scotland and I of England died, one of his last acts being to negotiate a marriage between his heir Charles and Henrietta Maria, sister of King Louis XIII of France. James had been positive about his position as king of both nations and had insisted upon being regarded as king of Great Britain. The marriage treaty was, therefore, far more British and French than Scottish and French, although it might have caused less problems for Charles if its application to England had been less marked. Despite its English overtones a Scottish and a French dynastic marriage had once again been contrived; once again it was hedged about with secret clauses and, once again, it led to disaster for the Stuarts. A Papal dispensation had been necessary for the marriage to take place since Charles was, at least nominally, a Protestant. In agreeing to the marriage James had been required to agree, secretly, that Henrietta Maria's entourage would be allowed freedom to worship as their faith and consciences demanded and that, henceforth, the persecution of Catholics in Britain which had continued since the Gunpowder Plot of 1605 would cease. It was also agreed that the children of the marriage would be instructed in the religion of the new queen's choice. Charles I was probably the most cultivated, civilised, gentle and agreeable of all the Stewart or Stuart kings; he was also immovably convinced of his Divine Right to govern, immensely stubborn, proud, arrogant and guileless. These latter qualities, together with some of the former and combined with the Catholic connection of the queen, contrived eventually to bring about the Civil Wars and their aftermath, which shook England and Scotland from the late 1630s until the Restoration of the Monarchy in 1660.

Seven years before Charles I married Henrietta Maria and became king a war had begun in central Europe that was to last, off and on, for thirty years and earn the historians' title based on its span. Apart from a brief period of conflict between Britain and France in 1627 over the Huguenot stronghold of La Rochelle there was little military activity for those in Britain who wished to win their spurs. The outbreak of the Thirty Years War in 1618, which was in many ways a continuation of petty squabbles in the Baltic from the previous decade, provided a source of employment for those whose ancestors had joined the forces of mercenaries and others in the continental wars of the fourteenth and fifteenth centuries.

The *condottieri* and the *Landsknechts* had not vanished at the end of the Hundred Years War; there was always enough killing and pillage to go round in Europe. Scots had, of course, continued to serve wherever there was someone who would pay, as had all the other nationalities who formed part of the mercenary companies. From the point of view of this narrative, the outbreak of the Thirty Years War is significant because the involvement in it of so many Scots, in the service of France, contributed not only to the martial development of Britain within the period covered by this chapter but also wrote an important paragraph in any introduction to any history of the British army.

Despite the union of the crowns in 1603 and King James's insistence upon "Great Britain", England and Scotland were still two separate kingdoms, with separate legislatures and churches. Charles I had contrived to alienate the Church of Scotland in the mid-1630s and caused a brief war between 1638 and 1640 before England's own Civil Wars began in 1642 and occupied his time. Scotland did not become involved in England's internal troubles to any great extent and certainly not on an official, government-backed, basis until 1644. Thus, prior to 1638 and between 1640 and 1644 there was not much going on in Britain in the way of fighting that could interest government-sponsored bodies of Scots: what individuals did was another matter.

In 1635 there were 19 'foreign' regiments – regiments composed of non-Frenchmen – in the service of France. Three of these were Scots in origin, although we cannot be sure that they were entirely and solely recruited from Scotland or composed of Scots. The first to be raised, in 1633, was the infantry regiment commanded by Sir John Hepburn, who had previously been in the service of Gustavus Adolphus, King of Sweden. Hepburn's regiment, or *le régiment d'Hebron*, was ordered to be raised on 6 March 1633 and to consist of a total of twelve companies, each of 100 men – divided into 40 pikemen and 60 musketeers. In addition, each company had a captain, a lieutenant, an ensign, two sergeants, a pay-corporal, a captain-at-arms, a quartermaster, a surgeon and two drummers, making a total of 111 men per company. The regimental staff consisted of the colonel, a lieutenant-colonel, an escorting liason officer (interpreter), a sergeant-major, the sergeant-major's assistant, a regimental secretary, a sergeant, the sergeant's assistant and a chaplain. Total regimental strength on paper was therefore 1,341 of all ranks, not counting the provost and his archers (unspecified number), the regimental surgeon, two armourers and a drum-major – perhaps 1,350 men all told. Rates of pay varied from 500 livres per month for the colonel, 300 for each of the twelve captains, 75 for the ensigns, 30 for the sergeants, 15 for the company surgeons, drummers and pikemen, to 12 livres per month for the musketeers. The Lords of Secret (Privy) Council in Edinburgh ratified Sir John Hepburn's warrant from the king of France in April 1633, King Charles having approved it on 28th March. The total initial cost of the regiment to the French exchequer was 27,332 livres per month.

Hepburn's regiment is said to have landed, 2,000 strong, at Boulogne in August 1633 and is certainly recorded as having that strength ten years later. In 1634 it served in the Lorraine campaign but Hepburn was killed in 1636, at about the age of 36, at the siege of Saverne; he is buried in Toul Cathedral. After his death the command of the regiment passed briefly to his brother, George (or James) Hepburn, before being given to Lord James Douglas, who held it until his death in 1645. Douglas's elder brother, later Earl of Angus and Ormonde, succeeded to the command, which he held – inactively – until 1655 whereupon his half-brother Lord George Douglas – later Earl of Dumbarton – succeeded and retained the colonelcy until 1688. *Le régiment d'Hebron*, later *le régiment de Douglas*, remained in the service of France until 1661 when, after the Restoration of the British monarchy, it was recalled temporarily to Britain to be mustered as the senior regiment of the British line. It returned to France in 1662 with a strength of 23 companies of 100 men each. In 1665 it again returned to Britain, since although serving the king of France, it was now a British regiment and not a French one, and Britain was then at war with the Dutch, temporarily allied to France. In 1667 the regiment returned to France, was augmented by recruiting in Scotland in 1671 and in 1673, when it was referred to as *The Scotch Regiment* in a document listing *English* (sic) *Troops in the Service of France and on the English Establishment*. A further 800 men were ordered to be recruited in Scotland in 1674, the campaigns in Germany under Marshal Turenne having taken a considerable toll, and its last campaign took place in 1677. In the following year the regiment returned to Britain to become a permanent part of the British Army; now 356 years old it bears the title The Royal Scots (The Royal Regiment) and is senior regiment of the British line infantry. Its history, and that of its commanders, are more fully dealt with elsewhere but we will encounter it again in the context of this narrative.

The other regiments of Scottish origin, commanded by Scottish officers and noted as being in the service of France in the 1630s were short-lived infantry and cavalry regiments commanded by two colonels called Forbes. The cavalry regiment, commanded by Colonel The Hon. John Forbes was raised in 1635 and passed to a Colonel Ruthworm in 1641. Colonel N. Forbes commanded an infantry regiment bearing his name between 1635 and 1638. There is no evidence to confirm that either regiment was composed of Scots.

In 1643, besides the *régiment de Douglas*, there were four other regiments of Foot of Scottish origin in the French service. Little is known about those commanded by Lords Gray and Lundy and a Colonel Fullerton, except that each had a paper strength of 1,000 men and that, in January 1643, half the strength of Fullerton's had disembarked at Boulogne.

Better known, represented by 2,000 men also disembarked at Boulogne by January 1643 and often confused with either the *Compagnie écossaise de la garde du corps du roi*, the *régiment de Douglas* or even the Scots Guards of the British Army – to name but

The monument in Toul cathedral to Maréchal de Camp Sir John Hepburn, 1st colonel of The Royal Scots (The Royal Regiment), who died in 1636.

George, Lord Gordon, son of the 2nd Marquess of Huntly, who served as his father's lieutenant in the 1st company of the gens d'armes and was killed at the battle of Alford in 1645. Artist unknown.

(The Duke of Hamilton and Brandon)

three – was the *Régiment des Gardes écossaises*. This regiment was raised in 1642 by the Earl of Irvine and comprised 30 companies, each of 150 men. The entire regiment had probably disembarked at Boulogne by the end of 1643. Generous promises were made by the French concerning both the pay and status of the regiment, which would be on the same footing as the two other French guards regiments of infantry – the *gardes françaises* and the *gardes suisses*. It was promised that the *gardes écossaises* would take precedence after the Swiss guards and before the senior French infantry regiment. It was also promised that one company would be attendant upon the king. None of these promises were kept. The regiment, in a state of near mutiny, was badly defeated at Tuttlingen in November 1643 and the lieutenant-colonel, Sir Robert Moray, and several other officers were captured. Moray was eventually ransomed and returned to Scotland to raise more recruits for the regiment. The supply had largely dried up, however, and he was unable to obtain more than half the number that he had promised to raise (800). This led to recriminations and, since he had been paid in advance for 800, accusations

The tomb of the Lord James Douglas, colonel of The Royal Scots (The Royal Regiment) from 1637 to 1645, in the church of St Germain-des-Près, Paris.

(M. J-C. Lemaire)

by France of fraud. The depleted regiment fought alongside the French guards at the battle of Lens in 1648 and, although the regiment continued in the French service until 1662, it was not utilised after the Peace of Westphalia ended the war. In 1662 the last colonel, Andrew Rutherford, Earl of Teviot, was appointed governor of Dunkirk and the regiment was disbanded, those soldiers who wished to do so transferring to the *régiment de Douglas*.

Two other Scottish regiments served France between the ending of the English Civil Wars and the expulsion of James VII and II in 1688. A regiment called *le régiment de Campbell, écossais* was raised by one N. Campbell in June 1653, fought in Catalonia and was incorporated in 1657 into the *régiment Royal-Irlandais*. It is probable, if this regiment was composed of Scots (as opposed to just being raised by one), that they may have been exiles from Cromwell's campaign in Scotland in 1653–54 which effectively stamped out Royalist opposition to the government there. In 1671 George, Earl of Hamilton and Abercorn, raised the other, *le régiment d'Hamilton*. It served in Germany and the Low Countries until 1678 when it was amalgamated with *le régiment Furstemberg*.

Charles II, less Scottish than any of his predecessors, succeeded his father on Charles I's execution in 1649. He had spent the greater part of the first ten years of his reign in exile, in France, Spain and the Netherlands and, although he involved Scottish forces at the battles of Worcester and Dunbar on his behalf in 1650, is not really significant personally to this story. His understanding with King Louis XIV of France, which developed into the "secret" treaty of Dover in 1670, made it possible for the 1st Regiment of Foot to serve in France without its presence there being thought so odd.

Charles's brother James, the last reigning Stuart king of Britain, spent his formative years as a soldier in the French service, fighting five campaigns in the 1650s under

Lord George Douglas, 1st Earl of Dumbarton, by Gascars. Lord Dumbarton was colonel of The Royal Scots from 1655 to 1688, in both the French and the British service, and went into exile with King James VII and II in 1688. He died at St. Germain-en-Laye in 1692.

(NGS)

Marshal Turenne. As Lord High Admiral of England he was a relatively successful sailor-commander after the Restoration and, in 1670, he sired a future Marshal of France by his mistress, Arabella Churchill – James Fitzjames Stuart, Duke of Berwick. In Scotland in the early 1680s he carried out a policy of savage persecution against the Convenanters, an extreme Protestant sect to which he, as a Catholic, was unalterably opposed.

James's accession to the throne, following his brother's death in 1685, was initially trouble-free although his Catholicism gave cause for concern since it was perceived as the religion of absolutism, in the French mould, and the English and Scottish parliaments were taking every opportunity to flex their constitutional muscles. James became gradually more intransigent about matters political and religious but his parliaments and councils continued to tolerate his behaviour. Only when a legitimate son and heir was born did the matter become desperate, since the existence of the infant James implied a continued Catholic succession, no hope of what was then perceived as constitutional government and a junior partnership in a French alliance. Secret negotiations were opened with Prince William of Orange, husband of the elder of James's daughters, Mary, and when William landed in England with an invasion force in 1688, by invitation, almost all of the senior military commanders who were Protestants rallied to him, as did senior clerics and politicians.

James had no option but to flee to France and the safety offered by King Louis XIV. For the century after James's expulsion in 1688 the word *Jacobite* would be used pejoratively and patriotically to indicate a supporter, real or supposed, of the Catholic Stuart succession to the British throne. The success or failure of all the attempts to reinstate James and his successors would depend, ultimately, on support being forthcoming from both France and Scotland; the support most needed was money and soldiers and so the Auld Alliance was to be invoked once more.

Chapter Three

Emigrations, Rebellions and Wars 1688–1746

THE ACCEPTANCE BY WILLIAM III AND MARY II OF THE THRONES OF ENGLAND AND Scotland in 1689, following the expulsion of Mary's father, James VII and II, began a period of conflict between Britain and France. While the Stuart monarchs (with few territorial ambitions) had been kings in Britain, especially when their religious faith had been sympathetic to that professed by the kings of France, the ancient enmity between the two countries had been kept under control.

Many Scottish and English Catholics had fled to France during the Commonwealth and Protectorate period in Britain, between the execution of Charles I in 1649 and the restoration of his son, Charles II, in 1660. As the power of France and strength of its monarchy grew under Louis XIV after his accession in 1643 (and especially after his attainment of his majority in 1651 and commencement of personal rule in 1661), so the position of religious minorities in France became less secure. Henry IV had allowed freedom of worship to his Protestant, or Huguenot, subjects by the Edict of Nantes in 1598 and thus gained for his recently sundered kingdom a considerable measure of internal stability. By 1685, when Louis XIV felt secure enough in France (yet insecure enough in the eyes of the Papacy) to revoke the Edict and thus pose as the champion of Catholicism, his Huguenot subjects had been having an increasingly hard time from Louis's government who were, among other things, afraid of the potential for a fifth column which the Huguenots were felt to represent. The revocation of the Edict sent many Huguenots into exile in Britain and in those Protestant states on the eastern borders of France. The expulsion of James from Britain in 1688 and the resultant ending of religious toleration for Catholics led to an evacuation of many Catholics from Britain, most of whom ended up – at least initially – in France.

These religion-based emigrations inevitably became bound up with the series of rebellions which periodically shook Britain, to greater and lesser extents, between 1689 and 1746. The rebellions, all of which were aimed at the restoration of the Stuart dynasty, the Catholic religion and personal monarchical government, became associated with the principal internal threat to the established British governments of those 57 years: Jacobitism. Taking its name from the last Stuart king's Royal Style and Title, *Jacobus Rex*, Jacobitism was far more than an anachronistic movement comprised of disgruntled and dispossessed Catholics. William III, the new king of Britain, was an avowed enemy of Louis XIV who had persistently aimed at extending France's frontiers at the expense of those of the Netherlands. William was also a Protestant and widely regarded as the champion of the Protestant cause in a Europe threatened by an expansionist, Catholic France. William had received little help from the last two Stuart kings of Britain and so when the opportunity came to become Britain's king, and therefore be able both to turn Louis's flank and to utilise the British army against France, he took it with such eagerness as his natural dourness allowed him to muster.

Throughout the Jacobite period, and certainly until after the rebellion of 1715, many influential people in Britain hedged their bets by attempting to maintain at least a

King James VII of Scotland and II of England, when Duke of York, by Sir Peter Lely.

(NGS)

correspondence with the exiled Stuart court, while also doing their best to appear loyal to William and his successors. Until the Peace of Utrecht in 1713 specified that the Stuart court should be evicted from French soil, France was the natural home for the exiled Stuarts. As the enemy of Britain, France was naturally the leading foreign protagonist of the Stuart cause, as much for reasons of continuing the wars by back–door methods as for actually wanting the Stuarts back on the British throne. The Stuarts were a Scottish dynasty, although Charles I and his sons had successively watered down the Caledonian connection. The greater part of support for the Stuart cause was found in Scotland, after William's murderously effective campaign in Ireland in 1690 had stamped out the Jacobitism which had been evinced there, and so, although there were cells of Jacobites in England, Scotland became inextricably associated with the Jacobite cause. This association was far stronger in the minds of non–Scots than among Scots themselves, who were – for the most part – either supremely indifferent or very well aware just how effectively the Jacobite movement had split Scotland at all articulate levels. Throughout French support for the Jacobite cause, there seems to have persisted in France – among those who were most vociferously pro-Jacobite – a belief that Scotland was wholly behind the Stuarts and just waiting for an opportunity to rise. At the same time, in Scotland and among a few hard-headed Jacobite protagonists, it was always believed that no rebellion could ever succeed without a strong measure of committed and uninterrupted French help.

One of the results of these essential yet basic misunderstandings between the two halves of the partnership was that Jacobitism was doomed to failure because the two forces that could make it succeed always failed to interrelate effectively. Part of the problem was that, throughout the period when Jacobitism was the most active threat, France was heavily committed elsewhere, usually against the British army. This brings us to the third part of the triumvirate of factors that influenced the relationship during the period under scrunity: wars.

By 1689 Britain had had a royal standing, or permanent, army for nearly three decades. Born, phoenix-like, from the New Model Army which had won the Civil Wars for Parliament, the new British army had grown in fits and starts from its beginnings in 1661. Regiments still came and went as occasions demanded but several regiments, of both Horse and Foot, had been raised – and remained in being – in the 1670s and '80s as internal troubles in England and Scotland had threatened the stability of the realm. The Scots Guards of the British monarch had been established in 1661, owing their beginnings to a regiment raised for service in Ireland two decades earlier. The 1st regiment of Foot had been brought back from France to be allocated its precedence number in 1661 but had not, as we have seen, become a permanent fixture on the English military establishment until seventeen years later. At the same time as the Royal Scots finally returned to England, so another Scottish regiment was raised, specifically to cow that part of the population in Scotland for whom the incipient Catholicism of the king and his brother was becoming just a little too overt; this regiment, ultimately twenty-first in the infantry precedence, subsequently became the Royal Scots Fusiliers. A fourth, or Scottish, troop of Horse Guards had been raised by Charles II and in 1678 Scotland got its own Dragoon regiment, the ancestors of the Royal Scots Greys. Like the Fusiliers, the Dragoons were raised specifically to hunt down and exterminate the extreme Protestants who called themselves Covenanters. These Scottish soldiers, none of whom wore kilts or any of the other 'Highland' impedimenta with which later generations have allowed themselves to become intoxicated, were part of the expanded British army that William took abroad in order to confront France. While a minority in Scotland still clove naturally to France to secure or restore its ancient privileges and dispossessed monarchy,

James Fitzjames, Duke of Berwick and Alba, Marshal of
France and natural son of King James VII and II and
Arabella Churchill. An engraving of 1693.

(NMS)

Prince James Francis Edward Stuart, the Old Pretender, from
the studio of A. S. Belle, c 1712.

(NPG)

a considerable majority was gradually moving inexorably towards England and sending
its young men to fight its former ally.

In France itself, after 1689 and the outbreak of war with Britain, many regiments found
themselves officered by exiled British Catholics and in several cases, the British contingent was not confined to the officer class. With Huguenots in the British army and
British Catholics in the French army, and with Scots on *both* sides, the series of conflicts
which began in 1689 assumed a character based upon politico–religious principles and
personal circumstances while contesting national boundaries and sovereignties. Admittedly, the old established Scottish corps of the French army, the Bodyguard and the 1st
company of the Gendarmerie, were by then almost wholly French – yet still with some
Scottish names – and were not threatened with either change of title or a loss of privileges
as a result of the wars against Britain; their position and loyalty seems by that time to
have been beyond question.

The British army welcomed Huguenots at all levels but there is no evidence to suggest
that certain regiments were particular favourites of these dispossessed French Protestants. By ridding France and the French army of the Huguenots after 1685, Louis
XIV had weakened both the nation and his army considerably. Britain gained as a result
and, during the next forty or so years, the first and second generation Huguenot
immigrants who joined the British army proved to be its backbone in terms of efficiency,
experience and, above all, loyalty. The Huguenot officers, unlike too many of their
British seniors, had nothing to gain by attempting to negotiate a furtive correspondence
with the exiled Stuarts and everything to gain by an overthrow of Louis XIV.

It is incorrect to interpret the conflicts, internal and international, of this period as
being ones in which questions of religion loomed large. Governments had always been
relatively cynical about considerations of faith and would continue to be so. The issue
of religious differences waxed and waned in a manner proportionate to the perceived
importance of other strands of political argument and should not at any time be confused

with more mercenary, personal or nationally aggrandising issues. There is no evidence to suggest that Huguenots, *en masse*, pursued any kind of religious vendettas against their Catholic opponents, either on the continent or in the Highlands of Scotland. Their interest in fighting for Britain was economic in origin and political in depth; having escaped persecution in France, for both their religion and their relative mercantile success, they had every reason to try and prevent it being exported to Britain. The Huguenot composition of the British army was never large, yet definitely noticeable, and it is to be doubted whether any Huguenots joined its ranks as part of a politico–religious crusade; in most cases it would have been simply in order to eat.

The primary Huguenot immigrations to Britain took place in 1686 and '87 and there were Huguenot soldiers in the British army prior to 1689. The advent of William brought more Huguenots in his train and five actual Huguenot regiments were created within the British army between 1689 and 1695. Three of them were regiments of infantry, all of which were raised betwen March and June 1689 and all of which took precedence (until their disbandment in 1699) over the two Scottish regiments of infantry which were also raised in 1689 and which (unlike many other Scottish infantry regiments of the period) survived: the King's Own Scottish Borderers and the Cameronians. Virtually all British regiments of William's reign were polyglot in composition and so, although the five Huguenot regiments had French officers, it is certain that the rank and file were neither uniformly French nor uniformly Protestant. The number of short-lived Scottish regiments that came and went between 1689 and 1697 implies, however, that there was no shortage of sources for Scottish recruits, but one must remember that all regiments, perennially starved of recruits, took their soldiers when and where they could, conditions and preoccupations of nationality entirely notwithstanding. However, whereas many English regiments are recorded as having Huguenot officers, there are no French names in the lists of officers of the Scottish regiments of the period. This did not continue to be the case and the occasional French name does occur in Scottish regiments of the 1730s and '40s; there were certainly officers of Huguenot extraction serving in the army in Scotland after the 1745 rebellion but by that time the process of their assimilation would have been complete and no significance can be attached to the fact that they were serving in Scotland. Scottish regiments served under supreme commanders who had Huguenot roots and, indeed, the two commanders on either side at the Revolution of 1688 both had Huguenot roots: Louis de Duras, Earl of Feversham, commander-in-chief of James's army (and nephew of Turenne), and Frederic, Duke of Schomberg, who was killed at the battle of the Boyne in 1690 and who had guided William's hand in 1688. In earlier life Schomberg had served in the 1st company of the Gendarmerie in France. A comrade-in-arms of Marlborough, and commander in Spain between 1704 and 1708, was Henri de Massue, Marquis de Ravigny et de Raineval, better known after his success in the Irish campaign of 1690–91 as Viscount Galway; he had begun his military career – as had so many other senior Huguenot exiles – under Turenne.

As matters were coming to a head in early 1688, James attempted to recall six British regiments then serving in the pay of the Dutch in the Netherlands and applied to his son-in-law, William, for their return. Three of the regiments were English and three Scots and many of the officers were religious or political exiles who had no desire to return to Britain to serve King James. A great many of the Scots other ranks were drawn from Covenanters who had fled religious persecution in Scotland in the 1670s. There were, however, a number of officers, English, Scots, and Irish, who were loyal to James and who chose to return to Britain in early 1688. Almost all of them were Catholics, who had been reluctantly given commissions by William in order to placate his father-in-law a few years previously. Aware that William presented something of a threat to his position, James was also keen to break up the Anglo-Dutch Brigade in order to deprive his son-in-law of a nucleus of British professional soldiers among his potential invasion forces. Therefore, whereas James – ideally – would have liked all six regiments back he knew that it was unlikely that all would agree to return, even if William allowed them to do so; at best, he could hope that such defections as could be engineered would affect the Brigade's stability. William's wishes fitted in neatly with those of his father-in-law: he had no wish to retain potentially disloyal Catholic officers or men (though there were few of the latter) and was eager to replace the Catholic officers who resigned their commissions with Huguenots or Irish Protestant officers who were in the Netherlands in the hope of obtaining commissions. Each regiment in the Brigade consisted of about 500 men so, potentially, James could have expected to find himself with a further 3,000 soldiers on his payroll. Unfortunately, having prorogued a Parliament because of its complaints about his policies, he had few sources of money with which to provide that payroll. Accordingly, he turned to the later Stuarts' traditional banker, Louis XIV, and asked if Louis would be prepared, as a *quid pro quo* for James having both weakened the Dutch forces and strengthened the Catholic section of the British forces, to pay for the upkeep of the regiments which left the Anglo-Dutch Brigade. Louis agreed. More than 100 officers left the Anglo-Dutch Brigade and three new regiments of Foot were formed, all paid for – at least initially – by King Louis XIV; one was English, one Scots, and one Irish, in terms of the nationality of the majority of their officers.

The Scottish regiment, commanded by Colonel John Wachop (or Wauchope), was raised on 11 March 1688 and, on paper, comprised 44 officers – including the quartermaster and surgeon-major – and 530 other ranks. Almost all the officers had Scottish names but it appears likely that a considerable portion of the other ranks were either Irish or were from Irish regiments. Few other ranks had left the Anglo-Dutch Brigade (most who wished to leave had been actively prevented from doing so) and so, unable to weaken William's forces in the Netherlands by inducing mass desertions, James was forced to diminish his own in Ireland by taking ten men from each infantry company stationed there in order to try and get his (and Louis's) new regiments up to strength. The regiments seem not to have reached their intended strength by the Revolution and Louis ceased paying for them after July 1688. The regiment must have been placed upon the Scottish military establishment (each kingdom having its own separate army organisation supported by its own separate revenue) since it is noted as being among the Scots troops ordered to march south in September 1688 in order to bolster the English forces once William's intentions had become clear. Its strength was noted in November 1688 as being 927 men, garrisoning the area named Clerkenwell in London.

As James's army disintegrated from within, following widespread desertions and in the face of William's inexorable march eastward from his landing at Torbay, so much of the Scottish army remained confused about its role and the king's intentions. Once William's success had been sealed by James's flight to the continent, those officers and men of the Scottish regiments who had marched south to defend James had to decide whether to follow their king into exile, or accept William as king, or retreat to Scotland to consider the matter. The disintegration of the army was so complete that these options became personal rather than regimental and, in many cases, officers voted with their feet, leaving their soldiers to shift for themselves. Known Catholics and supporters of James were relieved of their commands and some regiments appear either to have been disbanded or sent *en masse* into exile. The former procedure was applied to the King's Own Royal Regiment of Scottish Horse, whose Colonel was John Graham of Claverhouse, Viscount Dundee, but the latter – for lack of accurate information – seems to have been applied to Wachop's regiment. The regiment is noted as remaining in the service of France until disbandment in 1697, although Wachop and several of his officers served King James during his Irish campaign of 1690-91. The Earl of Dumbarton, who had been colonel of The Royal Scots since 1655, was forced to resign and followed James into exile: the colonelcy of his regiment was given to the Duke of Schomberg. Partly as a result of this, and partly through both confusion and a residue of loyalty to King James, the first battalion of the regiment mutinied in early 1687 and prepared to march north to join the Jacobite forces of Dundee then preparing to rebel in Scotland. The battalion was stopped in Lincolnshire, the ringleaders arrested and the remainder immediately shipped to the Netherlands, where the war was about to be renewed.

William faced a tripartite threat to his position by the middle of 1689: in Scotland, in Ireland and in France. These three areas and the conflicts that they represented directly reflect the title of this chapter. Scotland and Ireland rose together in rebellion as war broke out afresh in the continent; and both events were to involve dispossessed soldiers on both sides, individuals who, for reasons dealt with above, were emigrants. The campaign in Ireland brought French troops into the field on the order of James against the forces of William. The first Jacobite rebellion in Scotland flared up and was over as quickly; even had any French support been forthcoming, it would have arrived too late to be of any use.

The two operations began almost simultaneously in the early spring of 1689, although it would be stretching credibility to believe that such a combined assault on the new government of Britain was planned to be simultaneous. Ireland presented, as it had always done and would continue to do, an ideal springboard for an invasion of mainland Britain. The majority of the army on the Irish establishment, which had been weeded of Protestants by James's Lord Deputy, the Duke of Tyrconnel, was loyal to James. Only the Ulster towns of Derry and Enniskillen had declared in favour of William. A force that could swiftly capture Ireland and disembark troops from Ulster to Scotland would not only assist, and secure the success of, the Jacobite elements in Scotland but also, eventually, be able to threaten England on two fronts, not counting that presented by France from across the Channel. Louis XIV, all too aware of the increased strength of his arch-enemy, William, as a result of his combining of the British and Dutch armies, assisted James with his assault upon Ireland. The assistance, however, characterised the help that France was to give the Jacobite cause over the following six decades – too little and too late.

James's entourage was transported to Kinsale on the south coast of Ireland by a French squadron, unimpeded by the Royal Navy, in March 1689. Among his suite were his illegitimate son, the Duke of Berwick, and the Comte d'Avaux, ambassador from Louis XIV. A week after landing, James reached Dublin and began to plan the assault on the northern strongholds of Derry and Enniskillen. Estimates of James's initial strength vary. A French contemporary source listed 16 regiments of cavalry (Horse and Dragoons) and 44 of infantry, a rough total of 35,000. The majority of these were already on the Irish establishment and so had not accompanied him from France. Several of James's regiments had returned to Ireland from England after his flight to France, one of which – McElligott's – was the Irish regiment formed from the Irish Catholic officers of the Anglo-Dutch Brigade. Tyrconnel, however, estimated the Jacobite forces prior to the battle of the Boyne at only 26 Battalions, five of which would have been French. There were a few initial successes before siege was laid to Derry but its resistance, and that of Enniskillen, slowed down the campaign to the extent that its nature changed and it became possible to send only one regiment to join Dundee's forces in rebellion in Scotland.

This regiment, Purcell's Dragoons, landed at Duart, on the island of Mull, on 12 July

An officer of the 1st company of the gendarmerie, 1724,
copied in 1936 by Percy White from an original by A. de
Marbot.

(NMS)

1689 and, by forced marches, reached Dundee's troops just in time to participate in the one victory of the campaign, at Killiecrankie on 27 July. The arrival of the vanguard of William's forces in Ireland the following day raised the siege of Derry and the Jacobite forces in Ireland were pushed on to the defensive. Viscount Dundee had been killed at Killiecrankie, in the hour of his victory, and his rejoicing forces had been hacked to a standstill at Dunkeld, further south, a day or two later. Aside from a little rounding up of the Scottish rebels, the campaign in Scotland was effectively over and so William was able to concentrate on Ireland.

The army of Marshal the Duke of Schomberg landed unopposed and established his position in August 1689. Schomberg's army was composed of British and Huguenot regiments and, when reviewed in quarters at Dundalk in October 1689, consisted of eight full regiments of Horse, two of Dragoons, and 22 battalions of Foot, together with a company of miners. Among the 22 battalions of Foot were three Huguenot infantry regiments. These were commanded by Colonel Isaac de Monceau de la Melonière (who had commanded *le régiment d'Anjou* before 1686), Colonel François du Cambon (who had been a French officer of engineers until 1685) and Colonel Pierre Massue, Comte de la Caillemotte (who was to be killed at the battle of the Boyne). The Huguenot infantry regiments had all been raised between March and June 1689 and with them at Dundalk camp was a Huguenot regiment of Horse (really the commander-in-chief's personal Life Guards) called The Duke of Schomberg's Regiment of French Horse, which had been raised in March 1689. Most of the men of the Huguenot regiments, and certainly almost all of the officers, had had experience of warfare in Flanders and knew how to cope with the more rudimentary necessities of camp life. Consequently, the Huguenot regiments survived the winter of 1689–90 better than did their hastily raised English and Irish comrades who were ravaged by epidemics of disease brought on by poor (or even non-existent) sanitation and drainage at the camp site. "Dundalk camp" became a phrase indicating just how inefficient and amateurish the British army was at that time by comparison with its seasoned allies.

The opening of hostilities in the spring of 1690 was accompanied by a change in the field commander of the Jacobite forces. Antonin-Nompar de Caumont, Comte (later Duc) de Lauzun was a Gascon who had fought under Turenne and who, since James's exile, had made the Stuart cause very much his own. With Lauzun came the five French infantry regiments of Biron, Bouilly, Tirlon, Chémerault and Zurlauben (the latter formed of Swiss soldiers). Louis had promised 7,000 soldiers but five regiments would only comprise half that number, unless they were two-battalion regiments, and so it may be that, again, Louis had sold the Jacobite cause short. William himself landed at Carrickfergus on 14 June 1690 and had been preceded by reinforcements of English, Dutch, Danish and Brandenburg soldiers – all contracted to serve against the Jacobites. William also had Finns and Swiss fighting for him and so the resultant clash of the two armies, stiffened by professionals but swelled by raw and untrained recruits, at the battle of the Boyne on 1 July 1690, was very much an international affair. As the tide of the battle turned William's way so the French regiments and James's Irish Footguards covered the retreat in a way which would be necessary again, at Culloden, 56 years later. James left Ireland about a week after the first battle and was followed in September by Lauzun and the French regiments. Part of the deal whereby Louis had lent five French regiments to James for the Irish campaign was that James would let Louis have an equivalent number of his loyal Irish regiments for the French service. The loss of Ireland by the Stuarts meant that, unlike the French regiments, the Irish could not return home and so they remained in the service of France, forming a sizeable and loyal cadre within the French Army. Their story must, however, be read elsewhere.

James never returned to Ireland, and the campaign of 1691 finally finished active Jacobitism in Ireland. It was characterised by a rapid mopping-up operation conducted by Marlborough and involving – among other regiments – The Earl of Leven's Scottish Borderers (anxious, no doubt, to wipe out their defeat at Killiecrankie). Louis XIV refused to commit more troops to a war that he rightly perceived as lost but he sent three more military commanders to assist Tyrconnel and the Duke of Berwick in staving off defeat for as long as possible, Lieutenant-General de St. Ruth and Major Generals d'Usson and the Chevalier de Tessé. St. Ruth commanded at the defeat of Aughrim in 1691, where he was killed.

As Scotland and Ireland were gradually pacified and prevented from being a threat to William's government so the flood of exiled Jacobites to France increased. Many of these exiles had actually fought for the Jacobite cause, either in Scotland or in Ireland, and some had been ruined by their adherence to the Stuarts. The armed forces of continental Europe were to benefit from these emigrés for the next six decades after 1690,

An officer of the 1st company of the King's Bodyguard,
c 1740. A painting by Eugène Leliepvre, c 1970.

(NMS)

and especially after the Jacobite rebellions of 1715 and 1745. France, because of its shelter for the exiled Stuart court and general sympathy for the cause, was the natural home for exiled Jacobites, but there was a limit, even in the huge army of Louis XIV, to the number of commissions available for exiled Scots. Unlike the professional Huguenot officers gladly employed by William, many of the Scots who sought military service under Louis did not have years of professional military training behind them. Many, too, suffered in their candidature for commissions by not being of sufficiently noble birth, a prerequisite in almost all cases for a French commission.

Father Forbes-Leith lists the names of 94 Scots, whom he describes as officers, who had served under Dundee in Scotland in 1689 and who had left after the end of the rebellion to serve James in France. James's financial position was precarious despite Louis's unfailing generosity and he could not keep a growing court of indigent former rebels, however much he might have liked to do so. For the first four or five years of his exile in France James apparently maintained a household of exiled Scottish officers who had either fought for him between 1689 and 1691 or left with him in 1688. While there was still a reasonable chance of his regaining the crown, having a core of military support close at hand was a reasonable idea, even if expensive, but after a putative Jacobite invasion fleet was defeated by the British Royal Navy off La Hogue in 1692 all immediate hopes of a successful invasion vanished.

A number of sources confirm Father Forbes-Leith's tale of the 150 Scots officers who resolved to enlist as privates in the French army rather than be a burden on their king after the battle of La Hogue but all are so infected with the romance of Jacobitism that it is difficult to separate fact from wishful thinking. Most of the 94 officers listed by Forbes-Leith have profoundly Scottish names; there are 47 lieutenants, 40 captains, four ensigns, two colonels and a major. The two colonels have the same names as two officers of the Scots Guards, both former lieutenants of the grenadier company, both promoted to captain on 28 February 1689 (two months after James's flight to France) and both out of the regiment before 1691: Robert Somerville and William Davidson (or Davison). The major, Charles Erskine, was captain-lieutenant (senior lieutenant) in Wachop's Regiment – the Scottish Catholic regiment formed by James from the Anglo-Dutch Brigade in 1688. By comparing the remainder of the names on the list with those which appear in Charles Dalton's *English Army Lists and Commission Registers, Vol. II (1685–89)* (1894), some similarities can be traced, allowing for the occurrence of common Scottish names. If both lists, as reprinted in the late nineteenth century, are accurate and if the individuals on both lists *are* the same men, and do not just have the same name, of the remaining 91 officers on Forbes-Leith's list, noted as being in exile in France in the early 1690s, 19 previously held commissions in the British army. Since the others do not appear, one must assume that the remaining 72 individuals possesed commissions granted to them either by Dundee in Scotland or by James in Ireland or France after his exile. Only one of the 19 traced is listed by Dalton as a known Jacobite, Colonel Hugh Sutherland of Sir John Fenwick's Regiment of Horse. Sutherland had fought for James as a colonel of Horse in Ireland and had been wounded at the Boyne; in the 1690s he had exchanged a colonel's commission for that of a lieutenant in France. Two other officers had served with Major Erskine in Wachop's Regiment: Captain John Sinclair, a lieutenant in Wachop's, and Lieutenant Robert Maxwell, an ensign in Wachop's. Eight of the remainder had held commissions in the 1st Regiment of Foot (Royal Scots): Captain David Arneele (ensign), Captain Colin Campbell (second lieutenant), Captain John Hamilton (ensign), Captain Isaac Thrycle (Thelkeld) (ensign), Captain Robert Arbuthnott (ensign), Lieutenant Thomas Ogilvie (captain), Captain William Cunningham (ensign) and Captain William Robinson (ensign). The remaining officers who appear to have held British commissions prior to their exile were divided between other regiments, four of them having served in Scottish regiments: Captain James Innes (cornet, Royal Regiment of Scots Dragoons – Scots Greys), Captain Patrick Grahame (ensign, Buchan's Regiment – Royal Scots Fusiliers), Lieutenant Patrick Ogilvy (Lieutenant, 3rd Foot Guards – Scots Guards) and Captain William Innes (Captain, 3rd Foot Guards). In most cases, as can be seen, promotion was rapidly achieved by defection, not an uncommon occurrence.

Forbes-Leith also says that extra strength was added to the officers whom he lists by the addition of companies of soldiers who had defected from the British army, either in 1688 in England or in 1689 in Flanders or Ireland. He gives the name of two officers but implies that both served in the 1st Regiment of Foot. Andrew Rutherford certainly did, being lieutenant and adjutant in the 2nd battalion until his promotion to captain on 31 December 1688. John Foster, however (if, again, it is the same man), is listed as an ensign in the 1st Regiment of Foot Guards (Grenadier Guards) in November 1687 and so some confusion may have resulted in Forbes-Leith's mind between the 1st Foot and the 1st Foot Guards.

Finally, James Grant, perhaps the most romantic (and therefore the least reliable) of sources, in *The Scottish Soldiers of Fortune* (1890), gives the name of the commanding officer of the newly-formed "Company of Scottish Officers" as Thomas Brown, those of his lieutenants as Andrew Scott and Alexander Gordon and that of the ensign as James Buchan. The most likely candidate for the Thomas Brown is he who served as a captain in Wachop's Regiment in 1688. Andrew Scott cannot be traced as having held a British commission prior to 1689. Alexander Gordon may be the same man who was listed as a lieutenant in the 1st Regiment of Foot in 1687. We are on firmer ground with James Buchan, who was the nephew of Colonel Thomas Buchan of Auchmacoy, Aberdeenshire, and the second colonel of the 21st Foot (Royal Scots Fusiliers). Both Buchans remained loyal to James, the elder fighting in Ireland in 1689 and commanding the Jacobite forces in Scotland in 1690 until they were finally routed at Cromdale. James Buchan was captain-lieutenant in the 21st in 1688 and clearly followed his uncle's allegiance, managing to succeed to Auchmacoy on his uncle's death in 1720.

It may be that the 94 officers listed by Forbes-Leith are the residue of those who returned from Spain after forming an infantry company for the service of Louis XIV in his campaign there in 1692. They also fought in Alsace in 1697 but were disbanded at the Treaty of Ryswick in that year.

Disbandment of one of Louis's Scottish corps, his only remaining ultra-Scottish one, may have been a condition of the Treaty of Ryswick since William was known occasionally for his vindictiveness, and a soldier out of a job, dispossessed of lands at home and an outlaw was a very hungry soldier indeed. One of the conditions was certainly that the Duke of Berwick, James's natural son, be dismissed from his post within the French army, that of *maréchal de camp* – roughly equivalent to that of brigadier. William was aware of the gradual decay of the Stuart fortunes and did all he could to exacerbate the process.

James VII and II and William III died within six months of each other in September 1701 and March 1702. The defeat of the Franco-Jacobite fleet at La Hogue in 1692 and the policy of insubtle coercion in Highland Scotland, of which the "massacre" of Glencoe in 1692 is the most well-known – and exaggerated – example, combined severely to reduce the Jacobite menace to William and Mary's government. Mary had died in 1694 and her younger sister, Anne, succeeded William in 1702. The question of successions not only triggered off the next outbreak of war between Britain and France, it also closely involved the rebirth of active Jacobitism. In 1701 Louis XIV had recognised James III, the legitimate heir born to James VII and II in 1688, as rightful king of Great Britain. He had promised not to do this in the Treaty of Ryswick, which he clearly regarded as a much-needed breathing space for France, and so, while committing this diplomatic blunder, guaranteed to give William an excuse for re-opening hostilities, Louis may have thought that the time was ripe for a renewal of the war. What is more likely is that Louis, who had always regarded William as an usurper of the crown of Great Britain and the Stuarts as the rightful kings of England and Scotland, made the gesture as part of a grand design in order to proclaim his position as the defender of hereditary succession. He had already, earlier in 1701, proclaimed the right of his grandson, Philip of Anjou – second son of the Dauphin – to succeed eventually to the French throne. Philip had become King Philip V of Spain in 1700 and so the prospect loomed of a France and Spain eventually united under one king. More immediately, however, the prospect was of France and Spain, and Spain's possessions in the Netherlands, poised to fall upon Britain and anyone else who disputed the Spanish succession. The Papacy and the duchies of Savoy and Modena had all joined Louis and Philip in recognising James III as king of Great Britain. In the last six months of his life, William swiftly engineered an alliance between Britain and the United Provinces of the Netherlands and Austria.

In committing Britain to war, William had entirely ignored the Scottish parliament and after his death, his sister-in-law, Anne, continued the policy of insult by neglect. Scotland, as well as providing 20 new regiments of Foot and four of Dragoons for the war concluded in 1697, had not done well out of the previous hostilities and perceived them and any extension of them as expensive, unwise and wholly English in character and design. The Scottish economy had suffered severely between 1689 and 1697: trade with France had been disrupted, merchant seamen were conscripted for the Royal Navy on a damaging scale and the same Royal Navy had entirely failed to prevent depradations by French privateers on the Scottish coast, preferring to confine their activities to the English Channel. Denied protection and heavily taxed, the members of Scotland's parliament were infuriated when, in 1702, war was declared on their behalf against France by the English Parliament and the Scots Privy Council. The resentment by the Scots Parliament of not being consulted about the war, about the succession to Queen Anne or about the Act of Union of 1707 was successively interpreted by the parliament and monarch in England as being proof of the constant existence of Jacobite plots in Scotland. This was piling ignorance upon arrogance since all the English government did in ignoring Scottish opinions, advice and desires was to create or fuel Jacobitism where there had been none, or very little, previously. In doing this, the English government strengthened the position of the exiled Jacobites in France since Louis, through his agents in Britain, was able to see that Scotland, becoming more and more frustrated and enraged at the high-handedness of the English, might well present an ideal site for a second front in his war. France's aid to the Jacobite cause was always based upon expediency, namely what was in it for France, and her commitment to the Jacobite cause after 1702 reflected the extent to which she perceived a good chance of success initially or assessed the value of the annoyance factor to Britain as being sufficiently worthwhile.

Aside from the short-lived 24 regiments raised in Scotland for the war of 1689–1697, all the Scottish regiments which survived into the twentieth century, yet which were raised during the seventeenth, participated in the war. In Flanders they would have encountered both the 1st Company of the Bodyguard of Louis XIV and the 1st Company of the Gendarmerie. At Neerwinden in July 1693 both the 21st (O'Farrell's) and 26th (Munro's) Foot (Royal Scots Fusiliers and Cameronians) were part of Ramsay's Brigade, which was finally forced to retreat in the face of renewed and powerful French cavalry attacks. William III remarked upon the steadiness under an artillery bombardment of Louis's Household troops, among which were the Scots Company of the Bodyguard who participated in the later rout of the British infantry. Because of the tendancy of French writers to use the adjective *anglais* when referring to all male inhabitants of Britain, it is difficult to know whether General Susane means "English" when he lists the troops which composed a cavalry regiment raised for the French service by James VII and II in 1691. The regiment, known as *le régiment de cavalerie du roi d'Angleterre* (the King of England's Cavalry – or Horse), is said by Susane to have been composed of emigré Englishmen. It fought at Neerwinden, being commanded from 1691 by an officer called Dominic Sheldon, and was incorporated into the French cavalry of the line in 1698, ranking 56th in the order of precedence. It almost certainly rapidly became Irish in character since its first, second and third colonels all had Irish Jacobite roots, but in 1733 command of the regiment passed to Charles Fitzjames, second Duke of Berwick (and grandson of James VII and II) and it was as *le régiment de cavalerie de Fitzjames* that it participated in the last Jacobite rebellion. The Berwick connection was manifest too in

A trooper and a trumpeter of the 1st company of the King's Bodyguard, 1745. A print from a painting by Colonel Marcel Dugué MacCarthy, c 1970.

(NMS)

a regiment of Irish infantry raised in 1698 and commanded by members of the Fitzjames family, the first Duke of Berwick commanding from 1698 until 1713 and again from 1716 until 1718. The regiment, not surprisingly, was known as *le régiment de Berwick* but, despite its name, was always predominantly Irish.

For the eleven years of the War of the Spanish Succession, the forces of Britain and her allies were constantly in action on the continent with those of France and her allies. The principal areas of conflict were in Flanders and the Iberian peninsula and these wars, which were dominated for the British by the genius of John Churchill, Duke of Marlborough, produced a British army wholly different from the hopeless wretches who had died so apathetically in the squalor of Dundalk Camp a decade previously. The dispersal of Scottish regiments through the eleven year war reflects not only its geographical spread but also the strategy that the British governments of the period had to adopt in keeping Scotland quiet while fighting in Flanders and Spain at the same time. Of the Scottish regiments which still exist, four fought in Flanders and each was present at the British victories of Blenheim, Ramillies, Oudenarde and Malplaquet. At Blenheim in 1704, some of them would have played their part in crushing (General Susane says *écrasée*) the 1st Company of the Gendarmerie and would have met the, presumably rebuilt, Company at Oudenarde and Malplaquet too. At this last battle, in 1709, which was a pyrrhic victory for the British with horrific slaughter on both sides, few, if any, of the Scots of the Royal Regiment of Scots Dragoons, of the Royal Regiment of Foot, of the 21st (de Lalo's) Fusiliers or of the 26th (Preston's) Regiment of Foot would have realised that the young man who styled himself their rightful monarch was among the forces opposing them. Father Forbes-Leith describes him, styling himself the Chevalier de St. George, marching at the head of the Scots Bodyguard but, despite the fact that he was slightly wounded at Malplaquet, this account may be a little exaggerated. Eileen Cassavetti, in the latest account of the relationship between the Stuarts and France, *The Lion and the Lilies* (1977), describes James as leading a "company of horse" at Malplaquet, himself bedecked with the riband of the Order of the Garter and presenting, presumably, a tempting target for a musketeer in consequence. What exactly happened will probably never be known but it is clear that James, like most of the Stuarts, did not lack for courage – even if it was occasionally combined with rashness. James's courage may, on this occasion, have been the result of frustration at the failure of his attempts to regain his throne, attempts which had looked so promising two years before he first put himself in such danger at the battle of Oudenarde in 1708.

If Louis XIV, by recognising James VIII and III as rightful king of Britain in 1701, had played directly into William's hands by giving him an excuse to re-open hostilities and at the same time proclaim Jacobitism a creed tainted by treasonous association with France, then the government of Queen Anne had given the Jacobites and their Scottish disciples a propaganda gift by forcing through the Act of Union in 1707. The concept of a total Union of England and Scotland was not a new one in 1707. As we have seen, James VI and I had desperately wanted to unify far more than just the crowns of the two nations in 1603 but had been rebuffed by successive English parliaments. William's governments had taken the matter more seriously and were working on the necessary legislation, without necessarily consulting the Scottish parliament, when William died in 1701. The opening years of Anne's reign were also spent in consideration of the issue, which was perceived in Westminster as a tidying-up measure intended finally to reduce the basis of Jacobitism in Scotland and, although it was not admitted, gradually to anglicise Scotland to the extent that she could be ignored while the Westminster parliament proceeded to more important matters, like pursuing the war against France.

The Union of 1707 is probably more unpopular in retrospect than it was at the time since only the more realistic of Scots were then able to envisage, and not accurately, just how cynically successive England-based parliaments would regard and treat Scotland. Among the surviving Jacobite elements in Scotland, the nuclei of which were individuals with personal ambitions thwarted by the Whig oligarchy in London and Edinburgh and not thought worth bribing by that oligarchy to accept the Union, the Union was unpopular and they took every opportunity to exploit and proclaim its unpopularity, even going to the extent of sending a mission comprised of some of their number to France to urge that the time was ripe for a rebellion if only France would support it. Preceding this had been several years of intrigue between certain Scottish lairds and the exiled Jacobite court at St. Germain-en-Laye, the latter being disinclined to credit the former's stories about a Scotland ready to rise at the first sign of a French fleet.

The eventual rebellion of 1708, so much ignored by most historians of the period because it barely happened and yet so well analysed by John Gibson in *Playing the Scottish Card* (1988), came about purely because of Marlborough's crushing and unexpected victories at Blenheim in 1704 and Ramillies in 1706. These convinced the French military establishment that a second front had to be opened urgently against Britain. The government in London was all too aware of the rumblings in Scotland apropos the discussions over the Act of Union and also aware, through its own agents, its torture of Jacobite agents and information provided by self-seeking Jacobites like Simon Fraser, Lord Lovat – who would lie about anything if it suited his purpose – that a rebellion was likely. Accordingly it maintained forces in Scotland strategically situated to confront the rebellion when it came and this was why, with the exception of a battalion sent to Spain in 1709, the Scots Guards and 25th (Maitland's) Regiment of Foot spent the whole of the war in garrisons in Scotland. The Scots Guards even had a company of Highland soldiers, dressed and equipped as Highlanders, for a time. These acted as local scouts in the garrisons in the Highlands and supplemented the local Independent Companies who possessed the advantage of knowing their localities but the disadvantage of being related to many of the individuals most likely to be rebels.

The political background, personal chicanery, lying, cheating, humbugging, derring-do and what would now be called "shuttle diplomacy" that preceded the eventual Jacobite attempt at rebellion in 1708 is best read in John Gibson's pages since we are concerned here with the military reality which transpired in 1708 after at least four years of deferred decisions, changed minds, squabbles, jealousies and broken promises. The Memorial to Louis XIV drawn up in May 1707 by the disaffected Jacobites specified that 30,000 Scots would be in arms to support James as soon as he landed. They asked for munitions to fight with, money to subsist on and majors, lieutenants and sergeants to strengthen and discipline the more glamorous ranks of colonels, lieutenant-colonels, captains and ensigns which, it is clear, were already being eagerly apportioned. Louis's agent, Colonel Nathaniel Hooke, an Irishman of proclaimed ancient French lineage, scuttled round Scotland collecting signatures from the minor nobility, chiefly those who had not profited from the Act of Union, and getting prevarications and verbal promises from the great magnates. Hooke returned to France and, in concert with sympathetic French ministers, drew up the shopping list. Between 20 and 40 frigates were needed to transport the invasion force. 5,000 men, preferably of the Irish regiments in the French service, a siege-train, mortars, powder and grenades, together with 600,000 livres for expenses, were all specified. A decision was awaited from Louis and as weeks ran into months, so the potential rebels in Scotland began to think better of their hasty decisions and Louis, apparently unable to understand how Scotland had let itself become involved in the Union if it hated the concept so much, refused to be rushed. The government in England employed a Captain Ogilvy, who had been one of the French king's Company of Scottish Officers, and who, by 1707, was in need of money, to travel north and assess the situation. Using his Jacobite credentials well, Ogilvy confirmed London's fears that an invasion and accompanying insurrection was confidently expected. In December, prompted by his mistress, who had been approached by Queen Mary, James's mother, Louis agreed to support the Jacobites and send a fleet.

Command was given to the Comte de Forbin, a Provençal with a Scottish ancestor called Forbes or so he was told, who had become something of a naval hero in command of squadrons of privateers preying on British and Dutch shipping and operating from Dunkirk. From the start Forbin was not sanguine about the chances of success but found no one, from Louis downwards, who would listen. The Duke of Berwick, a newly created Marshal of France, shared Forbin's doubts and, clearly hoping to lead the expedition, had suggested how its military success might be accomplished: by a landing near Glasgow and a rapid march on Stirling and Edinburgh. Berwick was to be disappointed and the fleet eventually arrived off the east, not the west, coast. The fleet left Dunkirk on 6 March 1708 and comprised a total of 28 ships: 21 frigates of between 20 and 30 guns each, two frigates converted to transports and five ships of the line mounting between 40 and 60 guns each. Six two-battalion French regiments were aboard, the *régiments d'Agenois, d'Auxerrois, de Béarn, de Beaufermé, de Boulonnais* and *de Luxembourg*. Information had reached London of the massing of the invasion force and a fleet was assembled in the Downs at short notice to seek and destory it.

The first ship to arrive in the Firth of Forth was the 44-gun frigate *Le Protée*, commanded by *Lieutenant de Fregate* Rambures, on 12 March. *Le Protée* had been almost

75

totally de-gunned in order to transport troops and munitions and two of her fellow de-gunned frigates had been damaged in a storm and been unable to sail with the rest of the fleet. Rambures had to wait for the remainder of the fleet until the following day, when it arrived off the mouth of the Forth, having travelled too far north and been forced to turn south. As the rendezvous was effected so a British squadron, under Admiral of the Blue Sir George Byng, arrived from the south. Byng's force was four times larger than Forbin's but the Frenchman neatly sidestepped the British attempt to bottle him up in the estuary and sailed north, with the Royal Navy in pursuit. A running battle developed and the 50-gun *Le Salisbury*, captured five years earlier from the Royal Navy, was surrounded and taken. The remainder of the French fleet, with cleaner hulls and trimmer lines, escaped but were prevented from landing, as Forbin proposed to the increasingly frustrated James, in the Moray Firth by a persistent and strong off-shore wind. By 28 March the French invasion fleet was back in Dunkirk and the enterprise abandoned.

Scotland was ill-prepared to defend herself against the French invasion and, had it taken place, the Jacobites who relied on French aid for their rebellion would have risen and rapidly controlled Scotland. This would have necessitated a massive withdrawal of troops from Flanders and, had that happened, the newly conquered Spanish Netherlands would have risen against their Dutch masters. Queen Anne's government was saved from a serious threat to its stability by a combination of circumstances. The French government, with – like all governments – a strong sense of precedent and a particularly French sense of realism, would remember the failure of the attempt of 1708 whenever Jacobite plots again demanded their involvement. In Scotland the Jacobites who had signed the Memorial to Louis ran for cover and a sudden spate of diplomatic illnesses among the greatest in the land contrived to render them unavailable for questioning. A few minor Stirlingshire lairds who had been over-eager in taking horse, cloak, pistols and sword for Edinburgh when news of the arrival of the French was brought were arrested but a convenient lack of evidence against them prevented their punishment.

One of the conditions of the Treaty of Utrecht in 1713 was that Louis should cease to succour James and his suite and so James had to leave and take refuge in Bar-le-Duc in Lorraine. Overt support for the Jacobite cause was officially repudiated; covert support would continue, whenever expedient. The Jacobite court was split between Queen Mary, who remained at St Germain-en-Laye and James, who remained under the protection of Duke Leopold of Lorraine.

The embargo placed by the Treaty of Utrecht on French help for the Jacobite cause was observed in 1715 when the next attempt was made to restore the Stuarts to the throne of their ancestors. Sparked off by a refusal of both Scottish and English Jacobites to accept the Elector George of Hanover as King George I of Britain, the rebellion again had great potential, at least in Scotland, but, again, was mismanaged and ended in failure for the Jacobites. James himself only arrived in Scotland once the affair was almost all over. It had been principally the work of one man, John the sixth Earl of Mar, who had been ousted from his position at court by the new king and, deeply snubbed, attempted to raise support in Scotland for a renewed Jacobite invasion. Lord Mar was the Scottish Jacobites' only commander and ill-suited to the task. Failing to capitalise on early successes in the raising of large numbers of Highlanders and the easy capture of the city of Perth, he was brought to battle at Sheriffmuir, outside Dunblane, in November 1715. The battle was inconclusive but Mar retreated afterwards and continued retreating until meeting James at Peterhead a few days before Christmas that year. James had failed to bring any supporting troops, gold given him by the king of Spain had been lost in a shipwreck and Mar's army had dwindled from 12,000 to a quarter of that number.

In readiness for a rebellion after the accession of George I, the Jacobites in France

Lord John Drummond, 4th titular Duke of Perth and 1st colonel of the Royal Ecossais *with whom he fought at the battle of Culloden, 1746. By de Troy.*

(Duke of Roxburghe)

Francois-Antoine, Baron d'Andlau, an exempt officer from the 1st company of the King's Bodyguard, c 1745.

(La Sabretache)

had obtained 12 ships, moored them at Le Havre and stocked them with 12 cannons and ammunition, 4,000 barrels of gunpowder, 12,000 muskets and 10,000 swords; 2,000 French soldiers were also placed in readiness to disembark. The death of Louis XIV in August 1715 meant that his covert support for the Jacobite cause ended. The regent for his four-year old grandson, Louis XV, the Duke of Orléans, was not a Jacobite supporter and acceded to the demands of the British ambassador that the ships be unloaded. To add weight to the demands, Sir George Byng, who had been cruising up and down outside Le Havre waiting for the ships to put to sea, sailed into the port once the news of Louis' death had reached him and and trained his guns on the ships during their unloading.

Deprived of French support and with the rebellion rapidly collapsing around him, James left Scotland and returned to France. He was greeted with the news that he was no longer welcome, the regent being determined to support George I, and that because the Duke of Lorraine was so dependent upon French help he could no longer stay in Bar-le-Duc. As the states of Europe closed their frontiers to him, James travelled to Avignon, a Papal territory, and threw himself on the Pope's mercy. As a last gesture of gratitude to his Scottish supporters, who had begun their rebellion with no prompting from him, James sent five ships to rescue as many of his Scottish subjects as wished to join him in Avignon. Eventually his entourage exceeded 500 exiled Jacobites, most of whom had ruined themselves by their adherence to the Stuart cause. An Anglo-French alliance ratified in 1717 specified that even Avignon should be closed to the Jacobites and so James and his court moved to Italy, arriving in Rome in May 1717. Stuart fortunes had not been so low for 65 years and the death of Queen Mary at St Germain in 1718 terminated the connection of that palace with the *grande dame* of the Jacobite cause.

The Jacobite rebellion of the following year was a half-hearted affair, principally

Prince Charles Edward Stuart, the Young Pretender; an engraving executed while the Prince was in Edinburgh in 1745 and later published in Paris.

(NMS)

engineered by the Duke of Liria in concert with Cardinal Alberoni of Spain. Liria, the eldest son of the Duke of Berwick, had accompanied James to Scotland in 1715 as Earl of Tynemouth but had been banished to Spain on his return, deprived of his status in the French army – which included the colonelcy of the *régiment de Berwick* he had held since 1713 – and had taken over his father's Spanish lands and titles. Neither the Duke nor James went with the invasion fleet, the promised Swedish soldiers never arrived, and the rebellion disintegrated after a few shivering Spanish soldiers and the usual crew of opportunist Highlanders were soundly and predictably beaten at Glen Shiel in June 1719.

Although the 1720s and '30s were years of peace between Britain and France, France remained engaged in continental trials of strength with her neighbours. Few details are available but General Susane lists the campaigns in which the 1st Company of the Gendarmerie were involved during these two decades and notes them as being present at Metz and Thionville in 1719, in the Franche-Comté in 1721 and in the army of the Rhine in 1733. It was during the latter campaign that the Duke of Berwick was killed, at the siege of Philipsbourg where he was decapitated by a cannonball at the age of 64. His son, the Duke of Liria and second Duke of Berwick, took the young Prince Charles Edward Stuart on campaign in Italy in the same year and this provided the sum total of the young prince's military training; armed with which knowledge he was to command in the field in Scotland ten years later.

Despite, or perhaps because of, the period of peace between Britain and France, active recruiting for the French service continued, as it had always done, in the Highlands of Scotland and, as long as no threat or treasonous intent resulted, the government's representatives in Edinburgh chose to ignore it. They themselves had been actively recruiting in the Highlands since 1725 in any case, and in 1739 the Independent

Companies which had policed the Highlands after a fashion since the late seventeeth century were regimented into the Earl of Crawford's Regiment of Foot in the Highlands. This was not the first Highland regiment, nor was it the first to be entirely dressed in a military version of the dress worn by the average Highland Scottish male. Its distinction rests in the fact that, unlike its predecessors, it was the first Highland regiment to survive until the present day. Despite its formal title, which reflected its status and the name of its colonel, it retained the nickname that had been used to denote the Independent Companies and differentiate them, in their dark tartan plaids, from the red coated British infantry who also garrisoned the Highlands: the Black Watch or, in the language that all of the original soldiers and officers of the regiment spoke (some to the exclusion of English) *Am Freiceadan Dubh*. The survival of the Black Watch, initially numbered 43rd among the British line infantry, led to their imitation and numerous other regiments of Highlanders were raised later in the century, until their appearance came to be identified in the minds of many with all Scottish soldiers. The approach of war in 1740 changed the status of the regiment from that of a local police force to that of a fully fledged infantry battalion and the outbreak of the War of the Austrian Succession in 1741 eventually took it across the Channel with its fellow British regiments.

Memories of the '15 and '19 rebellions had faded in Scotland in the passage of a quarter of a century and a new generation was increasingly looking to the exiled Jacobites for leadership in overturning the government of King George II, who had succeeded his father in 1727. War between France and Britain was not actually declared until March 1744 but the armies of both nations had faced each other on the battlefield, notably at Dettingen in 1743, as allies of the opposing forces. The formal resumption of hostilities after thirty years rekindled the concept of the Jacobite second front against Britain and Prince Charles Edward Stuart arrived in Paris to live incognito while the French government made up its mind whether to renew open support for the Stuart cause once more.

Tacit support had been forthcoming in August 1744 when leave was given to the exiled Jacobite Lord John Drummond, later fourth titular Duke of Perth, to raise a regiment for the service of France. The regiment, titled the *Royal Ecossais*, seems to have been principally composed of Scots recruited in the Highlands but is known also to have included other nationalities in its ranks. Jacobite recruiting parties were increasingly active in Scotland in 1744 and 1745, prior to the landing by the Young Pretender, and it was for the *Royal Ecossais* that Alasdair Ruadh MacDonald, younger of Glengarry, was recruiting when he was noticed by government spies in the Highlands in June 1745. Drummond led his regiment at the battle of Fontenoy in May 1745, a battle at which the 1st battalion of the Royal Regiment and the 25th (Lord Rothes's) Regiment were also present. Drummond's elder brother, the third titular Duke of Perth, was a prominent Jacobite and owned vast tracts of land in southern Perthshire, based upon the family seat of Drummond Castle, near Crieff. This area was not far from Aberfeldy, where the Black Watch had first been mustered as a regiment in 1740, nor that distant from Glengarry's lands further north. This geographical closeness, together with family and social ties, gives credence to the story related of a meeting, and a dram or two, on the night before Fontenoy between Lord John Drummond, Colonel of the *Royal Ecossais*, one of his officers John Roy Stewart, and several officers of the Black Watch, one of whom is named as Lieutenant Lewis Grant of Auchterblair. Stewart had, himself, been an officer in the Royal Regiment of Scots Dragoons (Scots Greys) but had resigned from the army after failing to transfer to the Black Watch. His service in the *Royal Ecossais* was brief; he raised and led a regiment recruited in Edinburgh during the 1745 rebellion and was present at the battle of Culloden in 1746. The conviviality of the night before Fontenoy

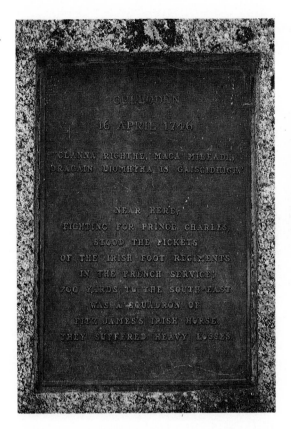

A model of the French light frigate Du Teillay *which delivered Prince Charles Edward Stuart to Scotland in 1745. Displayed at the National Trust for Scotland's visitor centre, Glenfinnan.*

(Author)

The memorial plaque on the stone which marks the centre of the Irish picquets' position on the battlefield of Culloden.

(Mrs J. Smith)

did not stop the Black Watch from fighting like demons the following day and one of their number, Private John Campbell, killed nine French soldiers with his broadsword before being incapacitated by a round-shot in the act of dispatching another. Notwithstanding the French victory at Fontenoy, or perhaps because of it, a French pamphlet published in Paris two weeks after the battle described the Highlanders' assault as being: "with more violence than ever sea did when driven by a tempest".

It was to be the turn of British troops in Scotland to experience the violence of the Highland charge on occasions over the next eleven months after Fontenoy. In the spring of 1745 Louis XV had finally decided to support a further Jacobite attempt upon Britain and the news had been entrusted to two Jacobite envoys, one of whom was Sir Hector Maclean, lieutenant-colonel of the *Royal Ecossais*, who took it to Scotland in March of that year. In July Prince Charles Edward left France aboard the French frigate *Du Teillay* with 12 companions and, proceeding via the Hebridean island of Eriskay, arrived at Glenfinnan to raise his father's Standard on 19 August. He had, he said to Alexander MacDonald of Boisdale - who met him on Eriskay and advised him to go home, come home.

Much of the rest is history so well-known as not to require repetition but there are one or two matters which are relevant to the subject of this narrative. As Bruce Lenman so assiduously points out, in his seminal treatment of the Jacobite rebellions, *The Jacobite Risings in Britain 1689–1746* (1980) Charles Edward came to Scotland by way of his French contacts, those Franco-Scots who still believed in the viability of rebellion and those Scots who maintained contacts in France and had little actual connection with the realities of the position in the Highlands. Charles Edward's efforts would come to nothing, though, without French gold and French arms and these, despite the Treaty of Fontainebleau signed at the end of October 1745 and representing the last Franco-Scots military alliance, were a long time in arriving and inadequate when they arrived. Had not Cameron of Lochiel arrived at Glenfinnan when he did, with 700 clansmen armed to the teeth, then even the prince might have changed his mind and gone back to France. The initial success of the rebellion was, it may be suggested, exactly as successful as those of 1708 and 1715 might have been had they been properly directed. The British government was widely unpopular in Scotland and the state of the country's defences deplorable. Fortunately, Charles Edward had military commanders, Lord George Murray in particular, who would amply capitalise on these factors, especially upon the latter. Nothing succeeds like success and the rebellion was carried along under its own momentum until it over-extended itself in England and allowed the forces of the government to regroup against it. Even then, powerful French naval support or an invasion of several crack battalions of French infantry could have tipped the balance in the prince's direction. Neither type of aid was forthcoming.

The French forces which came to the prince's aid came in two waves. The first, which landed at Montrose on 25 November 1745, was composed of detachments from the *Royal Ecossais* and from the French Irish regiments, those of Berwick, Bulkeley, Clare, Dillon, Lally and Ross; a total of about 800 men. By the time that they landed, the prince's forces were strung out between Carlisle and Penrith on their way south. The French detachment under the overall command of Lord John Drummond, colonel of the *Royal Ecossais*, marched to Perth where it recruited while Charles Edward's army continued into England as far as Derby. The Irish detachment, called the Irish piquets, was under the command of Brigadier Walter Stapleton, lieutenant-colonel of *le régiment de Berwick* and the *Royal Ecossais* were commanded by Lord Lewis Drummond as lieutenant-colonel. The arrival of this detachment, together with letters from Lord John Drummond to the prince, were contributory factors in making the Jacobite army retreat: they believed that all French help was likely to arrive in Scotland rather than in England and that the northern kingdom was, therefore, the place to regroup. Both sections of the first wave fought at the battle of Falkirk on 17 January 1746. During the retreat towards Culloden the *Royal Ecossais* took the coastal route via Aberdeen and Lord John Drummond, charged with the defence of the Spey valley, set up headquarters at Gordon Castle at Fochabers. The Irish piquets laid siege to Fort Augustus, which fell on 5 March 1746, before marching to Culloden.

The second wave of French support troops landed on 22 February 1746 at Aberdeen. The ship that docked on that day was one of three that had sailed from France on 10 February: two privateers, *Le Bourbon* and *Le Charité*, and a brigantine, *La Sophie*. The *Sophie* landed one squadron, about 70–75 men, of Fitzjames's Horse but the other three squadrons and more detachments from the Irish regiments of Berwick, Bulkeley and Clare, about 360 men in all, had been captured when the *Bourbon* and the *Charité* were taken by HMS *Hastings*, commanded by Commodore Knowles, on the previous day. The capture of the two privateers, temporarily fitted out as transports, not only sent the Comte de Fitzjames, colonel of the regiment, into captivity with three-quarters of his regiment, it also deprived the one squadron that got ashore of its horses, all of which were on the two privateers. In order to mount the squadron of Fitzjames's, the troop of Horse that had been raised by William, fourth Earl of Kilmarnock, was ordered to be dismounted and to serve as infantry.

None of the French regiments was actively involved in the fighting at the battle of Culloden. Fitzjames's Horse were placed on the right wing of the second line of the

Jacobite army and after the battle, as the prince retired from the scene, he was escorted by a troop of Fitzjames's for some way from the scene. As French subjects they surrendered to the government forces in Inverness, were made prisoners-of-war and eventually repatriated. The *Royal Ecossais* were on the left centre of the second line, to the left of the Duke of Perth's regiment of Highlanders; the Irish piquets were on the left of the *Royal Ecossais* and thus on the extreme left of the second line of the Jacobite army. Brigadier Stapleton commanded the second line of the army and Lord John Drummond the centre of the front line. Both detachments were treated as prisoners-of-war after the battle; one account estimates the number of foreign prisoners-of-war at 222.

For an account of the battle, together with its prelude and aftermath, one can do no better than to recommend the classic yet human treatment given by John Prebble in *Culloden* (1961). The *Royal Ecossais* and Irish piquets came into their own at the end of the battle, as the Highlanders broke and fled and were pursued by the government Horse. The French professional soldiers used to a governed retreat from a conventional battle, stood calmly, fired volleys that kept most of the Horse at a respectful distance and retreated by ranks until most of the Highlanders who could still run had left the field. Only then did Stapleton, terribly wounded, ask for and receive quarter for himself and his men. These professional soldiers, the servants of the king of France and not, therefore, whatever their nationality, in treasonable arms against the king of Britain, were the only ones in the rebel army to whom quarter applied. Most Jacobites who could be caught, and were not deemed important enough to be kept for ritual execution, were killed where they stood, lay or crouched.

Among the French prisoners-of-war were the Marquis d'Eguilles, ambassador to the Jacobites and in the uniform of a captain of the Marine Regiment, Charles William Douglas, captain in the Paris Militia, M. du Saussai, described as a French engineer, and two officers of artillery, M. d'Andriou and M. Charles Bodin. Six officers from the *régiment de Berwick*, three from the *régiment de Bulkeley*, eight from the *régiment de Dillon*, three from the *régiment de Ross* and six from the *régiment de Lally* were made prisoners and were accompanied by eight officers from the *Royal Ecossais*, including the lieutenant-colonel, Lord Lewis Drummond. Seven officers from Fitzjames's surrendered, as did three of the prince's French staff and liaison officers.

The prince's escape, after five months of pursuit and hiding in the mountains, caves, glens and islands of the north-west of Scotland, was made in October 1746. Several others had preceded him, among whom was Cameron of Locheil who had been among the first to welcome him to Scotland, who had been shot through the ankles at Culloden and who was to be given a French regiment as a reward for his loyalty. Less generously rewarded, after all the trouble that he took to hide the prince and move him around the Highlands and, especially, the islands after Culloden, was Neil MacEachen. MacEachen put himself outside the law as a result of his help for Charles Edward Stuart and took risks in concealing the prince that are best read in full in *A MacDonald for the Prince* by Alasdair Maclean (1982). MacEachen, son of a minor landowner from Howbeg on the island of South Uist, emigrated to France in the wake of his royal master and eventually became the father of one of Napoleon's favourite Marshals, Marchal MacDonald, Duke of Taranto. The exploits of this later MacDonald belong to a period of history in which there was little friendship between Scotland and France, an interruption to their long amity which made them temporary enemies.

Chapter Four

Temporary Enemies 1746–1815

David, Lord Ogilvy by Allan Ramsay 1745. Lord Ogilvy led his clan regiment at Culloden and escaped to France afterwards to become colonel of le régiment d'Ogilvie *in the French service.*

(Scottish private collection)

Donald Cameron, 19th of Lochiel, known as Gentle Lochiel, who led his clan throughout the '45 rebellion and escaped to France after being wounded at the battle of Culloden. He became colonel of le régiment d'Albanie *in the French service and died in France, being buried at Sancerre.*

(Sir Donald Cameron of Lochiel KT)

FOR 70 YEARS AFTER CULLODEN BRITAIN AND FRANCE WERE IN A FAIRLY CONSTANT state of war, both hot and cold, and each side took every opportunity to score points off the other, even when not at each others' throats militarily. Although the victory of the government forces at the battle of Culloden and the cultural genocide which followed effectively terminated the threat of Jacobitism, this termination was recognised by the French government long before the British government. Scotland assumed the status of an occupied nation for at least a decade after Culloden and Jacobite panics and rumours of further invasions were commonplace. The war for Empire known to European historians as the Seven Years War, and – in reality – the first genuinely global war, changed Britain's position in the world and had wide-ranging effects upon Scotland, which affected France as much as they did Britain.

Retribution for giving the British government a considerable fright in 1745 and 1746 was swift, savage, indiscriminate and meticulous in its cruelty. Much has been made after the event by romantic apologists for the Jacobite cause and it is no part of this

A wooden model of a British man-of-war, made by French prisoners in Edinburgh Castle in 1760 for the Duke of Atholl.

(The Duke of Atholl; NMS)

narrative either to take sides in an emotive argument or to attempt to referee it. The pacification of the Highlands, the ritual execution of those Jacobites deemed important enough or sufficiently implicated in the rebellion to be worth making an example of, the transportation of the others: all these punishments, individual as well as general, reflected not only the immense gulf that existed between the government in London and sections of Scottish society but also the cheapness in which life was still held in the mid-eighteenth century. The great magnates in Highland Scotland had been exercising judicial retribution over their subjects for centuries and had not thought twice about the odd pogrom when it was deemed expedient. The savagery of medieval feudal society lingered in north-west Scotland long after it had died out in regions further south and east, but a society that could still happily approve public executions, judicial butchery of the executed and a host of other everyday horrors could not be termed, using modern criteria, civilised.

The government in London, in sanctioning the genocide in post-Culloden Scotland and lauding the battle's victor as the Conquering Hero, regarded Highland Scotland with distrust, horror, distaste and disdain. It is worth considering the retribution that was meted out a century later in India following its mutiny and attempting to decide whether much development in the humanity of government had transpired in the intervening years. The population of Highland Scotland expected nothing less than carefully organised and calculated brutality following the defeat of Culloden; the lower orders of society had known little else and life would not have changed for them whoever had won at Culloden. British troops had policed Highland Scotland since after the English Civil Wars of the mid-seventeenth century. The barracks, garrisons, forts and battalions of clod-hopping redcoats with their scouts from the Highland Independent Companies were a regular sight and the local population had long since come to terms with the cultural gulf that separated them from the soldiers. The initial success of the '45 rebellion also contributed, in the long term, to the extent of its aftermath since, as its momentum swept it along, so more and more people became implicated by it and so, when it ultimately failed, there were more on the government's blacklist than after previous rebellions which had had nothing like the actual success of that of the '45, leaving aside their potential success. As a result, there were more people running for cover after the '45 and less people with valid or believable excuses. This explains not only the numbers of the Jacobite refugees who arrived on the continent, and their social status, but also why the government could sanction such indiscriminate retribution. Everyone was likely to be guilty who remained behind and if their native tongue made them incomprehensible this was little short of dumb insolence and tantamount to implication in rebellion. Lacking, for the most part, the wherewithal to escape, those who had always been on the receiving end of retribution – just or unjust – continued to occupy their traditional position. Those who fled were, in some senses, the lucky ones: lucky to be able to, lucky to survive, lucky indeed if they managed to subsist in exile.

Fortunately, the king of France was still at war with Britain and needed soldiers. As we have noted, recruiting for the French service in Highland Scotland had gone on uninterrupted by periods of peace or war since the seventeenth century and earlier; when a state of war existed between France and Britain it was just a little more clandestine and subtle. France's wars in Europe used up men in the mincing machine of Flanders at a horrifying rate, far more dying from disease and untreated wounds than in action.

The Highland Scots recruited either by French agents or by their masters before the '45 rebellion would chiefly have gone into one of the French Irish regiments, which also recruited fairly steadily from Ireland. A common, or relatively common, language between the Irish soldiers and the Highland Scots would have made inter-regimental communication easy and all the officers, Irish or Highland Scots, would have spoken Gaelic. The reason that the French service appealed to the Irish and the Highland Scots was principally bound up with religion. After the accession of William III no Catholic could be granted a commission in the British army and, in theory, Catholics were not allowed in the ranks either. The growing number of landed families who were attainted after each Jacobite rebellion meant that there was never a shortage of Highland Scots officers available for service in the French army. Virtually all would either be Catholic or prepared to convert and a great many, especially those higher up the social scale, would either have spent some time in France as part of their education or speak French sufficiently well to get by. Attainted or not, it was felt by most of the great families in Scotland that to have a member of the family in exile in France, either as a soldier or as a member of the Jacobite court or both, was a kind of insurance policy against a successful French invasion or Jacobite rebellion. Those were uncertain times and the magnates of Scotland, especially in Highland Scotland, had not achieved their power and status by committing themselves immutably to causes, but by assiduous fence-sitting and by dispersal of resources so that every eventuality was covered. Accordingly, wholly committed adherence to the Jacobite cause was indulged in only by the more ambitious, by those who had little to lose and much to gain and by the odd individual – such as the Duke of Perth or Cameron of Lochiel – whose unswerving loyalty to the Stuarts overran their normal good sense, at least in Lochiel's case. Thus, when the Earl of Airlie and Lord Lovat stayed at home during the '45 and sent their eldest sons to lead their clan regiments at Culloden they were carefully keeping a foot in both camps. Their sons, David, Lord Ogilvy, and Simon, Master of Lovat, both eventually became lieutenant-generals, Ogilvy in the French army and Lovat in the British.

As we have seen, the resumption of active hostilities between Britain and France in 1744 had enabled the French to legitimise, as it were, their recruiting in Scotland by the establishment of the *Royal Ecossais*. Lord John Drummond, the regiment's colonel, became fourth titular Duke of Perth following his brother's death after Culloden and ceded the colonelcy of the regiment to his kinsman, Lewis, Earl of Melfort in November

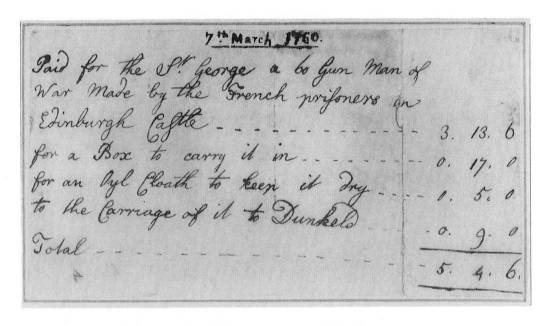

The invoice for the wooden model ship made by French
prisoners in Edinburgh Castle for the Duke of Atholl.
(The Duke of Atholl; NMS)

1747. In February 1747 two other Scottish regiments were raised in the French army. Both were said to have been largely formed from the debris of units that had fought at Culloden and managed to escape.

David, Lord Ogilvy, had brought his clan regiment largely intact away from Culloden and marched them south to Ruthven in Badenoch, where the order for disbandment was given. Ogilvy himself escaped to France via Norway, along with 12 others, six of whom had been officers in his regiment. Among the escapees was Henry Patullo, described as a Dundee merchant, who did not serve in Ogilvy's clan regiment but had been an enthusiastic Jacobite and had been appointed Muster-master of the Jacobite army. Patullo benefited, as did many other Jacobite exiles who had ruined themselves in the Stuart cause, from the *largesse* of Louis XV, receiving a gratuity of 4,000 *livres*. His later whereabouts are unknown unfortunately, but he may possibly have sought his kinsmen descended from the earlier Patullo who had made such a name for himself in Gascony three centuries earlier. Ogilvy also benefited from Louis' generosity and was commissioned to raise one of the two new regiments for the French service, *le régiment d'Ogilvie*. Consisting of 12 companies, it was principally officered by exiled Jacobite Scots who thus gained a salary; the extent to which the ranks were filled by Scots is unknown.

One of the officers of Ogilvy's French regiment was Neil MacEachen, the man from South Uist who had aided in engineering the Prince's escape from Scotland. MacEachen, who Alasdair Maclean suggests may well have been a soldier in the service of France prior to the '45 – either in the *Royal Ecossais* or, more likely, in one of the Irish regiments – had changed his name to MacDonald shortly after taking up permanent residence in France. The MacEachens of South Uist claimed to be descended, in any case, from the MacDonalds of Clanranald – although Alasdair Maclean makes a strong case for their descent from a sixteenth century Maclean – and so Neil MacEachen, finding that the French could not pronounce his surname and that the prince had a pro-MacDonald prejudice, had two good reasons for a change of indentity. A third may perhaps have

GARDE DU CORPS, 1750
PREMIÈRE COMPANIE (ÉCOSSAISE)

A drawing by Percy White, c 1936, of a trooper of the 1st company of the King's Bodyguard, c 1750.
(Christopher Allen Esq; NMS)

been that by adopting the relative anonymity of the MacDonald name he protected his kinsmen at Howbeg on South Uist from government reprisals. MacEachen's testimony of service, preserved in the archives of the *Service Historique de L'Armée de Terre* at the Château of Vincennes notes him as being first commissioned (or, in view of his possible earlier military service, re-commissioned) in *le régiment d'Albanie* on 23 December 1747. Albany's regiment was the other of the two new Scots regiments in the French army and it was raised, as was *le régiment d'Ogilvie*, on 28 February 1747.

Opinions differ about aspects of Albany's regiment. According to General Susane in his *Historie de l'Infanterie* (1876), it was raised by the *"comte d'Albany"*. This title, used by Prince Charles Edward Stuart in France as one of his aliases, tends to indicate that the regiment was raised by the prince. The Colour of the regiment bore the Royal Arms of Scotland encircled by what may have been intended to be the collar of the Order of the Thistle. Surmounting the shield, above the helm, was the royal crest of England, rather than that of Scotland and so the artist who painted the silk may have been badly briefed. That notwithstanding, the use of the Royal Arms tends to confirm the suggestion that it was the prince who raised the regiment. According to Father Forbes-Leith, the lieutenant-colonelcy, or perhaps the colonelcy, of the regiment rapidly passed to Donald Cameron of Lochiel, 19th chief of the clan, who had led his clan at Culloden and been severely wounded. Lochiel died in 1748, still in France, and the colonelcy may have passed to his son John – 20th of Lochiel – who was a captain in the regiment. According to General Susane the regiment was amalgamated into the *Royal Ecossais* on 1 March 1748 but Alasdair Maclean quotes from MacEachen's testimony of service to the effect that the *régiment d'Albanie* was incorporated into the *régiment d'Ogilvie* in 1749; certainly MacEachen transferred, as a lieutenant, from one to the other in that year. The date of 1748 may itself be significant concerning the position of Prince Charles Edward Stuart, since the Treaty of Aix-la-Chapelle which was ratified that year and which ended the War of the Austrian Succession specified that he should be expelled from France.

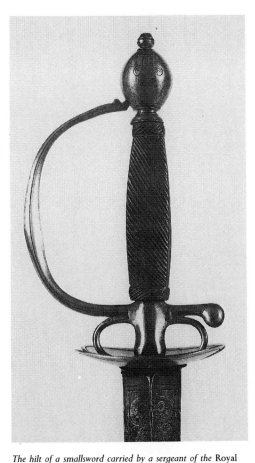

The hilt of a smallsword carried by a sergeant of the Royal
Ecossais, *c 1760.*

(Musée de l'Armée, Paris)

The head of a partisan carried by a gentleman of the
Gardes de la Manche.

(Musée de l'Armée, Paris)

He finally left, under considerable protest and only after having been arrested at the
Opera, in December 1748. The death of Lochiel in October and the prince's enforced
exit in December, together with the undoubted association of the regiment with the
Stuarts, may all have contributed significantly to its disappearance in 1748-49.

The remaining two Scottish infantry regiments lasted for a further 13 years in the
French army, until 21 December 1762 when Ogilvy's was incorporated into the Irish
regiment of Clare and the *Royal Ecossais* into that of Bulkeley. This incorporation, by
no means unusual at the end of a long and expensive war, would inevitably have led
to redundancies among the officers in the two Scottish regiments. Certainly, Neil
MacEachen was out of a job and trying to survive on a retired lieutenant's pension of
400 *livres* per year. In petitioning the Stuart court for a gratuity he sought the support
of his former colonel, who had succeeded his father as Earl of Airlie in 1761, and
managed to squeeze a present of 300 *livres* out of the Old Pretender. The following year
he apparently tried again, writing from Sedan, to which he had moved from St. Omer
where he had found a wife, and it was in Sedan on 17 November 1765 that his son
Jacques Etienne Joseph Alexandre MacDonald was born. The family soon moved to
Sancerre, where a considerable colony of Jacobite exiles had been established, and it

A gentleman of the Gardes de la Manche, *mid-eighteenth century. The court uniform of the corps remained largely unchanged throughout the century.*

(Musée de l'Armée, Paris)

was there that the future Marshal MacDonald spent his childhood and where, in 1788, Neil MacEachen died.

Recruiting for the French army continued in Scotland between the Treaty of Aix-la-Chapelle in 1748 and the resumption of war in 1756. As early as an unspecified date in 1746 punishments were being handed out to individuals trying to seduce recruits from Scotland, as Campbell-Maclachlan quotes in his *William Augustus, Duke of Cumberland* (1876):

> By order of H.R.H. Elizabeth Williams convicted of endeavouring to inveigle men to the French service, is to be put into a cart sitting backwards, so that she may see the punishment inflicted upon Peter McConachy who is to be tyd to the said Cart, stripd to his waste, with a Label tyd about his neck, specifieing his crime, & to be whipd for spreading false intelligence by the youngest drum of each Regt. from the South end quite thro' the Town of Strathbogie till over the Bridge beyond the Castle, when the Serjt. who conducts them is to dismiss them, & acquaint them tht. if they are ever seen among his Majesty's Troops, it is H.R.H. pleasure that they be hanged immediately without a Court Martial.

Four sword-hilts in the Highland basket-hilt style, but with French blades. Left to right: a horseman's sword, c 1740–50, at one time in the Gordon Castle armoury; a sword with a cheaply made hilt and French cavalry-style blade of c 1730; a French-made sword in the Scottish manner but with a cavalry-style blade, c 1760; a cheaply-made French sword in imitation of the Scottish fashion, c 1770.

(Marischal College, Aberdeen)

The occupied status of Scotland in the late 1740s and into the following decade, despite Britain being nominally at peace with France, meant that the occupying forces were constantly on the lookout for French agents, Jacobite spies or any combination of the two. As reports reaching the Commander-in-Chief, North Britain, indicate, French recruiting agents – who were, as they always had been, exiled Scots returning temporarily with bags of French gold – were as much of an obsession with his agents as were imagined bands of Jacobite partisans skulking in the impenetrable mountain glens and caves. The Commander-in-Chief, writing to the Secretary at War on 14 July 1753 provided the information that:

> four Highlanders in the French service are lately arrived in the Highlands from France. None of them are of any consequence except Clan Ranald's Brother. However I have given orders to the troops who are in those parts to be at all pains to lay hold of them.

Three days later one of his Adcs wrote, giving those orders, to one of the garrison commanders in the Highlands thus:

> The General has received Intelligence that Donald McDonald Brother to McDonald of Clanranald with another McDonald, a Cameron and a McKenzie all officers in the French King's service, are lately arrived in the Highlands from Abroad with an Intention as is said to (illegible) men for that service, that the first mentioned two are gone into the Island of Uist and that the latter is gone to Strath Glass.

The network of secret agents, of intelligence and counter-intelligence, which the government forces that were trying to keep Scotland quiet, loyal and free of Frenchmen or their agents were forced to employ, together with all the skulduggery and air of mystery that was so clearly both enjoyed and taken seriously by at least one Adc to the Commander-in-Chief, North Britain, is revealed in the following extract of a letter from an Adc to a Colonel Montague in 1752. This extract is, as are the previous two, from the letter books of Lieutenant-General George Churchill, preserved in the National Library of Scotland.

> Sir,
> The General has received information that one ... was a Serjeant in Hacket's Regiment in the Dutch Service (from whence he deserted and join'd Ogilvy's Regt. in France) is now enlisting men for the service of the French King in some place along the coast in Aberdeen – or Banff-shires. Enclosed are seals upon two half-cards, that mark'd Banff you'll be pleased to transmitt to the officer commanding there, the other halfs with the seals are in the hands of a friend, whose fidelity you may rely on. He will at a proper time apply to you, or to the officer at Banff, and upon his producing the other half of the card, in the persons custody to whom he makes the application, the most proper & speedy methods are to be taken for seizing the person of the said ... as well as any recruits he may have with him, taking care that they are not allowed to converse with each other after they are apprehended. Should ... be taken without recruits, no other crime is to be alledged against him than that of his desertion from Hacket's till the General is acquainted; and if with recruits the true reason is not to be assign'd unless you are oblig'd to it, by the interposition of his or their friends. The General is told there are others recruiting for the French service in the above counties, of whom the bearer of the half cards will acquaint you, and through whose means 'tis hoped you will be able to detect some of them.
>
> The General desires you will particular care that the person who will give you the information is at no time discover'd.

As has been already recorded, recruiting for the French service in the Highlands almost certainly continued, but to a gradually decreasing extent, until 1789. It would have received its most serious setbacks during the Seven Years War of 1756–63 and the American War of Independence of 1775–83, not necessarily because of the wars themselves, but rather because of the effects that those wars had upon Highland Scotland and its male population.

The Seven Years War really began, not in Europe in 1756, but in America in 1754. By then, it had become apparent that the French in North America had regarded the Peace of Aix-la-Chapelle of 1748 as no more than a truce and were busy consolidating and expanding their position in Nova Scotia and Newfoundland, which they called Acadia. The position of the Indians – principally represented by the tribes of the Six Nations whose lands occupied the area south of the Great Lakes – was ambivalent and that of the British settlers in what is now the north-eastern United States decidedly threatened, as much by their own pusillanimity as by the French and Indian threat. In 1755, aware of the likelihood of war in America, in India and in Europe, the British government had commissioned a survey of the population of Highland Scotland, in order to ascertain its fighting potential. Two years earlier, the last senior Jacobite had been captured and executed. Dr Archibald Cameron, brother to the Lochiel who had briefly been colonel of the *régiment d'Albanie*, was taken in the Highlands – to which he had briefly returned from France – while, it was believed in Westminster, attempting to assess the degree of support for another Jacobite rebellion. Cameron's arrest, and the proximity of the three-front war, convinced the government not only that a fourth front – in Highland Scotland – had to be avoided if the war was to be won but also that, perhaps, the potential fourth front might be turned against at least one of the other three. The idea was not a new one although its extent, when put into practice, was far greater than anything which had already been attempted in America. Highlanders, male and

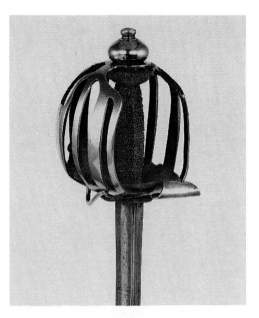

*A brass-hilted French heavy cavalry sword with a hilt of
basket form, possibly derived from Scottish hilts but not
markedly different to those carried by other European heavy
cavalry units, c 1760.*

(NMS)

*A cheaply made French sword in imitation of the Scottish
style, its hilt pre-fashioned from iron and brass flats, and
with a poor quality blade, c 1770*

(NMS; Kenneth Snodgrass Esq)

female, in enforced and voluntary exile, had been crossing the Atlantic since the 1650s.
Early in the 1740s Governor James Oglethorpe of Georgia had largely established his
infant colony with their assistance. With Oglethorpe's former Jacobite credentials and
later Hanoverian ones, he possessed exactly the right lack of scruple and evidence of
personal ambition to achieve what was wanted with the most available settlers on earth.

The reasons behind the raising of the two Highland regiments that were to fight in
America during the Seven Years War are too complex, and not sufficiently relevant to
this narrative, to be related here. They can be read in the most illuminating and enjoyable
detail in the penultimate chapter of Bruce Lenman's *The Jacobite Clans of the Great Glen
1650–1784* (1984), a book which, for many reasons, cannot be too highly recommended.
Of relevance, however, is the point that Lenman makes about what has been identified
as a palpable resentment against the French among those Jacobites who remained in
Scotland after the '45. There was, it seems, a powerful body of influential opinion which
ascribed the failure of the '45 – and probably that of the '08 and the '15 – to the lack
of committed French support. Apparently, one of the reasons that Malcolm Macpherson
of Phoiness joined the 2nd Highland Battalion, later successively the 63rd and 78th Regiment but usually known as Fraser's Highlanders, was simply to revenge himself with his
sword on the French. Macpherson got his revenge, bloodily, at the capture of Quebec.

The survey of the Highlands of 1755 indicated that, at that date, its fighting potential
– measured in terms of fit men between the ages of 18 and 56 – was of the order of
12,000: quite enough for a descent upon an unprotected England if necessary. The pro-
vincial militias in America were, curiously, more interested in fighting and squabbling
among themselves than getting stuck into the French who were threatening their northern frontier, and most of the Indians were addicted to fence-sitting. Indeed, from an
Indian viewpoint the French were preferable to the British in that – ostensibly – all they

The childhood home of Marshal MacDonald in Sancerre.
(M. J-C. Lemaire)

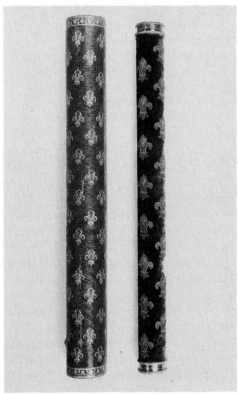

*The (Restoration pattern) Marshal's baton and case of
Marshal MacDonald.*

(Musée de l'Armée, Paris)

wanted to do was trade and not, as the British did, to settle. It was a pattern to be repeated by other Indians half a world away at the same time. Two things, particularly characterised by speed, made the two Highland regiments raised in 1757 notable: the speed with which they were raised and the speed with which they were dispatched across the Atlantic. The government, ever-mindful of the threat presented by bodies of Highlanders in arms, and – to be fair – with little time to lose in regaining lost ground in America, was not anxious to keep the new regiments hanging around in Scotland.

The 42nd (Black Watch) went to America too, and were appallingly cut up at Fort Ticonderoga, losing 314 killed and 333 wounded in an ill-judged assault against a strongly fortified French position; a second battalion of seven companies and 840 men was raised in Scotland in just a few weeks. Montgomerie's Highlanders, the 1st Highland Battalion, was a two-battalion regiment of 1,460 men, and campaigned initially in the Ohio valley, a campaign that resulted in the capture of the French Fort Duquesne and its renaming as Pittsburgh.

Fraser's Highlanders, many of whom had been at Culloden in 1746, were at the capture of Quebec in 1759. In command of them and the rest of the British army at Quebec was James Wolfe, who had faced Fraser's at Culloden as Adc to the Duke of Cumberland. Facing them at Quebec was the Chevalier de Johnstone, Adc to the French commander, the Marquis de Montcalm. Johnstone had been on the Jacobite side at Culloden and had last seen the whirling broadswords and the power of the Highland charge from behind. Wolfe had seen it from the receiving end and knew what it could do; it clinched his victory and the surrender of the basis of French power in North America. Finalised too, by this reversal of positions vis-à-vis the French and the Highlanders, might be said to have been the dissolution of the ancient friendship. Bruce Lenman says it in *The Jacobite Clans of the Great Glen.*

> When a French officer called Jean-Baptiste Roche de Ramezay surrendered Quebec to the British, he sealed the final demise of the Auld Alliance, that precarious and often bad-tempered alliance between Scotland and France which had persisted, off and on, and latterly more off than on, since the Middle Ages. Under its auspices his own Ramsay family appears to have emigrated to France around 1600, and his father had emigrated from Burgundy to New France in 1685 [another Huguenot?]. One of Jean-Baptiste's sisters, a strapping six-footer of a nun, was so passionately patriotic and given to co-operating with and informing the French army that she provoked James Murray, Wolfe's successor and governor of Quebec, into a waggish threat to conscript her into a grenadier company. Her stature would have been appropriate for a unit always composed of the biggest and strongest men in any given regiment, and she would only have been fractionally more reluctant to serve than many others of her comrades-in-arms.

1759 was known to British historians as the Year of Victories: Quebec in America, Minden and Quiberon Bay in Europe, Goree in Africa and Masulipatam, Wandewash and Badra in India. At Minden in August the Scots company of the French Gendarmerie fought for the last time; among their enemies on that day was the 25th (Lord Home's) Regiment, now the King's Own Scottish Borderers. The victory of Admiral Sir Edward Hawke over a French fleet off Quiberon Bay was equalled by another by Admiral Edward Boscawen off the coast of Portugal. Hawke's victory finally put paid to hopes of a French invasion of England and the regiments that had been massed in the French Channel ports, including the *régiment d'Ogilvie* and the *Royal Ecossais*, were sent elsewhere. The victories of the British and East India Company's armies over both the Dutch and the French in India in 1759 were followed by later victories in 1761, when Pondicherry was captured,

Marshal MacDonald, a portrait painted after the Restoration of 1816.

(Musée de l'Armée, Paris)

The tomb of Marshal MacDonald and his family in Père Lachaise cemetery, Paris. Unlike those of Napoleon's other Marshals, it is unmarked on maps and in guidebooks. Pilgrims will find it in the 38th division, on the east side of the Avenue des Acacias.

(Author)

and in 1764 at Buxar. A regiment of Highlanders, the 89th (Morris's) participated on both occasions. Like Montgomerie's and Fraser's in America, it had been raised specifically for the war and was to be disbanded at its close. Its major, Hector Munro, had been part of the forces of occupation in Scotland after the '45 and the governor of Pondicherry, General Lally, had been colonel of one of the Irish regiments in the French service, from whom a detachment had been taken to form the Irish piquets at Culloden.

By the close of the Seven Years War in 1763, France had been expelled from both India and America, Jacobitism had finally been killed and the concept of regiments of Highlanders had been established. The disbandment of all the regiments of Highlanders, except the Black Watch, after the war paralleled the reduction of the *régiment d'Ogilvie* and the *Royal Ecossais*. Massive armies were expensive to run and not needed in peacetime. Apart from Montgomerie's and Fraser's Highlanders, all the Highland regiments which were reduced were brought home to be broken; the two regiments in America were disbanded there and encouraged to settle.

The late 1760s and early 1770s, until the outbreak of the American War of Independence in 1775 and France's involvement in it on the colonists' side in 1778, was a period of peace between Britain and France, although the peace was rarely anything but uneasy. Both armies underwent periods of reform during the decade, building on lessons learned during the Seven Years War and generally pruning and rationalising in order to save expenditure.

The Scottish Company of the Bodyguard was at its peak of sartorial flamboyance and, as behoved the senior regiment of the Royal Household, outshone all other French regiments. An ordinance of 1737 (or 1739: sources disagree) had fixed its complement

Lit de justice de Vendôme *by Jean Fouquet, 1458. Painted*
as the frontispiece for an edition of Boccaccio's 14th century
work De Casibus Virorum et Feminarum Illustrium libri
IX, *a French version of which,* Cas de nobles hommes et
femmes, *was produced for Laurens Gyrard, treasurer to*
King Charles VII in succession to Etienne Chevalier. The
Gardes de la Manche *can be seen in the foreground, armed*
with glaives and entrusted with maintaining order in the
court, at the proceedings of which the Duc d'Alençon was
condemned to death.

(Bayerisches Staatsbibliothek, Munich)

Marshal of France Béraud Stuart, 3rd Seigneur of Aubigny-sur-Nère, 1482–1508.
A copy of a frescoe, originally painted in 1520, at the Château de la Verrerie, Aubigny-sur-Nère.
(The Comte de Voguë; M. J-C. Lemaire)

Marshal of France Robert Stuart, 4th Seigneur of Aubigny-sur-Nère, 1508–1543.
A copy of a frescoe, originally painted in 1520, at the Château de la Verrerie, Aubigny-sur-Nère.
(The Comte de Voguë; M. J-C. Lemaire)

A nineteenth century depiction of a French dismounted
archer and a mounted Scots archer of the Bodyguard of
King Francis I, c 1520.

(NMS)

A nineteenth century depiction of a member of the Swiss
Guard and two gentlemen of the Scots company of the
Bodyguard of King Henry II, c 1559.

(NMS)

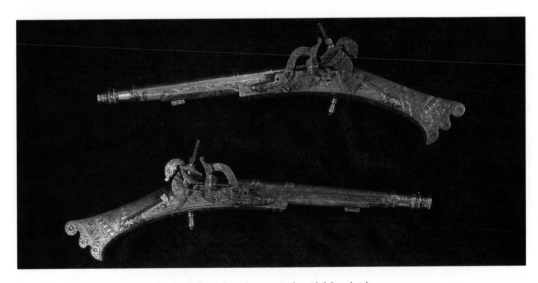

A pair of all-metal snaphaunce pistols, with left and right
hand locks, made by James Low of Dundee for King Louis
XIII and dated 1611.

(NMS)

A trumpeter of the 1st (Scottish) company of the gens
d'armes, *or gendarmerie, c 1724. A watercolour by Percy
White, 1938.*

(NMS)

*A basket-hilted broadsword dated 1731. This hilt is by John
Stewart of Glasgow and the blade of Solingen manufacture.
It was probably either assembled in Scotland using an
imported blade or reassembled in France to replace a broken
blade.*

(Musée de l'Armée, collection Brunon, Château de
l'Emperi, Salon-de-Provence)

The Black Watch at the battle of Fontenoy 1745. *Oil
painting by W. Skeoch Cumming 1896.*

(The Black Watch; Mrs J. Smith)

The regimental Colour of the Royal Ecossais, raised by Lord John Drummond in 1744. A watercolour copy by C. C. P. Lawson, c 1930, from an original in the Musée de l'Armée, c 1748.

(NMS)

A soldier of the Royal Ecossais and his wife, in camp. An original watercolour of 1752.

(Musée de l'Armée, Paris)

A nineteenth century depiction, with later colouring, of a soldier of the Royal Ecossais. Drawn by Major H. de Grandmaison.

(NMS)

The regimental Colour of le régiment d'Ogilvie *raised by David, Lord Ogilvy in 1747. A watercolour copy by C. C. P. Lawson, c 1930, from an original in the Musée de l'Armée, c 1748.*

(NMS)

The regimental Colour of le régiment d'Albanie, *raised by Prince Charles Edward Stuart for Donald Cameron of Lochiel in 1747. A watercolour copy by C. C. P. Lawson, c 1930, from an original in the Musée de l'Armée, c 1748.*

(NMS)

Two soldiers of le régiment d'Ogilvie *in camp. An original watercolour of 1752.*

(Musée de l'Armée, Paris)

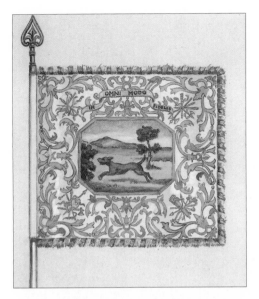

The Standard of the 1st (Scottish) company of the Gendarmerie, c 1762. A copy by Percy White, c 1936, from an original in the Musée de l'Armée.

(NMS)

A trooper of the 1st (Scottish) company of the Gendarmerie, c 1765. An unfinished watercolour by Percy White, c 1936.
(Christopher Allen Esq; NMS)

An officer of the 1st company of the King's Bodyguard, in full dress uniform, c 1775.
(Musée de l'Armée, collection Brunon, Château de l'Emperi, Salon-de-Provence)

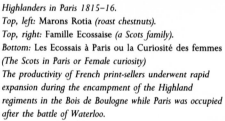

Highlanders in Paris 1815–16.
Top, left: Marons Rotia *(roast chestnuts).*
Top, right: Famille Ecossaise *(a Scots family).*
Bottom: Les Ecossais à Paris ou la Curiosité des femmes
(The Scots in Paris or Female curiosity)
The productivity of French print-sellers underwent rapid
expansion during the encampment of the Highland
regiments in the Bois de Boulogne while Paris was occupied
after the battle of Waterloo.

(NMS)

Captain James Alexander, 42nd (Royal Highland) Regiment by A. J. Dubois Drahonet, 1832.

(By gracious permission of H.M. The Queen)

An ensign of the 79th (Cameron) Highlanders at Chobham Camp by Eugène Lami, 1853.

(Victoria and Albert Museum)

Wounded French and Russian soldiers after the battle of the Alma in the Crimean War, 1854, by Orlando Norie, c 1860. One of the few depictions of French soldiers by a Scottish artist, it represents the ambulance of General Bosquet's 2nd Division. In the foreground are a wounded Zouave of the 3rd

Zouaves and a soldier of probably the 50th Infantry regiment. In the background a surgeon talks to a mounted staff captain. The soldiers in pale-grey greatcoats are Russians.

(Cavalry and Guards Club)

The charge of the French cuirassiers at Waterloo 1815
by H. F. E. Philippoteaux.

(Victoria and Albert Museum)

The charge of the Heavy Cavalry Brigade at Balaklava
1854 *by H. F. E. Philippoteaux.*

(The Royal Scots Dragoon Guards
(Carabiniers and Greys))

Soldiers of the 42nd (Black Watch) photographed after their return from the Crimea in 1856. Left to right: Colour-Sergeant W. Gardiner, Private D. MacKenzie, Private D. Glen. All three wear the Crimean War Medal 1854–56 and Private MacKenzie wears the French Médaille Militaire too. Colour-Sergeant Gardiner later won the Victoria Cross. Photographs in this series, Crimean Heroes, were to provide inspiration for both French and British military painters for the rest of the century.

(NMS)

A piper of the 42nd (Black Watch) in drill order by Edouard Detaille, 1879.

(NMS)

Portsmouth Dockyard or Entre les deux mon coeur balance (How happy could I be with either) by Jacques Tissot, 1877.

(Tate Gallery)

The Scots Guards return to barracks after an exercise,
preceded by their Corps of Drums, by Edouard Detaille,
1880.

(NMS)

The battle of Tel-el-Kebir 1882 *by Alphonse de Neuville,*
1883.

(NMS)

The stained glass memorial panel commemorating Captain Eugène Bourdon, Professor of Architecture at the Glasgow School of Art, killed in action on the Somme, 1916.
(Glasgow School of Art; Mrs J. Smith)

Citation for the award of the Croix de Guerre avec palme to Second Lieutenant D. M. Gill, 1st/5th Gordon Highlanders, 1918.
(The Gordon Highlanders; Mrs J. Smith)

The landing of the 13th Canadian Infantry battalion (The Royal Highlanders of Canada) at St. Nazaire 1915 by Edgar Bundy, 1918.
(The Black Watch: Mrs J. Smith)

The Regimental Colour of 6th battalion The Black Watch, decorated with the Croix de Guerre avec palme *in 1919 to reward the battalion's gallantry at Chambrécy in July 1918.*
(The Black Watch; Mrs J. Smith)

The King's Colour of 12th battalion The Argyll and Sutherland Highlanders, decorated with the Croix de Guerre avec palme *in 1919 to reward the battalion's gallantry at the battle of Doiran in Salonika, 1918.*
(The Argyll and Sutherland Highlanders; Mrs J. Smith)

The silver statuette presented in 1924 to Colonel C. Macleod Robertson, secretary of the committee, by the committee established to erect the memorial to the 51st (Highland) Division, 1914–18, at Beaumont Hamel on the Somme. The statuette was found in a field at St Valéry after the surrender of the Division in June 1940, and remained in French hands until being returned to Scotland in 1986. It is now the property of the 51st (Highland) Division Dinner Club. Made by Brook and Son. Hallmark: Edinburgh 1924–25.

(51st (Highland) Division Dinner Club; NMS)

The tenor drum of 1st battalion The Black Watch, left in Metz in 1940 and restored to the regiment in 1976.

(The Black Watch; Mrs J. Smith)

The tenor drum of 5th battalion The Gordon Highlanders,
left in Metz in 1940 and restored to the regiment in 1945.
(The Gordon Highlanders; Mrs J. Smith)

The tenor drum of 8th battalion The Argyll and Sutherland
Highlanders, deposited in the Banque de France in Metz in
1940, lost to the Germans, and eventually restored to the
regiment in 1975.
(The Argyll and Sutherland Highlanders; Mrs J. Smith)

Lord Adam Gordon, governor of Edinburgh Castle, and the Comte d'Artois, brother to Louis XVI, and later King Charles X, walking in Edinburgh in 1796. A drawing by John Kay.

(NMS)

at 330 men, 25 of whom continued to fulfil the function of *Gardes de la Manche*. The Company was divided into six *brigades*, each of which contributed four men to the *Gardes de la Manche*, the senior *brigade* also contributing the *premier homme d'armes*, who commanded the *Gardes de la Manche*. The three senior brigades were commanded by *lieutenants*, the other three by *enseignes*. Each brigade had two *exempts* (officers on the list but not actually serving with the Company), two *brigadiers* (corporals), two *sous-brigadiers* (lance-corporals) and one *porte-étandard* (standard-bearer). The senior *brigade* contributed a *timbalier* (kettle-drummer). The six *brigades* were grouped into two *escadrons* (squadrons). By 1766 the *Etat Militaire de France* (the French military list) noted not one Scottish name – unless heavily corrupted – in the Company. Since 1651 the captaincy had been the purlieu of members of the Noailles family, Dukes of Noailles and, later, of Ayen. Its last action had been at Laffeldt in 1747 and, until the Revolution of 1789 took it into abeyance until the Restoration of 1815, it continued to restrict its membership to the scions of French noble houses, all of whom had to be a minimum of five feet four inches tall. In 1776 a reduction was made in the Company which reduced it in size to 280 men and reduced the *Gardes de la Manche* to ten in number.

A model ship made from bone and a set of bone dominoes, the case and box in a type of primitive Tunbridge ware, made by French prisoners in Edinburgh Castle, c 1810.

(NMS)

A brass mantel clock in the Gothic style, made by French prisoners in Perth, c 1800.

(NMS)

The Gendarmerie was steadily reduced in size, first – in 1763 – from 16 to ten companies, the Scottish company retaining its premier position. This reduction was effected by amalgamating the six *chevaux-légers* companies, which had been separated in 1530, with the remaining ten companies of the Gendarmerie proper. In 1776 the ten companies were reduced to eight and in 1787 (or 1788: sources disagree) the remains of the Gendarmerie, including the 1st, or Scottish, Company, disappeared for ever.

The two Scottish companies left behind them something of a mystery however. Extant in many collections, private and public, are a number of basket-hilted swords, with hilts in the Scottish style, and with blades that are either unequivocally French or which bear French inscriptions, the most common being *Vive le Roy* (Long live the king). While some may well be 'marriages' of later blades with earlier hilts, not all can be and therefore some explanation for their existence has to be propounded. As far as it is possible to judge, the extant swords fall into three categories: those with undoubted Scottish-made hilts and traditional, yet non-Scottish in appearance, broadsword or backsword blades; those with hilts which could be either Scottish or French and with probably French blades; those with French-made hilts and blades – usually of very cheap quality indeed. A number of these different types are illustrated in this chapter in order to show the possible variations.

Because of the exiled Jacobite communities in France, the most prominent of which was at Sancerre, where Neil MacEachen settled and Donald Cameron of Lochiel died and was buried, it is by no means certain either that all the extant swords were used by one or other of the two Scottish companies or that the king referred to on the blades is Louis XV or Louis XVI and not James III or Charles III. It is in the nature of things that many of the Jacobite exiles, although from social classes in which ownership and carrying of swords were commonplace, would either have arrived in France without

*The 3rd Duke of Buccleuch and his family, by H. P.
Danloux, 1796. The two young men in uniform are Charles,
Earl of Dalkeith and later the 4th Duke and (bareheaded)
James, Viscount Stopford, later 3rd Earl of Courtown. Lord
Stopford was married to the Duke's eldest daughter – sitting
in front of him and holding his helmet on her knee – and
was lieutenant-colonel of the 1st regiment of Fencible
Cavalry; Lord Dalkeith was a captain in the regiment.*
(The Duke of Buccleuch and Queensberry)

Sergeant Mather, Grenadier company, Dumfries Militia, by H. P. Danloux, c 1798. Because of the connection of the Dukes of Buccleuch with the Dumfries Militia (Lord Dalkeith was its colonel from 1798) it is likely that this and a companion painting by Danloux were commissioned by the Duke.

(NGS)

Admiral Viscount Duncan of Camperdown, by H. P. Danloux, c 1800, After their victories at Camperdown and in the Mediterranean in 1799 and 1800, Admirals Lords Keith and Duncan – both Scots – were fêted and Danloux painted both of them.

(National Portrait Gallery)

them or have been forced to pawn or sell them. This may explain the cheaply made, all-French, swords with pre-fabricated hilts and blades of exceptionally low standard. Far too poor to have been used by either British or French soldiers, they may have been regarded as a cheap substitute by Jacobite exiles whose honour and self-esteem depended upon possession of a sword but whose purse would not stretch to a dearer one.

Many of the swords are unquestionably cavalry weapons, with the long, fullered blades, long ricassos and hilts which incorporate a ring on the inner side; the British heavy cavalry carried such weapons from the 1720s until the 1780s and, in the absence of evidence to the contrary, there is no reason to believe that their French opposite numbers did not copy them. The basket-hilt, in the Scottish style – with pierced and decorated panels – was not unique to Scottish infantry regiments since it provided excellent protection for the hand in a mêlée and did not interrupt the standard cavalry sword manoeuvres of the cut against a mounted opponent and the point against infantry. The fact that many swords with French provenances have Scottish-type basket hilts and blades with *Vive le Roy* on them should not necessarily indicate that they are connected with the Scots Bodyguard or Scots Company of the Gendarmerie; it may, but – equally well – it may not. Loyal slogans on sword blades were not the preserve of Household troops and the basket-hilt was not the preserve of Scottish units.

The final group of swords, which are exceptionally rare, are those with Scottish-made hilts and what appear to be French blades. The hilts are signed by Scottish armourers and the blades are in the French style, not the Scottish, and bear French inscriptions. It is conceivable that the few of these swords recorded are either the result of Franco-Scottish trade or examples of French cutlers replacing broken original blades in Scottish hilts. Since this type of sword was not confined to either soldier or civilian – a distinction itself uncommon in eighteenth century and earlier Highland Scottish male society – it is difficult to ascribe the few that exist to likely owners but, in these cases, it is more likely that the loyal inscriptions on the blade refer to Jacobite royalty rather than Bourbon royalty. This latter distinction may not be valid, however, since most exiled Jacobites would have been loyal to both.

There are, of course, swords with basket-hilts extant in France which have no connection at all with either Jacobite exiles or the Scottish companies in the French army and Royal Household. These are genuine all-Scottish, or all-British, swords, either carried by those officers of the Scottish infantry regiments in the French service who had managed to bring their swords with them, or relinquished by Scottish soldiers in or after battles against French troops. All ranks of the Highland regiments carried swords until 1784, at least in theory. The campaigns in America, however, did not lend themselves to the use of the sword and, in both the Seven Years War and the American War of Independence, orders were frequently given for private soldiers to lay their swords aside before embarking on a campaign.

The latter conflict brought Britain and France to war again, established the United States of America, taught the British army many salutary lessons and hastened the end of the Bourbon monarchy in France. French intervention in the war was essentially personal until 1778 when a formal treaty with the 13 states was drawn up, the Marquis de la Fayette having gone to America with other volunteers early on in the conflict. La Fayette's reasons may, themselves, have been partly personal since his father had been killed by the British at the battle of Minden in 1759. The capitulation of British forces under Burgoyne at Saratoga in 1777 persuaded the French king, Louis XVI, to listen to those of his ministers who urged intervention but not until 1780 did 6,000 troops under the Comte de Rochambeau arrive in America. By 1781 French land forces and American troops had bottled up a British force in Yorktown and the French admiral, the Comte de Grasse, had Yorktown blockaded by sea. The surrender of Cornwallis's forces at Yorktown in October 1781 effectively finished the war. Among the British troops who marched out of Yorktown to surrender was the second Highland regiment to bear the name Fraser's Highlanders. Also raised by Simon Fraser, now almost completely rehabilitated by his perceived loyalty to the Hanoverian succession, the regiment was numbered 71st in the British infantry precedence; it was disbanded after the war and was the only Highland regiment at the surrender of Yorktown. Together with some Scots in the Scots Guards detachment of the composite battalion of Foot Guards which also surrendered at Yorktown, Fraser's Highlanders would have been the only Scottish regiment to exchange shots with French troops on the American mainland during the war.

The French Revolution caused, it has been said, the hair to rise on the crowned heads of Europe. The French monarchy had been in financial decline and increasing difficulty throughout the eighteenth century and its decline was paralleled by a concomitant rise in the latter part of the century of concepts of equity and self-determination: the rights of man. The oppression of the pre-1789 French monarchy, especially when unfavourably contrasted by British caricaturists with the supposed freedoms existing in Britain, has been – and was – grossly overstated but the causes of the Revolution of 1789 form no relevant part of this narrative. The effect, in the short term, was a fresh batch of exiles needing to be accommodated, usually in Britain, and, in the long term, a period of almost continuous war between Britain and France from 1793 to 1815. Until a later, but much shorter, war assumed the title, the wars against Revolutionary France and then Napoleonic France were known to later generations as the Great War. The renewal of hostilities necessitated an increase in the army and, two years after the last vestige of a Scottish connection with the French king's Bodyguard had been purged – by the

Lithograph commemorating an event at the battle of Waterloo in 1815. In translation, the inscription reads as follows. The Old Guard vigorously charged a body of Scots. An ensign fell, mortally wounded, one of his comrades would have rescued the Colour but, being unable to reach it, lifted both the ensign and the Colour on to his shoulders and that way rescued both. The Guard stopped, cried, "Bravo, Bravo to the Scots", and gave the brave soldier time to rejoin his regiment.

(The Black Watch; Mrs J. Smith)

disbandment of the whole Bodyguard in 1791 – the foundations of the modern Highland regimental system were laid by the raising of the remaining regiments which existed into the current century. By the end of the 1790s the Seaforth, Cameron, Gordon and Argyll and Sutherland Highlanders had appeared in the British *Army List*: they have yet to leave it.

By the 1790s, however, recruiting in the Highlands was no longer the easy matter that it had been 40 years or even 20 years previously and there was great competition among minor landowners to raise regiments and among recruiting agents to enlist men for them. Not all landowners in the Highlands were keen to let their tenants go, since the policy of replacing people with sheep had hardly begun. In the Outer Hebrides the thriving kelp industry was very labour-intensive and the livelihood of, for instance, Mac-Donald of Clanranald depended upon keeping hold of his labour force. The nephew or great-nephew, of Neil MacEachen, and therefore cousin of Maréchal MacDonald, was arrested on the island of South Uist in 1804 when attempting to ship 150 of Clanranald's tenants abroad and into the Canadian Fencibles. Despite Ranald MacEachen's avowedly patriotic, but probably deeply mercenary, intent, Clanranald was not prepared to jeopardise his profits from the harvesting of Hebridean seaweed by allowing his tenantry to escape from the island. MacEachen's fate is not recorded but by 1804, when he was arrested, his cousin's star in France was momentarily in decline.

The future Marshal of France was destined to have a career little dealt with by British historians, perhaps because Britain was about the only one of France's enemies against which he never actually fought. Napoleon is quoted as saying that he had no wish to test MacDonald's legendary loyalty by putting him within the sound of bagpipes, an indication not only of the implied ubiquity of Scottish troops in Britain's armies but also of the profound impression that they and their music made upon the French.

MacDonald was born in Sedan on 17 November 1765 and moved, while an infant, with his father to Sancerre – home of an exiled Jacobite community. His parents apparently separated relatively soon after his birth. His military career began in 1784 when he joined the *Légion Irlandais* as a subaltern, transferring to the *régiment de Maillebois* in the following year in order to see action against the Dutch as a lieutenant. The regiment arrived too late to see action and was disbanded at the end of the short war. Determined to remain a soldier, MacDonald eventually secured himself a cadetship, a kind of volunteer status, in the *régiment de Dillon*, an Irish regiment whose colonel was to flee at the Revolution and raise a regiment of the same name – formed of French emigrés and Swiss – in the British service. By the time of the Revolution he had become a *sous-lieutenant* or second lieutenant in the regiment.

Guerrier Ecossais, *an engraving by Bertrand after Laby,*
published c 1815.

(The Black Watch; Mrs J. Smith)

A watercolour by N. D. Finart depicting a musician of a
Highland regiment, c 1815.

(By gracious permission of H.M. The Queen)

The point is made in MacDonald's own *Recollections*, edited by Rousset (1893), that throughout his career his loyalty remained to France and not to any one individual. This, naturally, led to accusations of coat-turning, of "trimming" and of putting personal survival above all else. Few knowledgeable about MacDonald would describe him as much else than dour and he certainly lacked the flamboyance of some other Marshals of France, notably Ney. Because of this, his professed and unshakeable allegiance to the country of his birth can be taken at its face value; on the few occasions that he intervened in politics he did so for what he believed to be the best interests of France. The fact that these, ultimately, became the best interests of MacDonald may be regarded as coincidental but, perhaps, prove the true value of patriotism – an indefinite concept at the best of times. Like many of his fellow officers, MacDonald thought about emigrating at the Revolution and was still thinking about it in 1792; the imminent arrival of his

La Graduation de la Famille Ecossaise, *a print published by Genty, Paris, 1815.*

(NMS)

La nouvelle Mode, ou l'Ecossais à Paris, *a print engraved by Blanchard after Finart, 1815.*

(NMS)

first child and his avowed – or professed – lack of interest in politics induced him to remain in France.

For the next 12 years his progress was meteoric. Promoted captain, he became Adc to General Dumouriez, commanding France's northern frontier, and accompanied him to the Army of the Ardennes where, after the victory over the Prussians at Valmy, Mac-Donald was promoted lieutenant-colonel. He fought at Jemappes in November 1792, was promoted *général de brigade* in August 1793, fought at Turcoing and Hondeschoote and was promoted *général de division* in November 1794. Until 1798 he remained in the Low Countries with the *Armées du Sambre-et-Meuse* and *du Nord*. In 1798, for a year he was a governor of Rome until, in 1799, the governing Directory of France gave him his first command, of the Army of Naples. Fighting his way north, to join the Army of Italy, under General Moreau, he took Modena in 1799 but was wounded in an engagement with Austro-Russian forces on the River Trebbia in June. MacDonald supported Napoleon in the military *coup d'état* that toppled the Committee of Five Hundred on 18 Brumaire (10 November 1799) and was rewarded by the new First Consul with the position of deputy to General Moreau on the Rhine and subsequently by command of the 2nd Army of Reserve, later known – once it had invaded Switzerland in August 1800 – as the *Armée de Grisons*. Crossing Switzerland through the Splügen Pass, MacDonald invaded Italy and fought a successful campaign in northern Italy against Austrian forces and severe weather conditions. In 1801 he was sent as ambassador to Denmark, a country then toying with an alliance with France. He remained as ambassador and military advisor for a year and returned to France at the truce of the Peace of Amiens in 1802. Then his former comrades Generals Moreau and Pichegru were arraigned on treason charges and MacDonald was implicated. Although nothing was proved, the

Infanterie Ecossaise, *a print drawn by St Fal, engraved by Alix and published by Noel, Paris, 1815.*

(NMS)

implication was enough to prevent him from joining the list of Marshals of France drawn up after the coronation of Napoleon as Emperor, but insufficient to prevent him from receiving the dignity of first *Commandeur* and then *Grand-officier* of the new *Légion d'Honneur*. He retired, in semi-disgrace, to his newly acquired property at Courcelles-le-Roi near his childhood home and remained there until being recalled to serve in Italy in 1809.

MacDonald assisted Prince Eugène Beauharnais, Napoleon's stepson, in winding up the Italian campaign and then led an army on a forced march, averaging 43 miles a day in the height of summer, to the battlefield of Wagram in Austrian territory. After an initial reverse on the first day of the battle, 5 July, MacDonald rallied and organised the troops under his command into a giant wedge of 24 battalions and 8,000 men and, although incurring colossal casualties, compelled the Austrian forces to break and retire. Napoleon, who had watched the manoeuvre with admiration at the bravery of the rigidly drilled troops, rewarded MacDonald by promoting him Marshal of France on the battle-field; he was the only Marshal of France to be so rewarded. His dukedom, of Taranto, and the Grand Cordon of the Legion of Honour followed in August 1809. Service in Spain followed in 1810 and 1811, and in 1812 he was given command of 10th Corps for the invasion of Russia. 10th Corps was placed on the French left and secured the Baltic provinces; it escaped most of the fighting and was spared the rigours of the Russian winter and retreat. As France's forces were gradually forced back by combined Russian and Prussian forces from the east, so MacDonald participated in the various holding operations at Lützen, Bautzen, Leipzig and Hanau in 1813.

Aware of the internal collapse of France in 1814 and correctly perceiving that the war was lost, with France hemmed in on all flanks, MacDonald was one of the marshals who

Militaires Ecossais, *a print by Debucourt after Vernet,*
1815.

(NMS)

persuaded Napoleon to abdicate in 1814. MacDonald remained in a position of influence, although by no means uncritically, to the restored Bourbon monarchy in 1814 and 1815 and saw to it that Louis XVIII was safely escorted out of the country when Napoleon returned from Elba in 1815. He took no part in the campaign of the 100 Days, which ended at Waterloo, and on the second return of Louis XVIII, he was made Arch-Chancellor of the Legion of Honour, refusing the position of Secretary for War. As commander of the Army of the Loire, temporarily, he was given, and executed, the task of its disbandment and so oversaw the final disappearance of the Grand Army. He was created a Peer of France and confirmed in his rank of Marshal of France by both Louis XVIII and, after the 1830 revolution, by King Louis-Philippe. He died at Courcelles in 1840 and is buried in Père-Lachaise cemetery in Paris.

In 1825 he visited the country of his father's birth and, as well as taking back to France some earth and some seed potatoes from the family property at Howbeg on South Uist, found time to visit the battlefield of Culloden. Communication with his kinsmen on South Uist was limited by the fact that the Marshal spoke little English and no Gaelic and his relations spoke no French and little English. The *Inverness Courier* of February 1875 reported his reactions when visiting Culloden:

> The marshal, having carefully examined the ground and position of the respective armies, asked 'Where was the artillery?' He was told that virtually there was no artillery. 'What! No artillery?' said the marshal, and then added, 'Where was the cavalry?' and was answered, 'There was no cavalry'. Upon which he became greatly excited, struck his forehead with his clenched fist, and exclaimed, 'Those idiots of generals, *les perruques*, if they had brought out these men on purpose to be slaughtered they would have done exactly what they did. They would have led them into these open moors without cavalry and practically without artillery against an army supplied with both'. Then, turning round and pointing to the mountains in the south-west, he continued, 'Why not occupy these fastnesses? Who can tell how long our brave Highlanders in their vantage ground might have kept the English at bay?'

106

Régiments Ecossais, a print published by Martinet, Paris, 1815.

(NMS)

The Restoration of the Bourbon monarchy in France in 1815 ended a period of 25 years of exile for the brothers of the executed Louis XVI. Although the elder, later Louis XVIII, spent his exile in England the younger, the Comte d'Artois, who would succeed to the throne in 1824 as Charles X, spent some time at the Palace of Holyroodhouse in Edinburgh. He arrived in 1796, together with his entourage, which included his son, the Duc d'Angoulème, and both royal princes were quickly taken up by Edinburgh society. Both, too, attended the regular military parades in the capital and the young duke was especially interested in the drills and musters of the Royal Edinburgh Volunteers, one of the many units of volunteer soldiers raised in the late 1790s to combat the threat of a French invasion.

There were other Frenchmen in Edinburgh at the same time. Although the Comte d'Artois only remained at Holyrood until 1799, returning briefly in 1830 after being deposed at the July Revolution, French prisoners-of-war languished in the dungeons of Edinburgh Castle and a camp was established at Penicuik for the overflow. Captured officers, who had given their parole not to try to escape, were interned in Selkirk and other inland Scottish towns. While the prisoners in the Castle and in the camps turned their hands to utilising available raw materials for the manufacture of saleable articles, the officers – at least those in Selkirk – appear to have enjoyed themselves baiting, and being baited by, the inhabitants. The officers continued to receive their pay of half a

Les Grapilleurs, ou Les Ecossais et les Anglais en
Vendanges, *a print published by Martinet and Charon,
Paris, 1815. A pun is intended on the words* grappe, *a
cluster, and* piller, *to pillage or loot.*

(The Black Watch; Mrs J. Smith)

Ecossais, a print published by Martinet, Paris, 1815.
(Musée de l'Armée, Paris)

guinea a week through Coutts's bank in London, which contrived to carry on transactions on their behalf throughout the period of the war. and so were able to live in comparative comfort. According to the reminiscences of an officer captured in Spain in 1811, Lieutenant Adelbert J. Doisy of the 26th French infantry, who was interned in Selkirk between 1811 and 1814, he and his fellow officers fished in the Tweed, organised a theatre and a café with a billiard table and an orchestra, visited Walter Scott at Abbotsford and countered the bell-ringing which celebrated Wellington's victories in the Peninsula by contriving their own celebrations and *vins d'honneur* at the news of Napoleonic victories in Russia.

Doisy makes a point of recording that the company of these French officers was generally shunned by local society in the Borders and so it is unlikely that the internees were visited by the likes of the Duke of Buccleuch. The 3rd Duke had, however, extensively patronised a countryman of Doisy's, Henri-Pierre Danloux, who had fled the Revolution in the early 1790s and brought his talents as a portraitist to London. The arrival of the Comte d'Artois and Duc d'Angoulème in Edinburgh in 1796 sent Danloux north to spend six months in Scotland between September 1796 and March 1797. Angoulème took Danloux up and was painted by him, as was Lord Adam Gordon, governor of Edinburgh Castle. Danloux, who had been welcomed into London society, soon caused Edinburgh society to wonder how they could have lived without him. In November 1796 he visited Dalkeith Palace, one of the seats of the Dukes of Buccleuch, and was commissioned to paint a family group, including the Duke's son and son-in-law in the uniform of their regiment of Fencible cavalry. At a later period, the Duke commissioned Danloux to paint two sergeants of his son's regiment, the Dumfries Militia. After Danloux's return to London he produced portraits of the Scottish Admirals Keith and Duncan, after their victories in 1799. Although Danloux was by no means the first French painter either to work in Scotland, to be attracted by the country or to become rapidly fashionable, he was among the first to produce military portraits of Scottish soldiers and, for that reason is considered sufficiently significant to be included in this narrative.

It has been no part of this narrative to dwell on the relatively short period, considering the timespan of the Franco-Scottish alliance in its various forms, during which Scottish and French soldiers were actively engaged in attempting to kill each other at the behest of each others' governments. As we have seen, the wars of the later seventeenth and early eighteenth century regularly brought Scottish soldiers into contact and conflict with French soldiers. Until Fontenoy in 1745, however, no kilted Highland troops had fought the French, simply because there were no kilted Highland regiments employed on the European continent prior to 1745. The reaction of the French to the Highlanders at Fontenoy has already been recounted and it was a reaction that was to be repeated continually throughout the wars against Revolutionary and Napoleonic France.

Although there are many Highlanders who would disagree, the fact is that there are few instances when Highlanders in Highland regiments fought consistently, conspicuously or continually better than their colleagues in less noticeable uniforms. The uniforms of the Highland regiments, which were not always kilted however, together with their distinct music, made them unique not only in the British army but also among the enemies of France in the period 1793–1815. Because of this unique appearance, together with a far from unjustified reputation for ferocity and steadiness in battle, the reputation of the Highland regiments tended to outstrip, often unfairly, that accorded to other British regiments not only by the French but also by the British. This reputation inevitably filtered back to the civilian population in France during the war and this, together with stories of the kilt and the bagpipes, made the Highlanders natural targets for curiosity when France was occupied by the Allied armies after Waterloo. Paris was full of outlandish foreign uniforms from 1815 to 1818 but few seem to have excited quite as much interest as the kilt, if the products of French print-makers can be taken as a yardstick of interest. The occupation of France, together with the good behaviour of the Highland troops relative to that of the Prussians and Russians, seems to have established the Franco-Scottish military alliance on an altogether different plane from that which it had previously occupied. The nineteenth century was certainly to mark the beginning of a French love-affair with the kilt and the bagpipes which was elevated to a *grande passion* during the century and continued through two world wars. Since France and Britain were not to fight each other, at least on the battlefield, after 1815, this change in the nature of the military relationship can be regarded as significant, not only for the military status of both nations but also for the gradually changing perceptions of war and the soldier.

*A private soldier of the grenadier company, 92nd (Gordon)
Highlanders, as he might have appeared in Paris in 1815. A
watercolour by Georges Scott, 1911.*
(The Gordon Highlanders; Mrs J. Smith)

Chapter Five

Allies and Artists
1815–1914

THE FINAL DEFEAT OF NAPOLEON SENT THE KINGS AND GOVERNMENTS OF THE states ranged against France into a kind of euphoria. Allies who, at various times, had been enemies or at least neutrals for the previous two decades, congratulated each other upon the defeat of the Tyrant – as Napoleon was persistently portrayed by hostile contemporary print-sellers. The success of absolute monarchy in the countries of continental Europe was secured and the actions of the returning Bourbons in France proved the truth of the saying that they had learned nothing and forgotten nothing.

One of the first actions of Louis XVIII on returning to his capital was to reinstate the Scots Bodyguard, which had gone into liquidation in 1791 by order of the National Assembly. Decrees of 1814 and 1815 resurrected all four companies of the king's Bodyguard and the Scottish company became known as the First Company of the Bodyguard once more. In January 1815, when the bodies of the executed Louis XVI and Queen Marie Antionette were moved from the cemetery of the Madeleine to the royal burial place in the cathedral of St. Denis, it was the 12 members of the First Company who conveyed and accompanied the remains, in line with their ancient privileges which Louis XVIII had renewed and confirmed. The First Company lasted as long as the restored Bourbons and vanished with them at the July Revolution of 1830 which installed Louis-Philippe as king of the French, France's first constitutional monarch. Extant records and sources do not indicate what happened to them during the 100 Days between Napoleon's return from Elba and defeat at Waterloo; it is likely, though, that they beat a tactful and hasty retreat with their Sovereign.

As might be expected, British and French historical sources – especially those among the latter which continue to regard the Emperor Napoleon I with a kind of patriotic awe – tend to disagree about the exact status of Napoleon's capitulation after the battle of Waterloo. Almost without exception, British sources – contemporary and modern – refer to it as a surrender. French sources, while not usually questioning his abdication in favour of his son, generally describe his embarkation from France aboard HMS *Bellerophon* on 15 July 1815, as a voluntary exile. Napoleon himself wrote the following letter from Rochefort on 13 July to the Prince Regent:

> Your Royal Highness,
>
> A victim to the factions which distract my country, and to the enmity of the greatest powers of Europe, I have terminated my political career, and I come, like Themosticles, to throw myself upon the hospitality of the British people. I put myself under the protection of their laws; which I claim from your Royal Highness, as the most powerful, the most constant, and the most generous of my enemies.
>
> Napoleon.

This letter had been written after protracted negotiations between members of Napoleon's suite and the captain of *Bellerophon*, Frederick Maitland of Lindores.

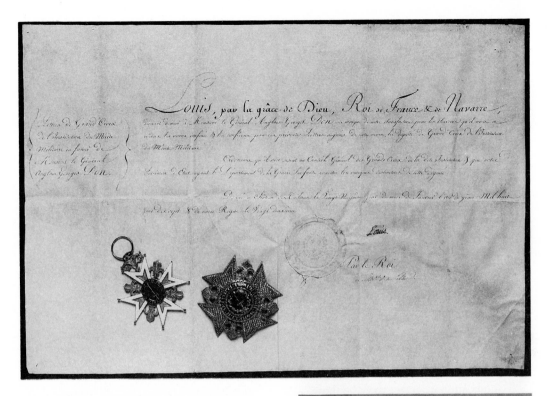

The Badge and Star of a Knight Grand Cross of the French
Institution of Military Merit, together with the warrant –
signed by King Louis XVIII – making the award to General
Sir George Don, 1817.

(NMS)

Lieutenant-Colonel Lord Arthur Hill, 2nd or Royal North
British Dragoons (Scots Greys) by A. J. Dubois Drahonet,
1832.

(By gracious permission of H.M. The Queen)

Maitland, a kinsman of the Earls of Lauderdale, came from a Scottish family with an impressive and extensive naval and military lineage. He was under the orders of Rear Admiral Sir Henry Hotham, who commanded a naval squadron based in Quiberon Bay which was charged, initially, with the task of blockading the French coast and, after the battle of Waterloo, with preventing Napoleon's escape. It is clear, from Maitland's own account, originally published in 1826 under the title *Narrative of the Surrender of Buonaparte*, that he – as an ordinary sailor – found the situation in which he was placed an odd one and one with which his previous experience had ill-equipped him to deal. That he was surprised by the engaging personal qualities of Napoleon is beyond doubt; he, too, must have been influenced by the print-sellers and the anti-Napoleon propaganda. It appears that he found his personal feelings, which in no way and at no time compromised either his patriotism or his loyalty, difficult to reconcile with his orders from Hotham, which had come straight from the Admiralty where, it is apparent, their lordships were unclear about how to deal with Napoleon should he be caught or give himself up. The orders on which he acted, transmitted from Hotham – who was flying his flag in HMS *Superb* – on 8 July, are both specific and procrastinatory; the relevant excerpts are as follows:

> . . . you are hereby required and directed . . . to keep the most vigilant look-out for the purpose of intercepting him [Napoleon]; . . . and if you should be so fortunate as to intercept him, you are to transfer him and his family to the ship you command, and there keeping him in careful custody, return to the nearest port in England . . . with all possible expedition; and on your arrival you are not to permit any communication whatever with the shore, . . . and you will be held responsible for keeping the whole transaction a profound secret, until you receive their Lordships' further orders.

Before Maitland agreed to receive Napoleon on board his ship he appears, by his own account, to have been punctilious about the terms on which the Emperor was to be received, treated and transported to Britain. He reports a conversation with the Comte de Las Cases, Councillor of State to Napoleon, apropos the terms and prior to the departure of Major General Baron Gourgaud, Adc to the Emperor, to Britain on board HMS *Slaney* with Napoleon's letter to the Prince Regent.

> I said, "Monsieur Las Cases, you will recollect that I am not authorised to stipulate as to the reception of Buonaparte in England, but that he must consider himself entirely at the disposal of his Royal Highness the Prince Regent". He answered, "I am perfectly aware of that, and have already acquainted the Emperor with what you said on the subject".

Since no instructions had been forthcoming about any honours to be paid to the Emperor, he was greeted on *Bellerophon* by the turning-out of the Royal Marines guard. He was treated as a general officer, since the British government recognised his status as a general but not as an Emperor, and given the whole of the after-cabin – the largest cabin on the ship – as his quarters. Discovering that Maitland was a Scot and related to Lord Lauderdale, Napoleon recalled Lauderdale, who had briefly been a joint-commissioner attempting to conclude a peace with France in 1806. On 16 July Napoleon briefly inspected the Royal Marines guard, commenting on the potential of a hundred thousand of such soldiers in a way reminiscent, now, of the statement by Maréchal Bugeaud, Duc d'Isly – who had fought against British troops, while a junior

Colour-Sergeant Alexander McDonald, 3rd Regiment of Foot Guards, by A. J. Dubois Drahonet, 1832.
(By gracious permission of H.M. The Queen)

Private John Rogers, 90th (Perthshire Volunteers) Light Infantry, by A. J. Dubois Drahonet, 1833.
(By gracious permission of H.M. The Queen)

officer, in the Peninsula – that *"l'infanterie anglaise est la plus redoutable de l'Europe. Heureusement il n'y en a pas beaucoup."* (The English [sic] infantry is the best in Europe. Fortunately there isn't much of it.)

Bellerophon anchored in Torbay on 24 July and on 26 July moved into Plymouth Sound where she was joined by the frigates HMS *Liffey* and HMS *Eurotas*, which provided guard boats that rowed constantly around *Bellerophon*, more to keep away onlookers in small boats from the shore than to prevent the escape of Napoleon or any of his party. Newspapers brought aboard, including the *Courier*, the semi-official mouthpiece of the government, were already predicting exile to St. Helena, and it appears that General Gourgaud had never been allowed off HMS *Slaney* in order to deliver Napoleon's letter to the Prince Regent in person. On the following day Maitland took Napoleon's letter himself to Lord Keith, the Scottish First Lord of the Admiralty, and was given instructions about

*A private of the 79th (Cameron) Highlanders at Chobham
Camp, by Eugène Lami, 1853.*

(Victoria and Albert Museum)

116

Fraternité d'armes franco-britannique sous Sébastopol, *a*
lithograph by Hippolyte Bellange, 1854.
(Musée de l'Armée)

Napoleon's treatment. The Emperor was to be treated according to his rank as a general, his suite was to be divided among the ships accompanying *Bellerophon*, no communication with the shore was to be allowed. Lord Keith met Napoleon on 28 July but, according to Maitland, was non-committal about the eventual fate of the Emperor. Maitland records that on 30 July, a Sunday, the cluster of small boats crowding as close to *Bellerophon* as the hard-pressed guard boats would allow was such that he estimated that close to 8,000 people were on the water and anxious to catch a glimpse of Napoleon. Lord Keith had, apparently, told Maitland – in as many words – that exile to St. Helena was to be Napoleon's fate but had sworn Maitland to secrecy, not told the Emperor and ordered that all sentries were to be doubled and other precautions taken to prevent any escape attempt. The news of his impending exile was broken to Napoleon by Lord Keith and Sir Henry Bunbury, an Under Secretary of State, on the last day of July and, although bitterly resented, did not – it seems – come as much of a surprise.

French sources refer often to the perfidy of the British government, and its representatives, in consigning the Emperor to St. Helena as a prisoner-of-war. Napoleon himself said that he would have preferred to have been surrendered to the Bourbons, or imprisoned in the Tower of London, rather than be exiled to an unfavourable tropical climate. With only Maitland's account to go on, and bearing in mind that – as he asserts – no promises were made to Napoleon by any British officer in respect of his reception in Britain, it is difficult to see how accusations of perfidy can be justified. On 7 August 1815, the day that Napoleon was transferred from *Bellerophon* to HMS *Northumberland*, commanded by another Scot, Rear Admiral Sir George Cockburn, Lord Keith wrote to Maitland saying that the Comte de Las Cases had complained of broken promises concerning Napoleon's fate. Maitland replied at length, reporting his side of the conversations with Las Cases prior to the Emperor joining *Bellerophon*, and was supported in written testimonies by Captain Sartorius of HMS *Slaney* and Captain Gambier of HMS *Myrmidon*.

Les Highlanders à Inkermann, *a coloured lithograph by V. Adam, c 1855. This depiction has to be deemed allegorical since no Highland regiments fought at Inkermann in November 1854.*

(NMS)

All three officers were firm on the point that no commitments or promises had been made concerning Napoleon's reception in Britain and that the Emperor, if he joined *Bellerophon*, did so of his own free will. Maitland also records that Maréchal de Camp the Comte de Montholon, Adc to Napoleon, went out of his way to reassure Maitland that the Emperor did not blame him for his government's decision and that Las Cases, who had been in charge of negotiations, was attempting to cover his own failure to obtain promises of safe conduct by inventing tales of broken promises and non-existent commitments. The overall impression, from reading Maitland's account, is that he was mightily relieved when Napoleon, and especially his entourage, left his custody for that of his fellow-countryman Admiral Cockburn. Maitland was scrupulous in refusing to accept a jewelled box set with a miniature of the Emperor but felt able to accept a glass tumbler from Napoleon's travelling canteen. Maitland's career continued after 1815 and he saw regular overseas service. He was promoted to Rear Admiral and knighted in 1830 and died at sea off Bombay in 1839. Napoleon's present, the glass tumbler, is preserved in the Scottish United Services Museum in Edinburgh Castle.

Admiral Sir George Cockburn, the Scot who took Napoleon to St. Helena in 1815 on board his flagship HMS *Northumberland*, had had a long and distinguished career prior to taking charge of Napoleon. He had had dual field command, with another Scot, Major General Robert Ross, under the overall command of yet another Scot, Admiral Sir Alexander Cochrane, of an expedition which attacked and burnt the United States' capital, Washington, in 1814. Among his troops were the 21st Royal North British Fusiliers and these soldiers and their naval and military leaders chased President Madison out of his house, ate his dinner, drank his wine and then torched the place. When it was rebuilt and repainted after the War of 1812, the colour chosen for the exterior gave it its name: The White House. Cockburn's account of the journey to St. Helena can be read in extracts from his diary, published in 1888, and in the relevant chapters of his biography by Captain James Pack RN (1987). It is clear that Cockburn found Napoleon's company uncongenial and was determined to treat him as a general who was also a prisoner-of-war; no special honours were paid and no recognition of his former Imperial status allowed.

HMS *Northumberland* anchored off the capital of St. Helena, Jamestown, on 15 October and, until the following August, when the new governor arrived to relieve him, Cockburn was charged with Napoleon's captivity. Cockburn handed over the command of the Cape of Good Hope station to yet another Scot – if of slightly more watered-down lineage – Sir Pulteney Malcolm, and the governorship of the island to Lieutenant-General Sir Hudson Lowe. Although the Scottish connection – in a naval sense – remained, the appointment of Lowe to command St. Helena might be interpreted as a calculated insult by the British government to their distinguished captive since Lowe had formerly been colonel of a regiment of emigré Corsicans in the British army.

The death of Napoleon in 1821 removed the most serious perceived threat to the security of the great European powers. Although Europe was far from peaceful internally for the next three or four decades, Britain would not fight again in Europe until 1854. For France the situation was much the same. She was involved increasingly in Algeria and occasionally and briefly in Spain and the Low Countries but, as with Britain, little significant conflict in or near to Europe galvanised the French in the years between Waterloo and the outbreak of war in the Crimea. Unlike Britain, however, there were crises of government and threats of outbreaks of revolution which, although serving to enhance Britain's legendary smugness by their non-occurrence across the Channel, underlined France's far more European status and, in any case, were only just avoided in Britain itself. Very little of Europe in the 1820s, 1830s and 1840s escaped some form of political turmoil but its seriousness, its outcome and its degree of national uniqueness varied widely. The British monarchy remained untouched and largely unthreatened by these convulsions. The victory of 1815, the eventual beginnings of Parliamentary reform, the size, apolitical nature and loyalty of the armed forces, the comparative prosperity of the middle and upper classes and the overwhelmingly Establishment view of the press all contributed to keeping successful revolutionary movements from being imported to Britain from the continent.

The nature of Highland Scotland had undergone profound change since the beginning of the wars against France in 1793. The acts of proscription against the outward manifestations of the Highland identity, such as the wearing of the plaid and of tartan, the playing of the bagpipes and the bearing of arms, had all been withdrawn in the 1780s. The much-published heroism of the Highlanders in the Seven Years War and American War of Independence had been followed by similar feats – real, exaggerated and mythical – during the wars against France and these three campaigns, together with the growth of evictions of Highland tenantry by their masters to make room for the more docile, profitable and useful Cheviot sheep, had rendered Highland Scotland a place – in English eyes – that one might consider visiting. Napoleon is recorded by Maitland as carrying a volume of the poetry of Ossian with him as part of his travelling library on board *Bellerophon* and he was not alone in being taken in by this fraudulent pan-Caledonian doggerel which purported to be of ancient Bardic lineage and yet had been produced in the post-1780s surge of interest in a mythical and invented Highland ideal. The invention of 'family' tartans, the writings of Walter Scott, the popularity of whisky during the lack of easy availability of French spirits all contrived, among so many other ephemeral factors, to make Scotland increasingly socially acceptable. Furthermore, Scotland was increasingly being identified with *Highland* Scotland, even by Lowland Scots – who knew a profitable bandwagon when they saw one – and the final seal of approval was applied

Episode de la bataille d'Inkermann: Episode of the battle
of Inkermann, *a coloured lithograph by F. Grenier, c 1855.
No such event is recorded and no Highland regiments fought
at Inkermann.*

(NMS)

to the whole process of the re-invention of Scotland by two royal visits and an eventual
royal residence. King George IV, whose romantic notions included ones associated with
the supposed Celtic twilight and who had been instrumental in the paying of a pension
by his father to the exiled Stuarts, visited Edinburgh in 1822. His niece, the young Queen
Victoria, repeated the process in 1840 and on several subsequent occasions and the pur-
chase and development of Balmoral, in an area of Deeside reminiscent to the royal
couple of Prince Albert's home at Coburg in Thuringia, finally confirmed the process
of adoption in the 1850s.

   Although Scott has been extensively blamed for his part in the reinvention process that
transformed Scotland during the nineteenth century, a lot of the blame is both superficial
and unfair. That admission notwithstanding, it is undoubtedly true that his writings,
when they reached a continental European audience, made him and the country of his
birth famous overnight. When his extensive series of "Waverley" novels came to include
Quentin Durward (1823) and *Tales of a Grandfather* (1828–30), the lionising that had
greeted him in Paris in 1815 grew to fever pitch among the French and, later, he came
to be acknowledged as a progenitor of the Romantic movement among French novelists
such as Hugo, Balzac and Dumas, for whom Scott's historical style proved so influential.
Quentin Durward, the tale of a young Border Scotsman in the service of the King of France
as part of his Bodyguard popularised Scotland and the Scots in France, and revived folk
memories of the Auld Alliance among a far wider audience than those few Parisiennes
briefly intoxicated by the sight of Highlanders camped in the Bois de Boulogne during

the occupation of the city. To those remnants of Napoleonic society who still recalled or yearned for past glories, the fictitious ones of Scott, as related about his own countrymen, struck a chord that still reverberates in France.

These glories of literature, and the fashion for tartan in civilian dress which swept Paris as a result of the Highland troops' presence during the occupation, provided a stimulus to Franco-Scottish relations. On a personal level these were continued among the classes of society which travelled and between monarchs, and contacts between Louis-Philippe, King of the French and, successively, King William IV and then Queen Victoria remained close. William IV, who – despite having been a career naval officer – shared his elder brother's interest in uniforms, commissioned a French portraitist, Alexandre Jean Dubois Drahonet, to paint a series of 100 small paintings depicting soldiers and sailors of all ranks in the Royal Navy and the army of 1832. Most remain in the Royal collection and are among the best evidence of the appeareance of the British serviceman of the 1830s. Dubois Drahonet, who had no reputation prior to 1832 – and his royal commission – as a military artist, painted various figures from the Scottish regiments of the time, not because they were Scottish but rather because they were a part of the British army of the period. He cannot be put into the same class as later French battle painters who seem to have found particular inspiration in the exploits and appearance of the Scottish regiments of the British army and so he should, perhaps, be thought of as a latter-day David Morier, the Swiss artist who had recorded the British army of the early 1750s for King George II.

The nearest that France came in the nineteenth century to recreating the glories of the Napoleonic epoch was during the Empire of the first Napoleon's nephew, Napoleon III, from 1852 to 1870. Louis-Charles Napoleon Bonaparte was the son of the King of Holland, who was Napoleon I's brother, and he had gone into exile in 1815 at the age of seven. He passed the next 33 years abroad, making two attempts at *coups d'états* in 1836 at Strasbourg and in 1840 at Boulogne. During his exile Louis Bonaparte paid at least one visit to Scotland, to participate with members of the British *jeunesse d'orée* at the Eglinton tournament of 1839. This occasion, seriously marred by bad weather, was held by the Earl of Eglinton on his estate in south-west Scotland and largely consisted of an attempt, using both genuine and reproduction arms and armour, to recreate what the Romantic movement perceived to be the joys of chivalry in the Middle Ages. Louis was elected, finally, to the presidency of the National Assembly in December 1848, having cemented his relationship with Britain by taking an English mistress and, more respectably, by enrolling as a special constable in London during the Chartist riots of 1848. After declaring himself Emperor in 1852 he married Eugénie de Montijo, a Spanish beauty with a Scottish grandfather in the shape of a Kirkpatrick of Closeburn. The new French Imperial family and the British royal family were to grow increasingly close, Queen Victoria being charmed by the Emperor – whom she was surprised to find scarcely *parvenu* at all – and finding great kinship with the Empress – who shared Victoria's abiding interest in the enchantment of Balmoral and its surroundings.

A year before Louis Bonaparte became president of France, the 79th (Cameron) Highlanders were subject to a visit by a son-in-law of one of the first Napoleon's brothers. Although Russian, Prince Anatole Demidov recounted his experiences of the Officers' Mess of the 79th in French, clearly spoke French in preference to Russian and, having been educated in France and worked as an attaché in the Russian embassy in Paris, was more French than Russian. His brief marriage to Princess Mathilde, daughter of King Jerome Bonaparte of Westphalia, cemented his French connections and so, for the purposes of this narrative – and especially because what he says of the 79th could just as easily have been said by a native-born Frenchman – he is worthy of inclusion here.

Ils savent combattre et mourir en frères: They know how
to fight and to die like brothers, *a lithograph by A. Adam,
c 1855.*

(Musée de l'Armée)

Visiting the 79th in Gibraltar in August 1847 he quickly made friends with the lieutenant-colonel commanding, Lauderdale Maule – brother of Fox Maule, later Lord Panmure, the Secretary for War in Britain – and was invited to dine in the Officers' Mess. The relevant extract from Demidov's reminiscences, published in 1858 under the title *Etapes Maritimes sur les côtes d'Espagne*, is quoted in full in the regimental magazine of The Queen's Own Cameron Highlanders of 1907. It is slightly abridged here but provides an insight into the impression that the ceremony of a Highland regiment's Officers' Mess made upon a relatively *soigné* young aristocrat with profound French connections.

> The 79th is one of the regiments which wears in all its singular beauty the costume of the Scottish Highlander, but the officers in undress are clothed in trousers. The officers are our hosts and we go to their mess table. The table is magnificently laid for twenty guests, the service is first-rate and the fare excellent. Suddenly, in the middle of dinner, the door opens, and a piper advances slowly with measured steps three times round the table. He plays airs consecrated to welcome and hospitality.

Le Vengeur, *a lithograph by C. Vernier, 1855. A*
Highlander protects, or revenges, a wounded Zouave in an
unrecorded incident.

(Musée de l'Armée)

—— Enfin , je tiens donc un Montagnard écossais .... il y a longtemps que je cherche
l'occasion de prouver à ces gaillards là que l'hospitalité se dôôônne et ne se vend jamais,
non non jamais , jamais , jamais .... je vas lui payer un grand p'tit verre !......

Nos troupiers en Orient, *No. 5, a coloured lithograph by
C. Vernier, 1855. This lithograph was "improved" in c 1935
by added colour in an attempt to render the Highlander
accurately portrayed as being of the 93rd (Sutherland)
Highlanders. The inscription may be loosely translated thus:
"at last I have got a Scottish Highlander . . . for a long
time I have waited for the opportunity to show these fellows
that hospitality is given and never bought, no never, never
never . . . I am going to buy him a drink".* (NMS)

Brothers in Arms, *a lithograph from* Punch *of 21 October
1854.*

(Punch)

They are obliged to explain their meaning to us, for it is only Scottish ears which
can interpret the significance or time in the midst of the shrill screams of the instrument and the bass humming; still it is a wild and grand music. After dinner the wine
is passed, a ceremony which, according to English [sic] custom, is rather a solemn
proceeding. Soon, however, under the influence of the excellent produce of France
[note, *not* Portugal], tongues are loosened; conversation waxes lively, and toasts, with
inevitable replies, succeeded one another. The last toast is given with a glass of
whisky, which is essentially the Scottish drink. But in order to use the 'spirituous'
occasion, the toast is drunk with one foot on the chair, the other on the table. The
hurrahs, nine times repeated which salute this supreme libation are in keeping with
the whole scene. After this enthusiasm we adjourn to the salon. A short pause ensues
which is devoted to sipping a cup of coffee; then one sees eight fine soldiers appear
to perform, in turn, the sword dance. The sword dance is called in the Scottish dialect
the 'Gill Calm' [sic], literally a young and vigorous man [Actually *Dannse Gille-Caluim*,
from the first two words of a tune to which it is danced. *Gille* is Gaelic for a young
lad and *Caluim* – the Gaelic for Malcolm – may have been, traditionally, a sprightly
or vigorous dancer.] This is what happens: two great swords, 'Claidheamh mhor'
[Gaelic for great sword – the origin of 'claymore'] are placed on the ground at right
angles. The dancer faces this way and that, with extreme agility performing many
and varied steps. The tune first played is called the 'Strathspeg' [sic] [Actually
Strathspey: a dance slower than a reel and, now, usually performed by four persons]
but the pace quickens and becomes 'Le reel'. The Highlanders consider this dance
the symbol of the most sincere and hospitable welcome. Needless to say the dance
is performed to the tune of the bagpipes.

Demidov also witnessed several parades, periods of drill and maneouvres while at
Gibraltar and commented with surprise on the presence of regimental mascots – animals –

*Colour-Sergeant of the Scots Fusilier Guards, 1856. He wears
the Crimean War Medal 1854–56 with clasps for the battles
of the Alma, Balaklava and Inkermann and for the siege of
Sebastopol, together with the French Médaille Militaire.*

(NMS)

125

Sketches by the French Capitaine Vanson of privates of the 79th (Cameron) and 93rd (Sutherland) Highlanders, together with a musician of the 93rd, in camp at Varna, July 1854.
(Musée de l'Armée)

at the head of the military bands. He records that, while at Gibraltar, the mascot of the 79th was a stag and wonders how it coped with the sound of the bagpipes.

The Allied army that went to the Crimea in 1854 exemplified the new friendship between Britain and France and, especially, the close personal respect between Victoria and Napoleon III. Not all the Scottish regiments eventually served in the Crimea but of those which did it is noticeable that, once again, the picturesque Highlanders stole the show. A comparison of British and French popular prints and magazines reveals an interesting and perhaps relevant, disparity. French illustrators, when seeking either to personify their British allies in the Crimea or to illustrate the *fraternité d'armes*, chose Highland soldiers almost without exception. A number of French prints (using the term 'print' to cover the wide variety of mass-produced illustrations of the period) exist which depict a Highlander and a French soldier in battle, the former usually defending the latter – often a wounded soldier of a Zouave regiment – against bloodthirsty and unchivalrous Russian soldiers intent upon finishing off the wounded and helpless Frenchman. Even in depictions not of battle scenes but of the long intervals of co-existence between conflict, the figure of the Highlander was clearly a popular one in France and instantly conveyed the impression of the British army to those reading the illustrated papers or buying the prints. The reason for this is not hard to find. Although it may stretch back to the experience of the French in the Napoleonic Wars or to that of Parisians during the occupation of their city, it is more likely to be more recent, to owe a great deal to the Romantic Celtic twilight of the 1820s, 1830s and 1840s and to the obvious fact that only the British Army had Highlanders and so they could not be confused with any other nation's soldiers by a public unfamiliar with the minutiae of military uniforms.

Oddly enough though, the converse does not appear to be the case. No such depictions appear in recorded British prints of the period, except where they are bilingual Franco-British ones, and *Punch*, for instance, has only one drawing of a Highland soldier in its pages for the whole period of the war; since it depicts a French soldier too it is reproduced in this chapter. This should surprise no-one familiar with *Punch*, the pre-occupation of which magazine with the *mores* of the south-eastern English middle classes is by no means new. Although it depicted British soldiers regularly during the Crimean war, when an allegorical figure representing the army was needed it was, with the one exception noted, always a Guardsman and usually a Grenadier. Since *Punch* was written principally for a London audience, or at least an audience familiar with the capital, and since it had long established – at least in terms of its attempts at humorous cartoons – a tradition of finding amusing anyone not of the south-eastern English middle class, the selection of a Grenadier Guardsman to represent the British army is by no means unusual; it might, indeed, be said to be as predictable as the rest of the magazine.

Few British prints of the Crimean War which depict French troops pay much attention to the Zouave regiments, which might be said – for a number of reasons – to be the Highlanders of the French army. The Zouave regiments were relatively new in the French army, picturesquely clothed, all volunteers and not conscripts – and therefore with greater enthusiasm for combat associated with a relatively remote and strange part of the French dominions and one with a reputation for the ferocity of its inhabitants. Although they had largely shed their association, in terms of their soldiers, with North Africa by the Crimean War, their intrepidity, élan and uniforms were to be widely copied after the war by the armies of other nations, notably the Army of the Union during the War between the States in America and by the British army for its West Indies regiments. A close relationship is said to have been established between the Highlanders and the Zouaves during the Crimean War but no Highland regiment's history makes mention of the event so assiduously represented by French illustrators. In the absence of proof to the contrary, or hard evidence to substantiate the event, one must assume that it is an allegory either of the general comradeship-in-arms or of the special relationship between the Highlanders and the Zouaves.

Four regiments of Zouaves were part of the French army in the Crimea, the three regiments of Zouaves of the French line and the Zouaves of the Imperial Guard. The latter regiment formed part of the *Division de la Garde Impériale* in the *Corps de Réserve* and was not formed until March 1855. The three regiments of Zouaves of the line were distributed through the first three divisions of the second French infantry corps commanded by Général de Division Pierre Bosquet. Bosquet's division, placed on the extreme right of the Allied forces at the battle of the Alma on 20 September 1854, succeeded in turning the Russian left and completing the rout of the Russian forces which were being forced back by the Allied forces to their front. The intrepidity of Bosquet's Zouaves in scaling apparently unclimbable heights above the river Alma made their contribution to the battle as newsworthy as the steady advance up the slope above the river of the British Highland Brigade. The arrival of Bosquet's division, with the 3rd Zouaves among other French troops in the vanguard, at the battle of Inkermann on 5 November 1854 saved the day for the hard-pressed British forces and Bosquet was personally

Two officers of the 42nd (Royal) Highlanders (Black Watch) sketched by Capitaine Vanson at Varna, 1854.

(Musée de l'Armée)

A lieutenant of a Highland regiment and a cantinière *of the French army sketched by Capitaine Vanson in the Crimea, c 1856.*

(Musée de l'Armée)

thanked by Field Marshal Lord Raglan, in command of the British forces, "in the name of England [*sic*]".

Initially, the Highland Brigade in the Crimea had consisted of just the 42nd (Black Watch), the 79th (Cameron Highlanders) and the 93rd (Sutherland Highlanders). By the end of the campaign, these original three Highland regiments had been joined by the 71st (Highland Light Infantry), the 72nd (Seaforth) and the 92nd (Gordon) Highlanders. In addition, the Scottish regimental presence in the Crimea was bolstered by the Scots Fusilier Guards (Scots Guards), the 1st Foot (Royal Scots), the 21st (Royal Scots Fusiliers) and 90th Foot (Cameronians). The 90th landed after the major battles of the Alma, Balaklava and Inkermann had been fought but the three other regiments distinguished themselves at Inkermann, where the day was saved for the Allies by the timely arrival of the French.

There were numerous occasions, in occasional skirmishes with the enemy and in the expedition to Kertch in the eastern Crimea in 1855, when Scots and French soldiers fought together but the only occasion when Allied troops became intermingled in the frenzy of combat was at the battle of Inkermann at which no Highland regiment was present. Since the Scottish regiments which were present at Inkermann looked virtually indistinguishable from other Guards or Infantry regiments of the period – except to the trained eye and in close-up – it is unlikely that the majority of French troops, in the heat of battle, realised that they were fighting alongside Scots. At the Alma and at the assault upon the Redan and the Malakov, the twin defensive fortresses of Sevastapol, British and French forces fought separately, the French taking the Malakov and the British – eventually – the Redan, and so, while a close relationship between the Highland soldiers and their French allies may well have been established in the period between battles, there was little opportunity for this to manifest itself in terms of actual combat.

E pour Ecossais, *a lithograph by V. Adam for a page from a French child's alphabet book, c 1856.*

(NMS)

E   Ecossais

The 2nd battalion of the Royal Scots was the only Scottish regiment to fight alongside the French in the only remaining Franco-British expedition of the nineteenth century: the expedition to China in 1859 and 1860. The battalion had been stationed in Hong Kong since 1858 and its officers had rapidly struck up a rapport with the officers of a French naval squadron also based there. As Major General Sir Alexander Tulloch recalled in his *Recollections of Forty Years' Service* (1903):

> We had many friends also amongst the officers of the French Squadron, several of whom belonged to the best families in France. Possibly the fact of our being a Scotch regiment had something to do with it. The French officers were well up in Scott's novels, and recognised that the forebears of the Royals had, in ancient days, been in the French service.

A detachment of the 2nd battalion accompanied a naval and military expeditionary force of French and British troops into the interior of China in January 1859 and the entire battalion contributed to a larger force which attacked the Taku Forts on the Peiho river in August 1860. The forts guarded the approaches to Peking and, once successfully stormed, the capital rapidly capitulated. The Franco-British force was under the command of Général Cousin-Montauban, subsequently Comte de Palikao, and comprised two French brigades of 8,000 men and a mixed naval and military British force of some 12,500 men.

If the expeditions to the Crimea and China were the only ones in the nineteenth century in which British and French servicemen participated together, they were by no means the only foreign adventures in which the Empire of Napoleon III became involved. For many years, British historians anxious to make comparisons between the Empires of Napoleon I and his nephew have written off Napoleon III's apparent attempts to emulate his uncle as fruitless, nay even ridiculous, strivings to attain *'la gloire'* for France – the need for which is thus supposed persistently to galvanise France at a moment's

The 2nd China War Medal 1857–60 and the French
Médaille de l'expédition de Chine 1860 awarded to
Private Joseph Crisp, 2nd battalion, 1st Regiment of Foot
(Royal Scots).

(NMS)

notice. Such simplistic views do their perpetrators little honour and misunderstand much about both Napoleons and the Empires that they and the people of France created, defended and, ultimately, destroyed. Before Napoleon's election as President of the Second Republic in 1848, Jules Grévy – a republican deputé – warned the National Assembly in tactful yet deliberately oblique terms against a resurgence of the spirit of Bonapartism. Alfred Cobban, in the second volume of his *History of Modern France* (1961), quotes Grévy's expressed fears:

> Are you sure that there will never be found an ambitious man, anxious to perpetuate his power, and if he is a man who had been able to make himself popular, if he is a victorious general, surrounded with the prestige of that military glory which the French cannot resist, if he is the offspring of the families which have reigned over France, and if he has never expressly renounced what he calls his rights, if commerce is languishing, if the people are in misery...will you guarantee that this ambitious man will not succeed in overthrowing the republic?

In the event, of course, Grévy's fears proved justified when Louis-Charles Napoleon Bonaparte became Emperor Napoleon III in 1852. Grévy, however, was finally triumphant and, after the exile of the Emperor following France's defeat by Prussia in 1871, he was elected as the first President of the Third Republic.

Napoleon's own interest in the Romantic movement prior to his election in 1848 was continued into the Second Empire and, very gradually, the spirit of that Empire began to embody, to reflect and partially to encourage a rebirth of interest in the glories of France's military achievement under Napoleon I. This growth in military power, despite the close personal relationships between the monarchs of Britain and France, inevitably made the British government feel uneasy, even to the extent of allowing an invasion scare of 1859 to get wildly out of control. There is no doubt that France's relatively successful intervention in the Crimea in 1854, wholly successful intervention in China in 1860, and rather pyrrhic involvement in the campaigns in Italy in 1859 and the 1860s gave the new Emperor and his state more global political confidence than France had had for several decades and nowhere was this better demonstrated, militarily, than in the splendour of the French army of the Second Empire and by the French military painters of the period.

For the whole of the nineteenth century, which – in many ways – is better regarded as the period 1815–1914 rather than 1800–99, France did not lack for artists who could convey, in a variety of ways, styles, media and treatments, the supposed glories and realities of the human, and usually the French, experience of war. From David, who might be described as Court Painter to Napoleon, to Detaille, who was virtually official artist to the French army during the Third Republic, the military history of Napoleonic France did not lack for artistic interpreters. Battle painters of the Romantic epoch, such as Raffet and Vernet had some common ground with Géricault, whose undoubted forte as a painter of horses led him to produce paintings of cavalry officers of the First Empire. The next generation were perhaps best represented by Meissonier and Philippoteaux, who were both exhibiting in the late 1840s but whose most relevant and best-remembered work belongs to the 1860s and 1870s. Although Meissonier never painted British military subjects, unlike Philippoteaux, it was he – regarded by many in the 1870s as the doyen of military painters – who observed that Britain had only one military painter, a woman. The extent to which this woman, Elizabeth, Lady Butler, was influenced by the various French schools of battle painting is examined at length in the relevant chapter of Jenny Spencer-Smith's excellent work *Lady Butler, Battle Artist* (1987)

L'Ecossais, *a piper of a Highland regiment by Edouard Detaille, 1879. The regiment depicted is probably the 42nd (Black Watch). The pose and many other details, allowing for the change in uniform, are very similar to that of Piper Muir of the 42nd, photographed in 1856 (see next picture).*

(National Army Museum)

Piper Muir, 42nd (Royal Highlanders), photographed after his return from the Crimea in 1856. It seems clear that Detaille used this depiction of a Highland piper, which was widely available, on which to base his painting L'Ecossais *(see previous picture).*

(NMS)

and the development of British battle painting in the nineteenth century is explored in laudable detail in Dr J. Hichberger's *Images of the Army: the military in British art 1815–1914* (1988). Since the Franco-Scottish connection is barely relevant in the context of British battle painting, it is to these two recent, well-researched and highly recommended works that those wishing to know more should turn.

Philippoteaux, born in the year of Waterloo, produced three battle paintings with British connections, two of which are relevant to this narrative and both of which were produced in the 1870s, the decade before his death. In *La Charge des cuirassiers français à Waterloo* (Victoria and Albert Museum, Apsley House, London) the artist depicts a square of Highlanders being set upon by a squadron of cuirassiers. The foreground is a carpet of corpses, human and equine, and the background, slightly elevated, is a mass of confusion as other French cavalry squadrons sweep up a slope and towards other British infantry squares. The repeated and ineffectual charges of the French cavalry against the British squares was, and is, well-known and admitted by French military historians. Philippoteaux, aware of this, may well have deliberately chosen Highlanders to represent the British, not merely because of their unique uniforms or rapport with his French audience but, perhaps to show the phlegm and stolidity of the British infantry –

A drummer of the 42nd (Royal Highlanders) by Edouard Detaille, c 1880.

(M. Jean-Claude Boyron)

as represented by one of its most respected sections – in contrast to the *élan* of the French cavalry. In his other painting which is relevant here, *Combat de Balaklava, le 25 octobre 1854* (Officers' Mess, The Royal Scots Dragoon Guards (Carabiniers and Greys)), Philippoteaux depicts another cavalry action, the Charge of the Heavy Cavalry Brigade at the battle of Balaklava. It, again, is a conventional battle treatment, the Royal Scots Greys being shown, having pierced the centre of the Russian cavalry, engaged in hand-to-hand combat with the Russians. The regimental butcher, in apron and without either jacket or headdress, is shown entering the mêlée (a frequently recounted story at the time). The action fades into the middle distance and the background, again on a rise, is of hills and the harbour of Balaklava. There are comparatively few French paintings of the Crimean War since later, and more uniquely-French, wars tended to overshadow the Crimea in the eyes of the successors to Meissonier and Philippoteaux.

Unlike Philippoteaux, the two most well-known French battle painters of the next generation – both of which, to differing degrees, are relevant to this narrative – have been the subject of brief but well-illustrated biographies.

Alphonse de Neuville, who died the year after Philippoteaux, in 1885 at the tragically-early age of 50, has been dealt with by Philippe Chabret in *Alphonse de Neuville: l'épopée de la défaite* (1979). Edouard Detaille, a pupil of Meissonier and the *éminence grise* of late-nineteenth century French military painting, has received similar treatment from

*The tomb of H.R.H. The Prince Leopold, Duke of Albany, in
the church of St. George, Cannes.*

(M. E. Lamy)

Dr. Jean-Marcel Humbert in *Edouard Detaille: l'héroisme d'un siècle* (1979). Both of these books should be required reading for anyone wishing to pursue the subject. De Neuville produced only one painting of relevance to this chapter, *La bataille de Tel-el-Kebir 12-13 septembre 1882* (Scottish United Services Museum but exhibited, 1989, at the Regimental Museum of The Black Watch, Perth). Painted in 1883, it depicts officers and men of The Black Watch, part of the Highland Brigade in Egypt in 1882, climbing out of the defensive moat around the Egyptian positions at Tel-el-Kebir. Ordered to attack with the bayonet, the Brigade suffered heavy casualties at this well-defended point and de Neuville has not shrunk from showing casualties and the brief desperation of the situation. He had employed a similar technique when depicting a similar hard-fought engagement, the defence of Rorke's Drift during the Zulu War of 1879. The bulk of de Neuville's paintings concerned the Franco-Prussian War of 1870–71 although he did produce a few illustrating actions in the Crimea and in the Italian campaign of 1859.

De Neuville's contemporary, Edouard Detaille, spread his coverage of military history much wider and lived longer (1848–1912). Detaille's historical paintings are principally concerned with the era of the first Napoleon but, like Philippoteaux, he did paint the well-known – and not quite apocryphal – incident of the French and British Guards saluting each other before opening fire at Fontenoy in 1745. Detaille had good personal reasons for painting evocative pictures seeking to capture the splendour of the First Empire. His grandfather had been a supplier of goods to the armies of both the Republic and the Empire and had been closely involved with all the developments of the Napoleonic military machine; Dr Humbert recounts how his grandfather's tales fired Edouard's imagination. Detaille's father, at the age of 5, had nearly been crushed by the Emperor's horse at the Camp at Boulogne in 1805. Napoleon had broken his bridle and, in order to miss the child, had reined in sharply, skidded on the wet road and been

134

Allied occupation of Tientsin 1908–09. A guard of honour found by 2nd battalion The Queen's Own Cameron Highlanders at the departure of the German detachment from Tientsin, June 1909. French troops from the garrison are in the right foreground.
(Queen's Own Highlanders; Mrs J. Smith)

thrown. Despite being bruised and covered in mud from his fall, the Emperor appears to have been more concerned that the son of one of his most reliable suppliers was undamaged. Needless to say the story was long remembered in the Detaille household.

Detaille first exhibited at the Paris salon in 1867 and, on the outbreak of the Franco-Prussian war in 1870, volunteered for service in a *Garde Mobile* battalion. This experience of war affected him deeply; it was to result in the mid-1870s in his finest paintings and other works dealing with the war, and influenced his treatment of war as a subject. Detaille is dealt with at length by Dr Humbert and, naturally, pre-eminence is given to the artist's French works. However, he – alone of all French military painters – was the one best known, justifiably, for his illustrations of Scottish military subjects. No case can be made for a particular preference by Detaille for Scottish – i.e. Highland – regiments over others of the British army since no written record exists of such a prejudice. However, his extant works on British military subjects are weighted in the direction of kilted regiments and even when painting his British patron, Edward, Prince of Wales, on manoeuvres at Aldershot in 1889 (the painting, a sketch rather than a finished work, is in the Musée de l'Armée, Paris) he contrived to place a company of Highlanders – either The Black Watch or Camerons – behind the Prince and his brother, Arthur, Duke of Connaught. The Prince of Wales is said to have provided Detaille with a pair of trousers, or trews, in Black Watch tartan and so it is probably fair to say that a degree of pro-Highland prejudice can be detected, when appropriate, in Detaille's work.

It seems, therefore, to be incontrovertible – although qualifiable – that the picturesque nature of the Highland regiments, together with their legendary fighting qualities, appealed to French artists to an extent disproportionate to the treatment meted out by those artists to other types of British soldier. Even Jacques Tissot, in no sense a 'military' painter and quite heavily anglicised, used a Highland soldier – a sergeant of The Black Watch – when searching for a suitable soldier to figure in his painting *Portsmouth Dockyard* (Tate Gallery, London) in 1877. In searching for a colourful figure, one imbued with virility and implied panache, in order to represent the idea of the painting, sub-titled unofficially *Entre les deux mon coeur balance* (How happy could I be with either?), Tissot –

135

*Allied occupation of Tientsin 1908–09. A tug-of-war in
progress between a French team and a team from 2nd
battalion The Queen's Own Cameron Highlanders at the
inter-regimental games of 1909. The Camerons team won,
after a pull of ten-and-a-half minutes.*
(Queen's Own Highlanders; Mrs J. Smith)

suggests Christopher Wood in his *Tissot* (1986) – may have selected the Highlander in
order less to offend Victorian morality than he had done in earlier paintings on the same
theme: one man between two women.

Franco-Scottish military relations remained on much the same plane until 1914 and
the global cataclysm that again brought together soldiers of both nations united against
a common enemy. As Victoria's children, and especially her sons, grew up and discovered France – and especially Paris, Biaritz and Cannes – so the mid-Victorian
Balmoralised view of Scotland and the Belle Epoque of *fin-de-siècle* France became
merged in the recreations of royal princes. One royal prince who exemplified the connection, and – in death – represents it still, was Victoria's youngest and shortest lived
son, Prince Leopold, Duke of Albany. Appointed colonel of the 3rd (Militia) Battalion,
the Seaforth Highlanders (Ross-shire Buffs, The Duke of Albany's) in 1882, he died in
Cannes in 1884 and is buried there. His effigy atop the tomb in the church of St. George
shows him in the full dress uniform, review order, of his regiment.

Franco-Scottish military co-operation continued into the first decade of the twentieth
century in China as international garrisons attempted to keep the sleeping giant asleep,
and occupied their time periodically by providing mixed guards of honour for arriving
or departing senior officers and in arranging athletics meetings; always good opportunities for a little healthy national rivalry. It is not recorded whether the tug-of-war team
of 2nd Battalion The Queen's Own Cameron Highlanders pulled harder in the ten-and-a-
half minutes that it took them to vanquish a French team in the Sports Day of 1909
in Tientsin because they had heard that, five years earlier in 1904, the British government, in arranging the formal *Entente Cordiale* with France, had formally and finally
abrogated the privileges of honorary nationality accorded Scots in France, and one
suspects that it would have meant as little to them as the privileges had done to most
Scots for more than a century. A considerable degree of mutual regard, notwithstanding
mutual incomprehension, was to continue despite the actions of London-based politicians, and this would be underlined in the two world wars which form the substance
of the next two chapters.

Chapter Six

Jocks and Poilus 1914–18

IN 1914 SCOTTISH SOLDIERS HAD NOT FOUGHT IN FRANCE FOR A CENTURY. THE WAR sparked off by the assassination of the Archduke Franz Ferdinand of Austria in Sarajevo at the end of June 1914 had actually been building for a generation. In the two decades between its end and the beginning of the next world war, very much its natural child, more books were written about the First World War, the Great War, than about any previous military campaign. That statistic alone indicates its impact upon more than just the generations which fought the war; its reverberations are with us still. It was a war which, in many ways, both defied statistics and yet spawned them. It killed more European soldiers than any war had ever done, it toppled ancient dynasties and it rewrote the map of Europe – never the most permanent of documents. The Scottish soldiers who disembarked in France in 1914 fought as part of the army of the largest, richest and most powerful Empire the world had ever seen, yet the British Expeditionary Force – small, professional and entirely made up of volunteers – was dwarfed by its allied French Army and its adversary, the German Army. It is no part of the function of this chapter to tell, yet again, the story of the war, its facts and its battles; this has been done, better and more exhaustively, elsewhere. Instead, with the aid of the copious illustrations that the war produced, an attempt will be made to study this new manifestation of the Auld Alliance as a series of vignettes, each reflecting some aspect of the relationship – principally from the Scottish angle – as it was developed and continued throughout the cataclysm.

The wars against Napoleon had been remarkable for the noticeable numbers of senior commanders in the British forces with Scottish roots. Although, in the twentieth century, this Scottish ascendancy was replaced by that of the Anglo-Irish, the First World War brought at least three Scots to positions of senior command. Pre-eminent, of course, was Douglas Haig. Less well-remembered, and desperately unlucky to be saddled with command of the unwinnable folly of Gallipoli, was Ian Hamilton. Almost entirely forgotten, except by students of the conflict and devotees of the history of the Royal Artillery, was Henry Horne. A field marshal and earl, a general and knight, a general and baron, these three Scots – in their differing ways – contributed considerably to the British effort during the war and, because of their positions, were in frequent contact with their French allies.

Haig has been the most regularly and assiduously dissected by historians. He has had his champions and his detractors. His most recent biographer, Gerard De Groot, in *Douglas Haig 1861–1928* (1988) goes to commendable lengths in establishing his position as the first objective biographer of the field marshal, a position occupied by his being, apparently, the first to be given full access to Haig's private diaries and letters and to use certain primary sources. It is, therefore, with a sense – one feels – of regret that Dr De Groot joins the camp of Haig's detractors and reveals him to have been undoubtedly great but inevitably flawed. It might be observed that few individuals, whatever their greatness, are without flaws and historians are as prone to these as great

D Company, 1st battalion The Cameronians (Scottish Rifles)
passing through Maretz on a route march, 20 August 1914.
(Imperial War Museum)

captains, if less required to hazard their reputations with the lives of their fellows and the destinies of their countries.

Haig was far more British than he was Scottish and, indeed, regularly fell into the English trap of writing 'English' when he meant 'British'; he may well have made the same mistake in conversation. As a conventionally educated, but in no sense intellectual, product of the British upper middle class, Haig's views on just about everything closely paralleled those of his peer group. His ambition, rarely effectively concealed, and his determination to succeed at his chosen profession marked him out, however, among his fellow cavalry officers and did not contribute to his popularity. In the years after the war, and particularly after his death in 1928, he would be widely accused of lacking imagination and there may be some justification for this in any analysis of his command decisions in the later years of the war. Before assuming supreme command, however, and with the exception of his apparent *idée fixe* apropos the permanent role of the cavalry, lack of imagination was not one of his characteristics. His opinions of France, the French and the French army were exactly what might be predicted from one of his background, especially one who so assiduously concealed a private warmth and humanity behind a carefully cultivated façade of British reserve and Scottish dourness. Although expressing his admiration of the professionalism and efficiency of the French cavalry, witnessed on manoeuvres in the Touraine in 1893, he was still able to write to his sister in 1900 that the French army of the Second Empire had been ruined by a policy of conducting small wars and awarding decorations lavishly. His admiration for the French cavalry – an admiration based more on the efficiency of the arm and the fact that it was cavalry than on the fact that it was French – did not extend to France or the French, unfortunately,

138

and his robustly expressed opinions sit uneasily in this narrative, concerned principally with the supposed friendship of the two nations.

This love-hate relationship, though, has characterised Franco–British relations throughout the twentieth century and, although periodically diplomatically suppressed during times of crisis, has been mutual and by no means confined – as we shall see in the next chapter – to the uneasy alliance necessitated by the First World War. There is every reason to believe that those French commanders who served alongside British commanders during the Great War found their Anglo-Saxon allies as mystifying, as annoying and as apparently unco-operative as British generals often found the French. The most common mutual recrimination concerned the apparent willingness of the British (or the French) to fight to the last Frenchman (or Briton) and neither ally appears ever to have been entirely free of the fear that the other would negotiate a separate peace.

In the light of this mutual incomprehension Haig's views may be seen as representative of those of his peers, rather than necessarily unique to him. Ironically, and providing yet another insight into his character, he was repeatedly assured by the spiritualists whom he occasionally consulted before and during the war that he and his career were being spiritually supervised by Napoleon. These mediums do not appear to have concluded whether Joffre or Foch were being looked after by Wellington. Dr De Groot notes that Haig's complaints about, and low opinion of, his French allies, first appearing in his diary as early as 27 August 1914, were to be 'repeated like a broken record over the next four years'. While it would be tedious, and unworthy, to repeat here what Dr De Groot has recorded as Haig's anti-Frenchisms, a few selected quotations may be appropriate.

'. . . one cannot believe a word they say, as a rule . . .'   August 1914

'. . . ever since we landed in France they seem ready to drain the last drop of blood out of the British force.'   November 1914

'These French leaders are a queer mixture of fair ability (not more than fair) and ignorance of the practical side of war. They are not built for it by nature. They are too excitable . . . they will not see a nasty situation as it really is . . .'
                    April 1915

'Some Frenchmen . . . find it hard to conceal their jealousy of Great Britain. They hate to think that the British Army is on French soil saving France. . . . The French are really very tiresome, but one has to keep on friendly terms . . . The truth is, we are too much of gentlemen for them . . .'   February 1916

'How difficult these "Latins" are to deal with! They mean to bleed the British to the utmost.'   April 1918

'Our troops are being used up to the last man in order to give the French courage . . . much of the French good name as efficient fighters was the result of newspaper puffs.'   June 1918

An uncompromising, unsympathetic and yet widely held belief, and one in which Haig remained resolute throughout the war, was that the French were inferior, their army poor quality and their leaders incompetent. As Dr De Groot points out, with gentle perspicuity, however, Haig 'consistently ignored the fact that French casualties in the war were nearly twice the British'. Had he not done so, it might be argued, he might have ascribed the higher casualty rate to the supposed inefficiency of the French commanders rather than to the tenacity, sacrifice and undoubted gallantry of the French soldier.

Soldat du regiment 'Black Watch' *a print from a drawing by Georges Scott, 1915.*

(The Black Watch; Mrs J. Smith)

Soldiers of The Black Watch advancing through a ruined village, a painting by H. Chartier, 1915.

(The Black Watch; Mrs J. Smith)

Dans la Tranchée, *a lithograph by Raoul Dufy, dated June 1915. Not shown in the photograph is the artist's inscription below the lithograph, of a thistle and the words:* Qui s'y frotte s'y pique *(he who rubs me will get stung).*

(Imperial War Museum)

A photograph from the album of Lieutenant G.S.M. Burton, 6th battalion The Black Watch, entitled Entente Cordiale, *taken in the winter of 1915 and showing a Highland soldier at a village pump with a local French girl.*

(The Black Watch; Mrs J. Smith)

141

Field Marshal Sir Douglas Haig, flanked by Joffre and Foch, leaving Haig's headquarters at Chateau Beauquesne on 12 August 1916 after luncheon with King George V.
(Imperial War Museum)

A trooper of the 2nd Dragoons (Royal Scots Greys), a painting by Raymond Desvarreux, c 1916.
(Musée de l'Armée)

Haig's relations with his French opposite numbers, despite awareness of the need – usually – to maintain an outward appearance of cordial co-operation, seem to have been constantly affected by his low opinion of their professionalism and social status. Avowedly distrusting the judgement of pro-French colleagues, such as General Sir Henry Wilson, Haig contrived to work with first Joffre and then Nivelle. He planned the Somme offensive of July 1916, designed to relieve pressure on the French at Verdun, with the former and initially expressed his respect for the latter. This respect, at least superficially, was also extended to Pétain, the defender of Verdun, and subsequently, if reluctantly, to Foch, under whose supreme command Haig was placed in the closing months of the war. Haig resentfully compared Foch to Napoleon because of what he perceived as his capacity for taking the credit for successes gained by British troops.

For a number of reasons, the near-contemporaries Douglas Haig and Ian Hamilton did not always agree. Hamilton combined a fluency in French with Francophile feelings that had first become manifest while he was in Germany during the Franco–Prussian War of 1870. He was also very close to Field Marshal Lord Roberts, the Grand Old Man of the British army at the end of the nineteenth and into the twentieth century, and neither Hamilton nor Roberts – nor, indeed, any of Roberts's 'circle' – had any time for traditional concepts of cavalry use, concepts which remained sacred to Haig. Hamilton, too, was a relaxed, ebullient and effervescent officer of Highlanders – the Gordons – and in many ways the antithesis of his fellow Scot.

Hamilton's attitude to his French allies was also antithetical to that of Haig. He was given command of the British forces for the Gallipoli expedition of 1915 and rapidly struck up a rapport with his French colleague Général d'Amade. Prior to the disembarkation of the Allied Expeditionary Force from Egypt for Turkey, d'Amade invited Hamilton to inspect the French contingent and, in his *Gallipoli Diary* (1920), Hamilton waxed

142

enthusiastically lyrical about the appearance and the apparent élan and panache of the French troops.

> '. . . the French trumpeters blew a lively fanfare which was followed by a roll of drums . . . I doubt whether the townsfolk [of Alexandria] have ever seen anything to equal the *coup d'oeil* engineered by d'Amade . . . the colours of the French uniforms, gaudy in themselves, ran riot, and the troops had surely been posted by one who was an artist in more than soldiering. Where the yellow sand was broken by a number of small conical knolls . . . there, on the knolls, were clustered the Mountain Batteries and the Batteries of Mitrailleuses. The Horse, Foot and Guns were drawn up, Infantry in front, Cavalry in rear, and the Field Artillery – the famous 75s – at right angles.
>
> Infantry of the Line in grey; Zouaves in blue and red; Senegalese wore dark blue and the Foreign Legion blue grey. The Cavalry rode Arabs and barbs [*sic*], mostly white stallions; they wore pale blue tunics and bright scarlet breeches.
>
> I rode down the lines of Infantry first and then . . . to the right of the Cavalry and inspected them, by d'Amade's request, at a trot, winding up with the six Batteries of Artillery.
>
> He then took command of the parade and marched past me at the head of his forces. Were all the Houris of Paradise waving lily hands on the one side, and were these French soldiers on the other side, I would give my cold shoulder to the Houris.
>
> The Cavalry swung along at the trot to the cadence of the trumpets and to the clink-clank and glitter of steel. The beautiful high-stepping barbs; the trembling of the earth beneath their hoofs: the banner streaming; the swordsmen of France sweeping past the saluting base; breaking into the gallop; sounding the charge; charging; *ventre à terre*; out into the desert.
>
> . . . No limit to what these soldiers may achieve . . .'

Although one can imagine that Haig would have shared Hamilton's regard for the appearance of the French cavalry, it is difficult to envisage the former sharing the enthusiasm of the latter, and particularly his optimism about their fighting qualities. Unfortunately, at least according to Hamilton's nephew, also Ian Hamilton, in his biography of the general, *The Happy Warrior* (1966), 'the Senegalese proved to be unreliable, especially at night, and the Zouaves were worse', but none of this was known in April 1915.

A brigade drawn from d'Amade's division of 18,000 men proved successful in the French feint against Kum Kale, on the southern shore of the Dardanelles, three weeks after Hamilton had inspected them but this success, as posterity knows, was short-lived and although French and British troops fought together at Cape Helles under their Scottish commander during the remainder of 1915 the expedition did not have the effect that its progenitors had hoped. The failure of Gallipoli, blamed by Hamilton on a persistent paucity of supplies of men and materials, did not weaken his regard for his French allies and he apparently regarded the withdrawal of a French division in September with relative equanimity.

In war, nothing succeeds like success and failure is often final. The failure of the Dardanelles expedition was, to all intents and purposes, blamed on Hamilton and, although he lived on until after the end of the Second World War, he was never re-employed in a combat zone.

The last of the trio of eminent Scots to gain distinction during the First World War, Henry Horne, was very much Haig's man and, a personal friend of the field marshal, shared many of his traits. Haig and Horne were both born in the same year, 1861, but Horne was an officer of the Royal Artillery and a Highlander from Caithness with family

A cartoon by G. D. Hamour, from Punch of 23 February 1916.

(Punch)

General Sir Ian Hamilton decorating Major Bertier de Sauvigny with the Distinguished Service Order, 29 September 1915. Lieutenants de la Borde and Pelliot await being decorated with the Military Cross. All three French officers formed the French military mission to Hamilton's head-quarters in the Dardanelles.

(Imperial War Museum)

connections with the Seaforth and Gordon Highlanders. Aside from a brief period between November 1915 and March 1916 spent in the Dardanelles and the Canal Zone of Egypt, Horne spent his entire war in France, but the lack of memoirs or a published biography result in one not being able to judge either what contact he had with the French army or what his opinions of it were. He is not mentioned in the memoirs of the French marshals of the period and seems to have enjoyed maintaining a low profile and merely getting on with the job in hand. He was credited with the invention of the 'creeping barrage' – a moving bombardment behind the curtain of which troops could advance – and, as commander of the 1st Army, successfully oversaw the Canadian assault on Vimy Ridge in 1917. As was normal after the war, he received his share of honours and was awarded the honorary degree of Doctor of Civil Laws by the University of Oxford on 30 June 1927, receiving his degree on the same occasion as did Marshal Foch. Both he and Foch died in 1929, a year after Haig.

If relations between British and French generals were not always of the most amicable during the war, those between ordinary soldiers often were. The nature of the war was that there were very few instances when Scottish soldiers and French troops actually fought side by side and their contacts were, therefore, principally when sectors were handed over by one nationality to the other, or on off-duty moments. Off-duty moments, of course, brought the Scottish troops into contact with French civilians as well and, as always, the power of the kilt exercised its undying fascination for the French. Although the gulf between the French conscript soldier and the Scottish volunteer (prior to conscription in 1916) was vast, and the culture-shock represented by the meeting of Caledonia and Gaul considerable, the experience seems to have been memorable for both parties. It generated acts of commemoration, excursions into verse and instances of humour – usually of the laboured and patronising *Punch* variety.

The acts of commemoration chiefly took place in the aftermath of the war, as memorials sprang up across the French countryside. These were in no sense restricted

144

Ecossais du 10th Gordon Highlanders. *Drummer Bromley and Piper Hastie in a photogravure after a drawing by Paul Sarrut, May 1916.*

(National Army Museum)

to Scottish formations but, because of the thrust of this narrative, only those relating to Scottish units are illustrated in this chapter. In some cases more personal instances of commemoration were contrived since it seems unanswerably true that the experience of combat inevitably heightens comradeship. A Scottish example of this occurred in 1936 when two earthenware urns, containing a mixture of earth from Brittany, from Picardy and from the foot of the monument at Aberfeldy which commemorates the first muster of The Black Watch in 1740, were exchanged between representatives of the 19th French infantry regiment and the 6th and 7th Battalions of The Black Watch. The exchange took place at La Boisselle on the Somme where, in 1915, the 19th French infantry had handed over a sector to the 6th and 7th Black Watch. One of the urns is preserved in the church at Folgoët in Brittany, the other is in the regimental museum of The Black Watch in Perth.

One of Britain's less well-known soldier-poets, Lieutenant E. A. Mackintosh MC, Seaforth Highlanders, who was killed in action in December 1917, wrote a poem at La Boisselle in 1915 which may well reflect the fact that Breton soldiers – distant cousins of those Celts remaining in the Highland regiments – were serving in the sector then. Entitled *The Undying Race*, it reflects not only distant memories of the Auld Alliance but also an undercurrent of the racism frequently encountered in both the propaganda and pro-war literature of both sides at the period; a racism based upon the romances of Malory but not without its touch of Scott.

Here in the narrow broken way
  where silently we go,
steadfast above their valiant clay
  forgotten crosses show.
Our whispers call to many a ghost
  across the flare-light pale,
and from their graves the Breton host
  stand up beside the Gael.

Year upon year of ancient sleep
  have rusted on our swords,
but once again our place we keep
  against the Saxon hordes.
Since Arthur ruled in Brittany,
  and all the world was new,
the fires that burned our history,
  burn in our spirits too.

One speech beyond their memory
  binds us together still,
One dream of home wherein we see
  river and sea and hill.
When in the night-time Fingal's peers
  fight their old wars again,
the blood of twice two thousand years
  leaps high in every vein.

Old songs that waked King Arthur's knights
  stir in our memory yet,
old tales of olden heroes' fights
  that we cannot forget.
To die as Fingal's warriors died,
  the great men long ago,
Breton and Gael stand side by side
  against the ancient foe.

The urge for commemoration, particularly in Highland regiments, is especially strong and uniquely reflected in their music, that of the great Highland bagpipe. Whereas Mackintosh chose to see the link in the dark days of 1915 as a romantic twilight view of Celtic solidarity against the flaxen-haired hordes and the men of 6th and 7th Black Watch decided to commemorate it by an exchange of earth – symbolic of both life and death – so the 8th Battalion the Argyll and Sutherland Highlanders, after taking over a section of trenches at Authuille from the Breton 116th Regiment, presented them with a pipe-tune. Composed by Pipe-Major William (Willie) Lawrie and entitled *The 8th Argylls' farewell to the 116th Regiment of the Line*, it was well-received by the Bretons, whose province of France remains the most Celtic and retains its own tradition of pipe music. Pipe-Major Lawrie also composed *The Cellars of Authuille* but one of his successors, Pipe-Major John McLellan, pipe-major from 1930 to 1935, composed three other pipe-tunes which directly reflect the battalion's association with France during the First World War: *The 8th Argylls' farewell to France*, *Buzancy* and *The taking of Beaumont Hamel*.

Aside from the ponderously English humour of *Punch*, other writers compiled what they considered to be amusing anecdotes about the Scots in France during the war. Chiefly centring on the language problem, and thus always good for a laugh by the

*Second Lieutenant Macleod, 2nd battalion The Black Watch,
when a prisoner-of-war in Fort 8, Ingolstadt, 22 August
1916. A pencil drawing by a fellow captive, a Frenchman,
who has annotated the paper with details of Macleod's
uniform, the information that he has been decorated with
the 4th class of the Russian Order of St. George and that he
was captured at Loos in 1915 after being wounded in the
arm and head by grenade fragments.*
(The Black Watch; Mrs J. Smith)

Piper A. C. Townsend, 1st London Scottish, a painting by Raymond Desvarreux, c 1916.

(Musée de l'Armée)

General Lord Horne and Marshal Foch in Oxford on 30 June 1927 to receive their honorary degrees as Doctors of Civil Laws from the University.

(NMS)

Tommy (to Jock, on leave). "WHAT ABOUT THE LINGO? SUPPOSE YOU WANT AN EGG OVER THERE, WHAT DO YOU SAY?"
Jock. "YE JUIST SAY, 'OOF.'"
Tommy. "BUT SUPPOSE YOU WANT TWO?"
Jock. "YE SAY 'TWA OOFS,' AND THE SILLY AULD FULE WIFE GIES YE THREE, AND YE JUIST GIE HER BACK ONE. MAN, IT'S AN AWFU' EASY LANGUAGE."

A cartoon by F. H. Townsend from Punch *of 26 April 1916.*
(Punch)

educated at the expense of the uneducated, these anecdotes have, in our sophisticated days, to be deemed apocryphal. True or false, they are always patronising and so only one will be retold here. Taken from a compilation entitled *Humourous Scottish War Stories* (selected from the *Daily Mail*) (1930) they were edited by one Allan Junior, glorified on the title page as having been the proud author of *Canny Tales Fae Aberdeen*. Most relevant, and perhaps least offensive, is the following:

> A Scottish and a French regiment were fighting near each other in France and the 'Scotties' succeeded in accomplishing a particularly fine piece of work, which filled the French with admiration.
> When the time came round for the mud-plastered 'Jocks' to go down the line, they found themselves surrounded by enthusiastic 'poilus' whose C.O. made a speech of congratulation to the impassive Scots, finishing up his harangue by exclaiming with emotion: 'Ah! vous Ecossais! Vous êtes tous couverts de gloire!' 'What's he saying, Sandy?' inquired one Scot of another. 'Och' replied Sandy, 'he's just saying that we're a' covered wi' glaur (mud)', and with a glance round at the mud-encrusted throng, 'Fegs! The mannie's no' faur wrang.'

149

Earthenware urn by M. Lacoste of Kergoël, Brittany,
containing earth from Perthshire, Picardy and Brittany.
Handed to representatives of 6th and 7th battalions The
Black Watch in 1936 by representatives of the French 19th
Infantry regiment to commemorate the handing over in
1915 of a sector at La Boisselle on the Somme. A similar urn
is in the church at Folgoët, Brittany.

(The Black Watch; Mrs J. Smith)

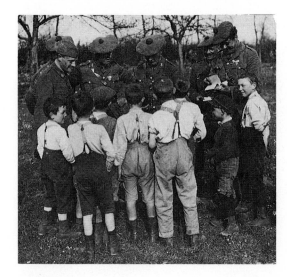

Distribution of prizes to French children by officers of The Black Watch after the children's race at the 7th Black Watch Sports meeting at Bailleul aux Cornailles on 10 May 1917.

(Imperial War Museum)

Le 14 Juillet sur le Front Anglais, *an engraving by Jean-Emile Laboureur dated 1917.*

(Imperial War Museum)

Soldiers of the 51st (Highland) Division washing and shaving
by the village pond in Flesquières during the battle of
Cambrai, 23 November 1917.

(Imperial War Museum)

"WE'LL NO GANG IN THERE, JOCK."
"FOR WHY, DONAL'?"
"MAN. IT'S GOT AN AWFU' GERRMAN-LIKE NAME, YON."

A cartoon by Fougasse from Punch of 5 December 1917.

(Punch)

Fortunately for the memory of both the fighting Scot and the modern manifestation
of the Auld Alliance, there are more tangible demonstrations of its existence in the shape
of two Colours in Scottish regimental museums, both decorated with the *Croix de Guerre*.
Twelve British units, of various sizes, were awarded the *Croix de Guerre* by the French
government during the war, the two Scottish units being the 6th Battalion The Black
Watch and the 12th Battalion The Argyll and Sutherland Highlanders. Both medals are
embellished with a bronze palm leaf, signifying the mention of the unit in an Army
Despatch, the highest grade of 'mention'.

The award to the 6th Black Watch was made in October 1918 and commemorated
the distinguished service of the battalion in the battles fought near Chambrécy between
20 and 30 July 1918. The Regimental Colour of the battalion was decorated with the
Croix de Guerre by the Military Governor of Paris, Général Berdoulet, at a ceremony held
in the Bois de Boulogne as part of the victory celebrations of 12 July 1919. The citation
for the award, in translation, reads as follows:

> This distinguished battalion, under the energetic command of Lieutenant-Colonel
> Francis Rowland Tarleton DSO, has given splendid proof of spirit and dash in the
> course of the hard fought battles between 20th and 30th July 1918. After seven days'
> bloody fighting, in spite of the exhaustion and the heavy losses caused by intense
> enemy machine-gun fire, it stormed a wood strongly fortified and obstinately
> defended by the enemy:
>
> Signed Guillaumat, General Commanding the 5th Army

The 12th Argylls, together with the 11th Cameronians and 8th Royal Scots Fusiliers,
were part of the 77th Brigade of 26th Division in 12th Corps in Salonika in 1918. Their
award of the *Croix de Guerre* was made for gallantry at the battle of Doiran on 19
September 1918, an action in which the Commanding Officer was mortally wounded

French patients at the Scottish Women's Hospital, Salonika 1917.

(Imperial War Museum)

The reverse of the French Médaille des Epidémies *awarded to Miss F. A. MacKenzie of the Scottish Women's Hospitals, 1917.*

(NMS)

A photograph taken near Locon on 10 April 1918 during the defence of Hinges Ridge; the soldier of the 51st (Highland) Division and the Frenchman have exchanged burdens.

(Imperial War Museum)

153

Marshal Foch inspecting the Guard of Honour formed of veterans of the 51st (Highland) Division at the unveiling of the Divisional memorial at Beaumont Hamel, Somme on 28 September 1924.

(NMS)

and the battalion sustained casualties of 299 men out of a strength of 517. The citation, in a French Special Order of the Day, reads as follows:

> A splendid battalion of a magnificent regiment, whose valour and spirit are traditional. On 19th September 1918, gallantly led by Lieutenant-Colonel R. Falconer-Stewart in person, and animated by an admirable spirit of self-sacrifice, it boldly attacked an enemy position formidably organised and defended by concentrated machine-gun fire. It stormed the position, killed or made prisoner all its defenders, and heroically resisted counter-attacks in spite of the loss of its Commanding Officer (who fell mortally wounded) and of the heavy casualties which it suffered. The battalion only withdrew when ordered to do so and had given a most brilliant example of determination in attack, and of tenacity in maintaining conquered positions.

> Signed Franchet D'Esperey, General Commanding in Chief,
> the Allied Armies in the East.

Britain does not indulge in decorating the Colours of its own or other nations with medals but it does reciprocate in the awards of honours to individuals of other nations. In 1916 the award of the newly founded Military Cross was made to Captain Eugène Bourdon, serving on the staff of the French 78th Brigade. Captain Bourdon had also received the *Croix de Guerre* in 1915 and been created a *Chevalier* of the Legion of Honour in the same year. This was not, in itself, that unusual an occurrence and were it not for its Scottish connection it would have gone unremarked here. Eugène Bourdon was

154

The memorial to the dead of the 51st (Highland) Division,
1914–18, at Beaumont Hamel on the Somme.
(Commonwealth War Graves Commission)

The memorial to the dead of the 8th battalion, the Argyll
and Sutherland Highlanders, 1914–18, at Beaumont Hamel
on the Somme.
(Commonwealth War Graves Commission)

born in Paris in 1870 and in 1914 immediately enlisted in the French army, being successively promoted to corporal and sergeant and then commissioned. It is likely that his
award of the British Military Cross reflected liaison duties between the French and the
British staffs, duties that would have been rendered easier since Bourdon spoke English.
When he was killed in action in 1916 it was 12 years since he had been appointed the
first professor of architecture at the Glasgow School of Art and his page-long obituary
in *The Scots Pictorial* of 29 July 1916 dwells, unsurprisingly, far more on his contribution
to the study of architecture in Glasgow than on the laurels that he won as a soldier of
France. The present, relatively new, architecture building of the School of Art in Glasgow
has been named in Professor Bourdon's honour and his services to Scotland and to
France are commemorated by a stained glass panel in its foyer.

As was said at the beginning of the chapter, the First World War became a statistician's
delight and the figures produced after the war which concerned the expenditure of men
and materials filled several thick volumes. Although, as is widely recognised, any given
set of statistics can be modified or distorted to represent any given point of view,
especially if handled by a politician, there are figures available which indicate, fairly
firmly, that Scotland's contribution to the war was not only disproportionate to its
population but also, *pro rata*, greater than that of any other part of the United Kingdom.
During the four years of the war, 557,618 Scots males enlisted into the British army.
This figure represented 41.4% of males between the ages of 15 and 49 in Scotland and
23.7% of all males in Scotland. During the period to January 1916, at which date conscription was introduced, Scotland's voluntary recruits exceeded, per head of male
population between 15 and 49, those of England and Wales together. Scotland's losses,
in terms of men killed, represented one-fifth of Britain's total dead. About 147,000
Scotsmen were killed during the war, in effect about a quarter of those who served and

*The memorial to the dead of 1st battalion The Black Watch
and 1st battalion The Queen's Own Cameron Highlanders at
Bois de Fourceaux (High Wood), Longueval, 1914–18. The
inscription about the Black Watch is on the side not shown.*
(Commonwealth War Graves Commission)

taken from a population of about 5 million in 1914. By contrast, from a 1914 population
of about 39 million, France's losses in manpower approximated 1.3 million men.

The number of women killed on active service was tiny by comparison, as might be
expected with the women's services in their infancy. The movements for women's
suffrage had, generally, seized upon the war as an opportunity to make a contribution
that would prove their right to vote and, ultimately, they were successful when limited
female suffrage was granted in Britain in 1928. Women in France had to wait for another
war before being able to exercise their democratic rights. Although official bodies of
women's services quickly came into being in Britain relatively rapidly after the beginning
of the war, the one of most relevance to this narrative was initially unofficial and privately
organised. Drawing its strength directly from the Scottish Federation of Women's
Suffrage Societies, the Scottish Women's Hospitals were organised in August 1914 by
the secretary of the Federation, Dr Elsie Inglis.

Voluntarily funded, the SWH eventually raised just under £½ million by the end of
the war and took mobile hospitals, staffed principally by Scottish women, to the battle
zones in France, Serbia, Corsica and Salonika. Dr Alice Hutchison was the first representative of the SWH to go to France, arriving in Calais in November 1914 in time to
help deal with an outbreak of typhoid in the Belgian army. Although the SWH effort
in Calais only lasted until the end of the epidemic in March 1915, two other SWH
hospitals were established in France, at the Abbey of Royaumont in December 1914 and
at Villers-Cotterets in the spring of 1917. Both were under the control of Miss Frances
Ivens, from Liverpool, who was to be decorated with the *Croix de Guerre*, was created
a *Chevalier* of the Legion of Honour and received the *Médaille d'honneur des Epidémies*
for her work in France. The Royaumont hospital, although under the auspices of the
SWH, was absorbed into the French military medical system under the title *Hôpital*

The memorial to the dead of the 15th (Scottish) Division, 1914–18, at Buzançy. The memorial also commemorates the sacrifice of the 17th French Division and the inscription reads: Ici fleurira toujours le glorieux chardon d'Ecosse parmi les roses de France (The glorious Scottish thistle will always flourish here amid the roses of France).
(Commonwealth War Graves Commission)

Reverse of a silvered bronze medallion presented to the Military Band and Drums and Pipes of 1st battalion the Gordon Highlanders by the Ecole Supérieure de Guerre (the French staff college) to commemorate a concert on 20 June 1937.
(The Gordon Highlanders; Mrs J. Smith)

Auxiliare de l'Armée No. 30. The wards at Royaumont were named after famous women: *Blanche de Castille, Jeanne d'Arc, Marguérite d'Ecosse, Queen Mary,* and so on. Royaumont was visited by President Poincaré in September 1916 and received regular visits from French generals and doctors who seem, from the account in *A History of the Scottish Women's Hospitals* (1919), to have been consistently amazed that hospitals – especially for soldiers – could be run efficiently and in a disciplined manner by women. At Villers-Cotterets the hospital was established in a hutted camp and, dangerously close to the fighting during the German spring offensive of 1918, was evacuated in May 1918.

As well as providing hospital care for wounded French soldiers, the SWH established canteens in the summer of 1917, at Soissons, Creil and Crépy-en-Valois. These provided hot meals and coffee for large numbers of French soldiers; that at Soissons serving 1681 meals at a maximum cost of one franc each in the seven weeks from June 1917, despite being under fairly constant German bombardment. The canteen at Creil found itself, like the hospital at Villers-Cotterets, too close for safety to the German advance in 1918 and had to be evacuated in June 1918. All the extant reports of the work of the canteens and the hospitals mention at length the colourful diversity of the French army and contrast the differing uniforms and ethnic types with the consistent appreciation of the contents of the *marmites* of soup and coffee.

As has been seen, there were many ways in which the shared experience of the First World War brought Scotland and France together. Indeed, when Scotland and the Scots were recognised by the French as being distinct from England and the English there seems to have been little difficulty in establishing an immediate rapport. The years between the wars were ones of retrenchment, of commemoration of sacrifice and of resolve never to repeat the experience suffered between 1914 and 1918. As the treatment of the Auld Alliance in the next chapter will attempt to show, however, the experience of 1914–18 not only made that of 1939–45 inevitable, it also made the events of 1939–40 deeply traumatic and, in a sense, predictable for both partners.

*A drummer of the Gordon Highlanders, painted by Albert
Brenet, 1937.*

(Musée de l'Armée)

Chapter Seven

Hosts and Liberators 1939–45

IT IS AN OVERWORKED MAXIM THAT GENERALS ARE ALWAYS ABLE TO FIGHT THE LAST war and never the present one, but in an age when wars may be likened to examination questions – with matters of precedent overriding intelligence and the caution of mediocrity taking the place of the brilliance of innovation – it is easily said and still more easily believed. In 1939 none would doubt Britain's lack of preparedness for war in almost all areas; from Britain, France was perceived as well-prepared and entrenched behind her Maginot Line.

That the First World War, or rather its result, caused the Second is beyond question. Germany had been humiliated by the peace settlement, had collapsed internally, had lost nearly three million men and had been forced to pay swingeing reparations; it was easy for these realities to become accompanied by the fictions that she had been stabbed in the back by her Jewish population and that her army had never been defeated on the battlefield. France and Britain had emerged victorious but shattered and determined never to repeat the process. In France, enlarged by the return of Alsace and Lorraine, this determination took the form of aggressive defence and an anti-German vindictiveness which is easily understood but, in retrospect, hardly excused, because of its effect. The shadow of Verdun fell across conventional French military thinking and the popular reaction to its defence policy for a generation, and as complacency replaced vindictiveness in the 1930s so the collapse of 1940 became understandable if not predictable. In Britain, basking in imperial twilight, deprived of a generation of young men and determined to commemorate their sacrifice in stone throughout the Empire and in the countries where they had died, a considerable war debt, an overstretched economy and worldwide policing commitments led once again to a policy of ignoring or belittling the concept of a European war until it was too late properly to prepare for one.

From the point of view of this narrative, the war divides neatly into two sections, that ended in the summer of 1940 and that begun after the Armistice of 1940 and ended by the Liberation of 1944. It was a very different war from the one waged by a previous generation, and yet when the British Expeditionary Force crossed the Channel in 1939 – as it had done 25 years before – it was very much less altered in equipment, training and tactical concepts than its adversary, the rebuilt German army.

Although the BEF and the French 1st, 7th and 9th Armies remained on the Franco-Belgian border, north of where the Maginot Line would have been if it had been extended along the Belgian frontier, initial fighting in Europe between the Allies and Germany began in Scandinavia. Both sides were interested in Norway, because of its strategic position and its iron ore resources. The Allied expeditionary force which captured Narvik on 18 May 1940, a month after the German invasion of Norway and Denmark, comprised British, French and Polish troops, the 1st battalion of the Scots Guards being among the British contingent and some Chasseurs-Alpins among the French forces. The strength of the German forces was such, however, that the Allies could not hold on in

Two officers of 51st (Highland) Division headquarters at Béthune in February 1940 making friends with three French children who have had bonnets knitted to look like glengarries. Left is Captain McDonald, GSO III, Argyll and Sutherland Highlanders, right is a Lieutenant in the Black Watch, who was assistant Camp Commandant.
(Imperial War Museum)

Soldiers of 5th battalion the Gordon Highlanders sorting potatoes for a French farmer, Béthune, February 1940.
(Imperial War Museum)

The Headquarters staff of 51st (Highland) Division, Béthune, March 1940. Seated in the centre of the front row is Major General Victor Fortune, the Division's commander.
(The Argyll and Sutherland Highlanders; Mrs J. Smith)

Norway and were evacuated at the beginning of June. Most of the expeditionary force returned initially to Scotland and the bugles and horns of the Chasseurs-Alpins band were heard, after their return from Norway, on at least one occasion in Glasgow's Kelvingrove Park.

A week before the Allied capture of Narvik – on 10 May 1940 – German forces attacked neutral Holland and Belgium, sweeping aside resistance with ease and penetrating into France at Sedan three days later. This lightning advance on all fronts by the Germans, combined with the rapier-like thrusts of the armoured columns of Rommel and Guderian, forced the Allies back and bisected their forces. Either side of Guderian's thrust that captured Sedan on 13 May were the two Scottish components of the British forces in France, the battalions – mainly the regular battalions – in the BEF placed between the French 7th and 1st Armies and the soldiers – mainly Territorial soldiers – of the 51st Highland Division. The 51st had arrived in France in January 1940 and been stationed alongside French troops on the Belgian frontier, occasionally

160

The massed Pipes and Drums of the 51st (Highland) Division play in Béthune during the visit to the Division of General Lanquetot, commander of the French 21st Division, based at Hazebrouck, March 1940.

(Imperial War Museum)

Two soldiers of 51st (Highland) Division take a French child for a walk, Béthune, March 1940.

(Imperial War Museum)

A pipe-major of 51st (Highland) Division shows his bagpipes to two French soldiers, Béthune, March 1940.

(Imperial War Museum)

161

4th battalion The Queen's Own Cameron Highlanders take
over a section of French defences near Bailleul and a piper
plays for some French soldiers, March 1940.
(Imperial War Museum)

changing sectors and generally being involved in strengthening the almost non-existent border defences. In March 1940 the Division had been stiffened by the addition of three regular battalions, the 1st Black Watch, 2nd Seaforths and 1st Gordon Highlanders and in April the Division was moved, *en bloc*, to occupy the areas forward of the Maginot Line in the sector adjacent to the Saar. They were there when the Germans invaded on 10 May.

The 51st were the only British division to be based in the Maginot Line and, because they were Highland Scots – most of whom were still kilted – they were a popular sight in France both before and during their time in the Line. Pipes and drums were in constant demand between January and April 1940 and the ceremony of Beating Retreat seems to have held a never-ending fascination for their French hosts. Many soldiers of the Division have left reminiscences of their experiences in France during the latter part of the 'Phoney War' and a uniform impression remains of the friendliness of the French civilians towards the Highland soldiers. In contrast, and sitting uneasily in these pages, is the almost uniformly poor impression made on the Scots by the French army. Experiences of the First World War were revived by encountering the evidence of different attitudes to sanitation – especially, apparently, in the case of French colonial troops – and there are few instances of Scottish soldiers being satisfied with the defences which they took over from French troops. Sir Derek Lang, who was adjutant of the 4th Camerons in the 152nd Brigade of the Division, talks in *Return to St Valéry* (1974) of the most forward of the outer lines in front of the Maginot Line – the *Ligne de Contacte* – as being more like grouse butts than properly prepared entrenched positions.

It seems, from all accounts, that where the Maginot Line existed it was regarded as impregnable and that its two forward lines and one rear line were regarded by the French as not worth taking too seriously; it was the Verdun philosophy writ large. Behind the

Ligne de Contacte, in the Saar sector about seven miles forward of the line itself, was the *Ligne de Recueil* – where troops would collect to be marshalled. Behind the Line itself, was the *Ligne d'Arrêt* – the stopping point of any advance. An idea of how seriously these lines, and especially the *Ligne d'Arrêt*, were taken is illustrated by a story concerning Major General Victor Fortune, who commanded the 51st Highland Division. Visiting a rear area one day he saw some French soldiers digging in a field; on asking what they were doing he received the reply that a general was imminently expected to inspect the *Ligne d'Arrêt* and so they were digging it.

There was fairly constant skirmishing along the *Ligne de Contacte*, made easier for the Germans by the fact that their troops were locally recruited and so knew the ground far better than did the Scots opposing them. Prior to the arrival of the Division their French predecessors had developed a 'live-and-let-live' attitude to their opponents – an attitude not dissimilar to that conducted on some fronts in the area 25 years earlier and one which had enraged Douglas Haig – but the 51st went over to the offensive, with varying degrees of success, during the six weeks or so that they occupied the sector. Attack became defence and then retreat after the German invasion in May and the Division was withdrawn on 20 May, moving to Varennes, west of Verdun, five days later. By that time, the Germans had encircled the Allied forces in the north-west of France and had closed any escape route. Operation Dynamo, the evacuation at Dunkirk, began on 26 May and eight days later, when it finished, 338,000 men, one-third of whom were French, had been lifted off the beaches.

The success of Operation Dynamo, mounted from the south of England and snatching a small victory from the yawning jaws of a potentially massive defeat, has tended to obscure what happened to the 51st Highland Division, at least, it appears, in the minds of the many English historians who have dealt with the period 1939–40. The fighting withdrawal of the 51st, from its position on 25 May east of Paris to its eventual surrender at St Valéry-en-Caux on 12 June, has been documented meticulously by Eric Linklater in *The Highland Division* (1942) and later by authors less restricted by censorship who were with the Division as it moved, by road and rail, westward through France to the sea. For the first nine days of the manoeuvre, until the battle of Abbeville on 4 June, neither retreat nor surrender were certain and, initially, the 51st moved to support French forces commanded by Brigadier Charles de Gaulle intended to stop the Germans on the Somme. With virtually undisputed mastery of the air and being constantly reinforced from the east, however, the German forces were too strong for the Allies and the 51st and the French were forced inexorably back from the lines that they had attempted to establish on the Somme. The 51st suffered almost 50 per cent casualties in the battle of Abbeville and for the next eight days, until cornered at St Valéry-en-Caux, all battalions fought increasingly fragmented and individual rearguard actions, sometimes alone, sometimes in brief alliance with retreating French troops.

Although the French army was gradually disintegrating under unrelenting German pressure, several of its units fought tenaciously and in a manner that aroused the admiration of their Highland allies. Some units contrived to reach the coast and were evacuated in small numbers by hovering destroyers, and 154 Brigade, which had retired to Le Havre, was eventually lifted off, first to Cherbourg and then to Southampton. The remaining brigades, support troops and French units that had been boxed in at St Valéry all surrendered on the morning of 12 June. Last to surrender, it seems, was a small force of French Chasseurs-Alpins and 1st Battalion The Black Watch who were surrounded in the village of Houdetot, near St Valéry, and who did not capitulate until 11a.m., by which time 33 men of the original 150 men had been killed and the ammunition had run out. Their defence of Bocquet's farm in Houdetot is now commemorated by a

During a ceremony near Bailleul at the end of March 1940 two Cameron Highlanders from Inverness (one with a censored divisional patch) explain the ceremonial to a Frenchman.

(Imperial War Museum)

granite monument, on which appears the *cor-de-chasse* of the Chasseurs-Alpins encircling the Scottish thistle.

The surrender of St Valéry was not the end, of course, but at the time it struck a powerful blow at morale in Scotland; Linklater himself compares it to Flodden in its impact. Most other Scottish units not in the 51st Highland Division got away at Dunkirk, although theirs was a fighting withdrawal too, the 1st battalion of The Royal Scots distinguishing themselves in the defence of Le Paradis on 27 May 1940 and suffering heavy casualties in the process.

Aside from leaving the bodies of their dead comrades in France, the battalions of the 51st Highland Division left regimental property too. Hurried withdrawals inevitably involve the jettisoning of non-essential items, and the most cumbersome of battalion property tends to be its drums. Three tenor drums and two side drums now repose in regimental museums in Scotland; these drums were left in France in 1940 and have made their way home by various routes. The three tenor drums were all left in Metz as the Division withdrew from that sector in May. The 8th battalion of the Argyll and Sutherland Highlanders entrusted theirs to the *Banque de France*, the 1st Black Watch and 5th Gordons may have done likewise. The 5th Gordons were the first battalion to get their drum back; taken by the Germans, it was found in Germany in March 1945 by an American officer and restored to the battalion at a ceremony in Munich in June of that year. The drum of the 8th Argylls, who escaped from France from Cherbourg, was found in an antique shop, bought by a French collector of military antiquities and given back to the regiment by him in 1975. The drum of the 1st Black Watch was found in Metz, in the possession of the widow of a Polish soldier, by an ex-soldier of the Seaforth Highlanders who was looking for drums of the 4th Seaforths which had also been left in the city. Alone, it appears, of the battalions of the 51st, the 4th Cameron Highlanders retained their drums as far as St Valéry and the two side drums now in the regimental museum at Fort George were hidden before the surrender by the Pipe-Major, Donald MacDonald, on the orders of the adjutant, Derek Lang. One, of which only the brass shell remains, was sunk in a pond, the other thrust hastily into a hedge. In 1987 when the towns of Inverness and St Valéry were twinned, the story of the missing drums was publicised and the two drums were produced by a French family; they had been rescued before being appropriated by the Germans.

The twinning of St Valéry and Inverness had another result a year prior to the discovery of the drums. Visiting Inverness on a preliminary visit in September 1986, one of the assistant mayors of St Valéry, Mme Maggy Savoye, showed a photograph of a silver statuette first to Lieutenant-Colonel Angus Fairrie, regimental secretary – and curator of the regimental museum – of the Queen's Own Highlanders (Seaforth and Camerons) and then to Sir Derek Lang. Colonel Fairrie recognised it as the silver statuette, copied from the memorial to the 51st Highland Division at Beaumont Hamel on the Somme, which had been presented in 1924 to Colonel McLeod Robertson in recognition of his work as secretary of the committee established to set up the memorial. In 1986 the statuette belonged to a fisherman in St Valéry, who had bought it from the son of a farmer, living near St Valéry, who had found it in 1940: in 1986 it was returned to Scotland and now belongs to the 51st Highland Division Dinner Club.

More work remains to be done on how the silver statuette, presumably donated or bequeathed to the mess silver of one of the battalions of the Division or of the Divisional staff, came to be in France in the first place and where it was discovered. The full answer will probably never be known. Similar research might be done on the officers and men of the Division who decided that the defeat of the Division was not the end for them and who subsequently escaped captivity. Some melted quietly into the French countryside, like Lieutenant Richard Broad of the 2nd Seaforth Highlanders, some escaped on the line of march from St Valéry to captivity, like Captain Derek Lang of the 4th Camerons. Others escaped from German prisoner-of-war camps, like Lieutenant Chandos Blair of the 2nd Seaforths – the first British officer to make a 'home-run' from Germany in the Second World War. The story of the escape of Lieutenant Blair, now Lieutenant-General Sir Chandos Blair, has yet to be written but those of Derek Lang and Richard Broad are available for consultation in detail and are especially relevant here since both involved escaping through France.

Richard Broad took seven men of his platoon with him on his escape and, as he himself says, it was the discipline innate in the group which made the escape both possible and successful. They survived, armed and in uniform, in France only with the help of the embryonic French resistance movement and because of aid from individuals unconnected with the 'official' resistance and yet sympathetic to their plight. In fact, it is noticeable that one of the things which the escapes of Broad and Lang have in common is that the helpfulness of the French was often in direct contrast to the lack of helpfulness of the British consular officials in Spain, in Broad's case, and American consular officials in Marseilles, in Lang's case. In some cases, as Sir Derek Lang relates, the helpfulness and enthusiasm For the escapers by the French was such that their actual security was often compromised. Despite the relevance of the escapes of Richard Broad and Derek Lang to this narrative, there is no evidence to suggest that they were especially favoured by their French helpers because they were Scots and, indeed, it seems certain that any British escaper would have been helped to the same extent by the same brave and loyal French people who helped them. In times such as those, considerations of humanity and beating the Germans came before more profound concepts of historical friendship. The books dealing with the escapes of Richard Broad and Derek Lang are noted in the relevant section of this volume; they can be read with ease, enjoyment and – occasionally – amazement.

On 16 June 1940 General de Gaulle arrived in London. Two years and one week later, on 23 June 1942, he made a speech in Edinburgh in which he constantly alluded to the Auld Alliance and made special reference to the gallantry of the 51st Highland Division. The conduct of the Division's soldiers in the battle of Abbeville, he said, helped him make the decision to leave France and continue the fight from Britain. Because of its direct relevance to this narrative, de Gaulle's speech is here quoted in full from his *War Memoirs*, volume one, (1955):

Cadet J. Thouvenin, one of the French liaison officers
attached to the Lothians and Border Horse, 1939–1940.

(NMS)

I do not think that a Frenchman could have come to Scotland at any time without being sensible of a special emotion. Scarcely can he set foot in this ancient and glorious land before he finds countless natural affinities between your country and ours dating from the very earliest times. In the same moment, awareness of the thousand links, still living and cherished, of the Franco-Scottish Alliance, the oldest alliance in the world, leaps to his mind.

When I say 'Franco-Scottish Alliance', I am thinking, firstly, of course, of that close political and military *entente* which, in the Middle Ages, was established between our ancient monarchy and yours.

I am thinking of the Scottish blood which flowed in the veins of our kings and of the French blood which flowed in the veins of your kings, of glory shared on past battlefields, from the siege of Orléans, raised by Joan of Arc, to Valmy, where Goethe recognised that a new age was dawning for the world.

In every combat where for five centuries the destiny of France was at stake, there were always men of Scotland to fight side by side with men of France, and what Frenchmen feel is that no people has ever been more generous than yours with its friendship.

Yet in our old alliance there was more than a common policy, more than marriages and fighting deeds. There were not only the Stuarts, the Queens of France and Scotland, Kennedy, Berwick, Macdonald, and the glorious *Garde écossaise*. There were also a thousand ties of spirit and soul. How could we forget the mutual influence of French and Scottish poets, or the influence of men like Locke and Hume on our philosophy? How could we fail to recognise what is common to the Presbyterian Church of Scotland and the doctrines of Calvin? How could we hide the influence which the great Walter Scott has exercised over the receptive mind of French youth? How could we ignore all the exchanges of ideas, feelings, customs and even words so frequent between two peoples joined by a natural friendship, a friendship of which a visit to Edinburgh affords such ample proof?

This friendship and understanding which Frenchmen have found in Scotland throughout history are today more precious than ever. Undoubtedly, they are mingled at the present time with the joint aims, efforts, and ideals which go to make up the alliance between France and Great Britain. But I think I can say, without giving cause for offence, that although mingled, they are not lost in the mingling, and they retain their special character, just as in a bouquet a single flower still keeps its own perfume and colour.

That the soil of France enfolds lovingly the thousands and thousands of Scots whose blood was shed with that of our own soldiers during the last war, I can affirm. The monument to their memory on the hill of Buzancy has, I know, never been more frequently bedecked with flowers than since the new invasion. If the roses of France are blood-stained today, they still cluster round the thistle of Scotland. For my part, I can say that the comradeship of arms, sealed on the battlefield of Abbeville in May-June 1940, between the French armoured division, which I had the honour to command and the gallant 51st Scottish Division under General Fortune, played its part in the decision which I made to continue the fight at the side of the Allies to the end, come what may.

We live at a time when every friendship counts, especially those which have lasted longest. That which you extend to us in the difficult task my comrades and I have undertaken affords comforting proof that, like your forefathers, you know where the real France stands and you have kept your faith in her future. We, like our forefathers, will know how to repay.

And that is why, in thanking you for the truly touching reception which you have given me here, I close by quoting the old motto of the *Compagnie écossaise: 'Omni modo fidelis.'*

Two side drums, one just a shell, left by 4th battalion The
Queen's Own Cameron Highlanders at St Valéry and restored
to the regimental museum in 1987.

(Queen's Own Highlanders; Mrs J. Smith)

Free French soldiers under General Leclerc's command and
Scottish soldiers of the re-formed 51st (Highland) Division
sharing cigarettes after the liberation of Tripoli, February
1943.

(Imperial War Museum)

The granite memorial in the village of Houdetot, near St
Valéry, commemorating the last stand of Chasseurs-Alpins of
the 5th demi-brigade and 1st battalion, The Black Watch,
12 June 1940.

(M. Georges Dickson OBE)

Captain Charles Trepel, officer commanding No. 8 troop of No. 10 Commando, at Achnacarry, July 1943.
(Imperial War Museum)

By the time of de Gaulle's speech the concepts of Free France and the Free French were well-established. In the same month that de Gaulle spoke in Edinburgh, No. 10 Commando had been formed; a unit which contained ten Troops, Nos. 1 and 8 Troops being formed of Free French soldiers. There had been Free French commandos in the other Commando units since 1940 but the formation of No. 10 Commando, with its polyglot composition of soldiers from most of the Allies, and especially from countries under Nazi occupation, gave a sense of identity and of purpose to the Free French commandos. Like all Commando units. No. 10 Commando underwent basic training at the Commando depot at Achnacarry near Fort William, the ancestral home of the Camerons of Lochiel. No. 1 Troop of No. 10 Commando was commanded by Philippe Kieffer, a naval captain from Alsace who had originally served in No. 4 Commando, and was chiefly composed of French soldiers who had escaped at Dunkirk or Breton sailors who had escaped to Britain by fishing boat. No. 8 Troop was originally commanded by Captain Charles Trepel, who died in a raid on the Dutch coast early in 1944, and subsequently by a former French naval officer, Captain Alexandre Lofi; its men had principally been sailors, *fusiliers marins* and soldiers of the French colonial infantry who had served in the Free French forces in Syria and North Africa. The original links of the Free French commandos with No. 4 Commando were maintained and the two Free French Troops of No. 10 Commando were attached, under command, to No. 4 Commando for D-Day and for a later attack on Flushing. The Highlands of Scotland provided the training ground for these Frenchmen and when the Free French commandos attached to No. 4 Commando went ashore at Ouistreham in Normandy on D-Day (or *Jour J* in French) the training and experiences that they had undergone in Scotland represented yet another link in the military chain of the Auld Alliance which stretched back 500 years to another time when Scottish troops had embarked in France to defeat a common foe.

A Franco-Scottish link with the Special Air Service was forged in 1941 when the Scottish founder of the SAS, Colonel David Stirling, persuaded General de Gaulle to allow him to recruit Free French parachutists into the 1st SAS regiment. These Free French parachutists in the SAS eventually spawned the 3rd and 4th SAS regiments which were formed, respectively, from the 2nd and 3rd *régiments de Chasseurs-Parachutistes*. The 3rd and 4th SAS were part of the SAS Brigade, commanded by Brigadier R.W. McLeod, which

The pipes and drums of the Commando Depot, Achnacarry, leading a detachment of Free French commandos past the saluting base where Lieutenant-Colonel Charles Vaughan, Depot Commander, takes the salute, July 1943.

(Imperial War Museum)

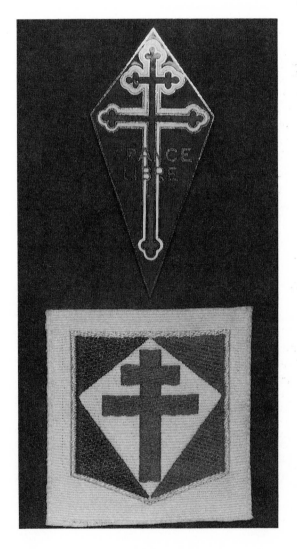

Badges worn by Free French commandos. The metal (upper) badge was worn on the chest and the embroidered badge on the beret.

(Sir Donald Cameron of Lochiel KT; NMS)

The Commando Memorial, Spean Bridge, Inverness-shire.
(Mrs J. Smith)

The grave of Mecanicien R. L. Pineau, mort pour la France 14 December 1942, in the Western Necropolis, Dundee.

(Author)

The grave of Merchant seaman S. Y. Amadou, mort pour la France 28 July 1943, in the Sandy Mount cemetery, Glasgow.

(Author)

trained in Ayrshire and parachute-trained at Prestwick aerodrome for the three months prior to D-Day. Operating behind German lines during the campaign in France throughout 1944, the 3rd and 4th SAS are credited with the expulsion of the enemy from Brittany and in two operations, codenamed *Haggard* and *Moses*, with the capture of 18,000 German prisoners. The 4th SAS operated in the Ardennes in January 1945, under American command, and with 3rd SAS in Holland in April, dropping 694 men and, supported by 268 Belgians of the SAS, killed, wounded or captured 600 Germans in return for 160 of their own casualties. At the end of the war the 3rd and 4th SAS returned to the French army but retained their historical link with Scotland by preserving their first pennant (or *fanion*) in the 'modern red' tartan of the Grant family. This *fanion*, with its fringed border and yellow silk backing, is charged, on one side, with the Cross of Lorraine on a *Tricouleur* shield and, on the other, with a winged parachute supporting another Cross of Lorraine. No extant records seem to exist to explain why a Grant tartan was chosen, since neither Brigadier McLeod nor Colonel Stirling would have claimed it as their own, and so – since it is principally red with a bold green cross-stripe – it may have been chosen simply for its dashing appearance.

Free French forces were manifest elsewhere during the war, other than just in the Special forces who trained in Scotland and fought alongside Scottish troops in North Africa and Italy. In North Africa they accompanied the rebuilt and reformed 51st Highland Division and the 51st, together with General Koenig's 1st Free French Brigade, fought at the battle of El Alamein in 1942, the battle which turned the tide of the war in North Africa and, ultimately, that of the war as a whole.

Almost four years to the day that he had left France, Charles de Gaulle returned. Landing in Normandy on 14 June 1944 with other representatives of the Free French forces, he was greeted by a Scottish officer. Major Louis Sanderson MC, of the King's Own Scottish Borderers, was a liaison officer at the Tactical Headquarters of the 21st

172

The memorial to the sailors of Free France on the Lyle Hill,
overlooking Gourock, Greenock and the Firth of Clyde.
(Author)

Army Group – the headquarters of General Sir Bernard Montgomery, commanding the land forces of the Allies in France. Montgomery had invited de Gaulle to luncheon and to inspect, during the course of a day, what progress had been made in liberating France. Montgomery chose Sanderson, whom he had known well and trusted as an Adc since before the war, because he spoke some French, because he was senior of the liaison officers and because he believed that Sanderson would be able to handle a potentially delicate situation well. The situation was perceived to be delicate by the British and American governments because they were concerned, among other things, that General de Gaulle would attempt to establish a Free French government in France before military operations in the country had been concluded. Although they may well have shared de Gaulle's expressed concern that the lack of a firm and rapidly established government in a liberated France might well lead to a communist takeover – based upon the communist-led cells of the Resistance movement – they were not, it seems, prepared to countenance what they regarded as de Gaulle's interference in purely military affairs by, as they saw it, attempting to make political capital out of the success of Anglo-American operations in Normandy. Little of the politics is relevant to this narrative but the views of that Scottish officer on de Gaulle and his visit may be, and since that officer, now Lieutenant-Colonel (retired) Louis Sanderson OBE MC, has been kind enough to furnish them at some length they are here published, unabridged, for the first time.

> General de Gaulle was invited to come to France and for security reasons to bring only three or four others in his party. He was invited to lunch with General Montgomery. This he accepted belatedly but, when he arrived off the beaches one-and-a-half hours late for his appointment for no apparent reason and certainly without any apology, he then declined. Incidentally, on landing about a dozen high-ranking

173

Pipe-Major J. Massie, Royal Scots Fusiliers, entertains women
and children on the pipes, St Croix-Grand-Tonne, Normandy,
6 July 1944.

(Imperial War Museum)

French Officers disembarked from the DUKW. De Gaulle did however visit Montgomery at his Headquarters and then went to Bayeux where he made a very inflam-
matory speech, including words to the effect that 'without the French people, the
invasion could never have taken place'. Without in any way wishing to belittle the
very important part the French Resistance played, or their incredible courage, it was
a sweeping and rather ungracious remark in the circumstances.

Two orders were issued for his safety. The first was that the vehicle he was travelling
in should not fly a flag, and the second was that he should be back on his destroyer
and clear of the French coastal area by early evening. Both orders were given in the
interests of the Allied cause and were lawful orders from the C-in-C. He refused to
heed either one, and used his military rank to force me to disobey both orders given
to me personally by General Montgomery, a discreditable performance as a soldier
and as a politician a singular lack of co-operation or understanding of the problems
facing a very hard-worked general during the most crucial period in the battle of
Normandy.

General Montgomery's orders to me were very specific, quite likely following
instructions from General Eisenhower or Sir Winston Churchill or both because
there was a possibility that once de Gaulle had set foot on French soil he might take
it upon himself to remain and establish himself and his Free French Government in
exile as the legal government of that part of France occupied by the Allied Armies.
That could only have led to untold problems at a time when our Armies were
involved in more than enough troubles following the heavy storms which had upset
the administrative build up over the open beaches. Our Intelligence Staff had
obviously been alerted to this threat. Hence the reason for restricting the size of de
Gaulle's party to no more than four in all, restricting publicity, no ceremonial
welcome, no flags to be flown; and the party to be clear of the beaches by 1600 hours.

I therefore arrived at the beach near Courseulles in good time just in case de Gaulle
should arrive early, driving my own jeep with a second one with a driver as back
up, and reported to the Beachmaster (I think Commander C. Maud, RN), who was
in radio contact with all ships using his beach area and also Monty's Tac HQ. De
Gaulle's destroyer *La Combattante* had not announced its arrival at that time, nor
did it do so until it was a couple or so miles offshore when it had been in sight for
some time. I am not prepared to say categorically that contact was initiated by the
Beachmaster, but I seem to remember that that was the case, the first discourtesy,

Especially since de Gaulle was already over an hour late for his lunch appointment with Monty, whom I had – of course – kept informed through the Beachmaster's radio.

The DUKW sent to pick up de Gaulle's party, the composition of which was still unknown to anyone ashore, yet another lack of courtesy when invited to lunch, eventually disgorged de Gaulle, followed by one Frenchman after another to my horror and consternation. I welcomed de Gaulle and was met by something that passed for a ceremonial smile, but I could sense that he was looking around for the real reception party befitting the occasion and his rank and status. Whilst I was trying to explain that we expected no more than four, and only had transport for that number, I was surrounded by (so far as I could assess) a dozen excited Frenchmen, all at least VIPs in their own eyes, and all talking simultaneously in strident voices, seemingly wanting to know where their transport was. I managed to ease de Gaulle aside and towards my jeep. His face grew longer when he saw his means of transport and no flagstaff. I explained that Monty, for security reasons, had ordered that no flag should be flown but he flouted that order, produced a flag, and insisted that it should be flown. With the greatest of disgust I looked around for a solution, found some driftwood and ultimately tied that to the edge of the windscreen and mounted his flag. We were joined by General Koenig and Admiral d'Argenlieu and with a sigh of relief I set off for Tac HQ leaving the remaining jeep and Frenchmen who were waiting to go to Bayeux to their own devices.

The meeting between Monty and de Gaulle could hardly have been more frigid. In the circumstances and the absence of an apology it was not surprising that Monty felt slighted and annoyed by de Gaulle's arrogance and bad manners, and his displeasure was abundantly clear. Had de Gaulle observed the customary punctuality and behaviour becoming an officer of his rank the meeting could at least have been cordial and have lasted an hour or so, including a social lunch and 20 minute briefing – a lot of time for a busy C-in-C to give up when fighting crucial battles for someone who could contribute nothing to their successful outcome. I hazard a guess that de Gaulle was piqued at not receiving a rapturous hero's welcome with due ceremonial when he first set foot on French soil, was displeased with the subdued reception on the beach and lowly form of transport, and was thus expecting these matters to be rectified on his arrival at Tac HQ. De Gaulle lit a cigarette on alighting from my jeep and before being invited into Monty's HQ caravan, only to be told sharply 'Put that thing out', before being allowed in. Within five minutes de Gaulle emerged and Monty hastily pointed at me saying, 'He will take you to Bayeux', and there the meeting ended, in the same chilling atmosphere as it had started.

I then drove de Gaulle and his two Officers to the Mairie in Bayeux, with hardly a word passing between any of us, where he was met by the Mayor and some of the remainder of his party who had made their way in my second jeep and other transport from the beach. They had busied themselves spreading the word that de Gaulle would address a meeting in the square, a fact that I discovered by chance because when de Gaulle left me he had given me no instructions, and as events showed I was only able to discover his intentions by following him in my jeep when he walked from the Mairie to where he made his speech, on which I have commented above. His audience was of moderate size, when account is taken of the short notice where and when he would be speaking, and their reaction was generally apathetic apart from the occasional voluble shouts of 'Vive la France!' rather than 'Vive de Gaulle!' which one sensed he was hoping for. However in mitigation for any lack of fervour on the part of his audience, it should be remembered that the French residents were still stunned by shock as a result of their liberation largely through annihilation, although Bayeux escaped the worst of the bombing and shelling.

When de Gaulle returned to the jeep I advised him that it would be after 1600 hours if we went straight to the beach near Courseulles and that General Montgomery had ordered me to ensure that for security reasons he and his party were

The Pipes and Drums of 5th battalion The Black Watch, led by Pipe-Major Sinclair, Piper Yardley and Pipe-Sergeant McGregor, entertain the villagers of Le Deliverande, Normandy, July 1944.

(The Black Watch; Mrs J. Smith)

Piper McNally of Lochee and Piper Yardley of Kirkcaldy, 5th battalion The Black Watch, with some of the inhabitants of Le Deliverande, Normandy, July 1944.

(The Black Watch; Mrs J. Smith)

to embark no later than that. He ignored that, even after I had repeated myself. He dismissed my remarks with an angry wave of his arms and said 'What matter? To Isigny!' It was some 32 kms west of Bayeux and over 55 kms from Courseulles. I had only three options. One was to ignore his order at my peril and drive him straight to the beach, which would doubtless have created an international furore. The second was to get out of my jeep with the key and leave him and his minions to find their own way back, which would certainly have led to an even greater scandal. The last resort was to ignore his disobedience to a superior's order, and illegal order to me, and to face up to the consequences of Monty's wrath when I eventually got back to Tac HQ. His arrogant and thoroughly unpleasant demeanour up to that time instinctively made me feel like dumping them but discretion ruled otherwise. Little did I know that worse examples of this offensive character were yet to show themselves. We then set off westwards, followed by the second jeep with three of his uninvited senior officers. Here are two examples of the reception that de Gaulle received and of his attitude to his own people.

Much of the very small part of France that had been liberated at that time had been done so virtually through annihilation, an unfortunate necessity. That those Frenchmen who survived promptly hung out the Tricolour despite everything was a genuine mark of patriotism, yet de Gaulle complained very bitterly and in the most scathing terms that the Croix de Lorraine was conspicuous by its absence. How petty and lacking in consideration for his own countrymen, especially so when the people were still dumbfounded by the shock of the invasion and were just beginning to recover sufficiently to be horrified by the cost to themselves of being freed from the German occupation.

On another occasion I stopped the jeep at his request so that he could speak to some farmers by the roadside. We had passed them by the time we halted but the second jeep loaded with some of his entourage were beside them. Those general officers, all of whom were in uniform, were given a warm welcome and, obviously embarrassed, kept pointing to the leading jeep saying 'De Gaulle! De Gaulle!' Puzzled at being almost pushed away from embracing those in the second jeep, they moved forward and, when they saw a general and an admiral in the back and only a major-general in the front, they set about giving the former a welcome in the best French style. Once again their ardour was damped brusquely and they were directed to the major-general in the front with the words, 'De Gaulle!' Bewildered, they moved to speak to him, and were greeted by a frigid look and the minimum words of welcome before I was ordered to drive on. In the mirror I could see the French farmers looking upset and mystified until they sprang to life when the second jeep loaded with generals passed them. Glancing over my shoulder, I could see de Gaulle scowling and furious that he had not been recognised by name or in the flesh. It seemed that, once again, his countrymen had offended.

At Isigny, in the heart of the United States sector at that time, I once again emphasised the need to return to the beach but my pleas were cast aside and for some reason unknown to me we headed northwards towards Grandcamp on the coast. Having reached a village seemingly of no significance en route, I was at last told to turn around and return to the beach. The reason for this deviation into the American sector was never apparent because hardly a word was exchanged all day between de Gaulle and his two lieutenants in the back. General Koenig, who was responsible for the Free French Underground Army, had a notable sense of humour and chatted a lot to the less effusive Rear Admiral d'Argenlieu, who commanded the Free French Navy. However, being in the back seats of an open jeep, the wind generally carried their voices away and with my impaired hearing I could catch only parts of their conversation. The jovial general in the back and the sullen-faced and largely silent one sitting beside me were certainly in marked contrast.

On arrival at the beach the Beachmaster told me that Monty had been asking where I was (the wireless set normally mounted in the back of the jeep had of course been removed to allow room for two passengers, and I therefore had no means of communication with Tac HQ) and required me to report back to him immediately! De Gaulle's goodbye was as lukewarm as was his duty-bound thanks. Not so my back-seat passengers, whose farewell came from their hearts. Fortunately the remainder of de Gaulle's party had been waiting for his arrival for some time and so, in a few minutes, all were aboard the DUKW and into the sea heading for *La Combattante*, and I left at speed for Tac HQ. I cannot recall the time, but the sun was low in the sky so it must have been about 1900 hours and I went straight to Monty's HQ caravan.

It was obvious that Monty was worried and for the first and only time in my experience he showed anger. The conversation went something like this. 'Where have you been and where is de Gaulle?' 'He insisted on going to Isigny, although I explained your orders and reason for being clear of the beaches by 1600 hours. He is now on his destroyer.' 'How do you know he is on the destroyer?' 'I saw him and his party in the DUKW enter the water heading for it and, because of your order to return immediately, I came back as soon as possible thereafter.' 'Then why has he got a room booked in the *Lion d'Or* in Bayeux?' 'I did not know that because I have been on the road since four o'clock apart from a few minutes on the beach and, because of your message, I came straight to see you. I cannot explain the booking.' 'Are you absolutely sure he is on the destroyer?' 'As certain as I could be without waiting to actually see him board her.' 'Alright, thank you', and that ended our meeting.

Unbeknown to me whilst I was driving round a large area of Normandy, one of de Gaulle's party who was to be left behind had gone to the *Lion d'Or* to book a room, only to find that all were taken by the Press. He had obviously used de Gaulle's name hoping to, and succeeding in, influencing the owner of the hotel. Our intelligence staff had picked up the story but drawn a false conclusion. The lines of communication between Monty and Eisenhower and Churchill, and likewise between Eisenhower, Roosevelt and Churchill, then became red hot to reach a decision on what action should be taken against de Gaulle and what would be the repercussions of any such action. Should he be arrested and deported or what? These were conversations and decisions of which I cannot record anything but they do explain Monty's concern when quizzing me. At length I managed to put the whole affair behind me and to get my first drink and bite of food since breakfast 12 hours previously, thanks to de Gaulle. His visit was of course an interesting experience; but I have no regrets that our paths never crossed again.

Lieutenant-Colonel Bradford DSO MBE MC, commanding 5th
battalion The Black Watch, lays a wreath in the cemetery at
St. Valéry, December 1944, where the dead of June 1940
are buried. Lieutenant-Colonel Derek Lang, then
commanding 5th battalion The Queen's Own Cameron
Highlanders, stands at extreme right.

(Imperial War Museum)

The memorial at St Valéry, unveiled in 1950, to those of the
51st (Highland) Division who died during the period
1939–45.

(Commonwealth War Graves Commission)

This narrative is not the place to argue the pros and cons of de Gaulle's treatment by
the British and Americans in the years 1940 to 1944 but a case may, perhaps, be made
to the effect that the apparent mutual incomprehension and difficulties of those years
did much to colour the behaviour of de Gaulle towards Britain and the United States
in the post-war period.

As Colonel Sanderson has said, the enthusiasm of the French people for their liberation
was considerable. Among these – as we have seen – were their own Free French forces
in the shape of the 3rd and 4th SAS in Brittany. The troops of General Leclerc's 2nd
Armoured Division advanced on Paris from the south, having landed on the Mediterranean coast, and Paris capitulated to Leclerc on 25 August. After some weeks of stalemate
in Normandy, a break-out was eventually successful in mid-August and St Valéry was
liberated in early September. On 10 December 1944 ceremonies were held in St Valéry
to commemorate the events of June 1940 and wreaths were laid in the cemetery where
Scottish and French soldiers lay buried. A granite memorial to the original 51st Highland
Division of 1940 was unveiled at St Valéry in June 1950, ten years after the Division's
surrender. The memorial bears inscriptions in English, Gaelic and French, the French
inscription being in poignant testimony to the memory of the Auld Alliance.

> A la memoire de ses glorieux enfants, officiers, sous-officiers et soldats de la 51e
> Division, l'Ecosse a élevé le monument sur le sol de son antique allié.
> (In memory of its glorious children, the officers, warrant-officers and soldiers of
> the 51st Division, Scotland has raised this monument on the soil of its ancient ally.)

In June 1988 a memorial window was installed in the church at Ouistreham, where No.
4 Commando and the Free French commandos under Commandant Philippe Kieffer
landed on D-Day. Paid for by an anonymous benefactor and designed by the artist
Raymond Bradley, the window commemorates all the component parts of the 51st

*Major Louis Sanderson MC, King's Own Scottish Borderers,
welcoming General Charles de Gaulle back to France, 14
June 1944. Behind General de Gaulle are General Koenig
and Admiral d'Argenlieu.*

(Imperial War Museum)

Highland Division which landed in Normandy in 1944. While commemorating the
services and the sacrifices of the Division, the window is also intended to represent the
sacrifices of the French people who suffered and died prior to the Liberation and after
it; as Sir Derek Lang said on the occasion of the window's dedication in 1988, 'we know
from the war memorials that more French citizens were killed after the invasion than
during the whole of the German occupation'.

The occupation of France had been such, and the fighting of the Liberation so long
drawn-out, that some French people had difficulty in believing that their war would ever
be over. Among these was the novelist Colette, living in Paris with her husband Maurice
Goudeket, as Leclerc's tanks rumbled down the Avenue d'Orléans on 24 August. As
Goudeket recalls, in *Près de Colette* (1956), despite his assurances that Paris was liberated
and full of French and Allied soldiers, she refused to believe that anything had changed.

179

Visit of the Fanfare à cheval de la Garde Républicaine *to Edinburgh for the Military Tattoo of 1952. The band of the Garde about to leave Edinburgh Castle, Scots Guards in the background.*

(W. A. Thorburn Esq)

'' 'Je n'y croirai vraiment que lorsque tu m'auras amené ici un major écossais.'

'En kilt?'

'En kilt.'

'J'y cours.'

Je traversai le jardin. Sur la place du Palais-Royal, en face du Louvre, des troupes britanniques stationnaient précisement, et je tombai tout droit sur le plus écossais des majors, kilt et petit moustache en brosse. J'engageai la conversation, et il m'apprit que sa fonction était de ravitailler Paris.

'Bonne nouvelle,' lui dis-je 'nous avons plûtot besoin de vous.'

'Oui mais en attendant, je n'ai rien mangé depuis vingt-quatre heures. Nos voitures ont dû se fourvoyer.'

'Qu'a cela ne tienne. Venez déjeuner chez moi. Je vous présenterai à ma femme.'

J'eus, en rentrant avec mon major, le succès qu'on devine. Nous ouvrîmes une grande boîte de corned-beef, perle du marché noir, et mise en réserve pour les grandes circonstances.'

'' 'I shall not really believe it until you have brought me a Scottish major.'

'In a kilt?'

'In a kilt.'

'I shall run and get one.'

I crossed the garden. In Palais-Royal square, opposite the Louvre, the British troops were positioned and I at once found the most Scottish of majors, with a kilt and a small bristling moustache. I spoke to him and he told me that his job was to provide Paris with fresh supplies.

'That is good news,' I said to him, 'we rather need you.'

'Yes, but all the same, I have eaten nothing for twenty-four hours. Our vehicles have got lost.'

'Don't worry, come and lunch at my house. I will introduce you to my wife.'

I had, on returning with my major, the expected success. We opened a large tin of corned-beef, a pearl of the black market and kept for a special occasion.

180

Visit of the 7th Spahis to Edinburgh for the Military Tattoo of 1957. An officer of the Spahis leaving the bottom of the Castle esplanade.

(W. A. Thorburn Esq)

Un charmant major éccossais, ma foi! L'occasion s'étant recontre de lui dire que Colette était un ecrivain français d'une certaine notoriété, il se fit épeler avec soin son nom.

'Ma femme lit beaucoup,' dit-il, 'Elle doit savoir.'

Puis il partit pour ses obscurs devoirs, kilt, moustache en brosse, et remerciements émus.

C'est ainsi que nous donnâmes l'hospitalité à un Ecossais et que, démunis de tout, nous ravitaillâmes celui qui était chargé de nous ravitailler.'

What a charming Scottish major! When he was told that Colette was a French writer of some note, he wrote down her name, spelling it carefully.

'My wife reads a lot,' he said, 'she must know of you.'

Then he left to his duty, kilt, bristling moustache, and overcome with gratitude.

That's how we were hospitable to a Scot and how, lacking everything, we fed the man who was in charge of feeding us.'

The years following the end of the Second World War have been noted for Franco-British military co-operation, a co-operation necessitated by the occupation of Germany, the stationing of Allied troops in Berlin, the Korean War and the policing duties carried out in the world's trouble-spots under the aegis of the United Nations. France and Britain both withdrew from their empires in the 1950s and 1960s, not without the attendant troubles, and those of France in Indo-China and North Africa meant that she could only spare one infantry battalion for service under the United Nations in Korea and, since it fought under American command, it is unlikely that it made much contact with the four Scottish infantry battalions which, successively, fought there too. France's

181

Visit of the Batterie fanfare de la Garde Républicaine *to Edinburgh for the Military Tattoo of 1977. The band of the Garde marching south along King's Stables Road.*

(W. A. Thorburn Esq)

An exchange of platoons between 1st battalion The Black Watch and the French 46th Regiment of Infantry, Montgomery Barracks, Berlin, 1989. Lieutenant-Colonel Richard, commanding the 46th Regiment, inspects the Black Watch platoon, followed by Captain David Denholm, platoon commander.

(The Black Watch; Mr M. Klineg)

withdrawal from NATO (or *OTAN* in France) naturally reduced the number of Franco-British military contacts and, aside from ceremonial ones, these are now generally restricted to those necessary to maintain the garrison in Berlin.

Scottish soldiers, and particularly kilted pipers, remain popular in France still and a sizeable Scottish contingent was among the British troops which were invited to Paris to participate in the Bicentenary celebrations of 1989. The interest is mutual of course and the bands, mounted and dismounted, of the *Garde Républicaine* have appeared on the esplanade of Edinburgh Castle on two occasions, in 1952 and 1977, to participate in the Edinburgh Military Tattoo. In 1957 a detachment of the 7th Spahis lent a touch of North African glamour to the Tattoo.

1989 marks the bicentenary of the French Revolution. It also marks the tercentenary of the beginning of the Jacobite rebellions and of the raising of the regiments that were to become the King's Own Scottish Borderers and the Cameronians. It is now six years short of 700 years since the first formal treaty of alliance was concluded between Scotland and France, and probably longer since close relations were established. For nearly seven centuries the two nations have had common interests and common foes; at times they have disagreed and have fought each other. While the Auld Alliance has been manifest in a variety of permanent ways, principally cultural and aesthetic, these have only existed because of the profound military underpinnings of the ancient friendship. Although Britain and France have not, quite, fought each other since 1815, an appreciable distance still lingers between England and France in many unfortunate ways. To an extent, this distance also exists between England and Scotland, two nations and neighbours in a partnership that remains uneasy and occasionally fraught with mutual incomprehension. All three nations are now contributors to a community, the strengths of which are that it is bigger than concepts of nationalism and yet can absorb many nationalities, races and faiths while not destroying any of them. Nationalism, racial hatred and differences of faith are the things that have caused past conflicts and while the military link between Scotland and France should never be forgotten – in any of its manifestations – it is to be hoped that it may now remain a memory as part of a more productive and wide-ranging partnership of European nations.

Suggestions for further reading

Introduction

Donaldson, Gordon, *The Auld Alliance: the Franco-Scottish connection*, Edinburgh: Saltire Society & L'Institut Français d'Ecosse, 1985

Fenwick, Hubert, *The Auld Alliance*, Kineton: Roundwood Press, 1971

Holmes, Richard, *The world atlas of warfare: military innovations that changed the course of history*, London: Mitchell Beazley, 1988

Hope, Annette, *A Caledonian feast*, Edinburgh: Mainstream, 1987

Kay, Billy and Maclean, Cailean, *Knee deep in claret: a celebration of wine and Scotland*, Edinburgh: Mainstream, 1983

Meikle, H. W., *Scotland and the French Revolution*, Glasgow: Maclehose, 1912

Royal Scottish Museum, *French connections: Scotland and the arts of France*, Edinburgh: H.M.S.O., 1985

General

Cassavetti, Eileen, *The lion and the lilies: the Stuarts and France*, London: Macdonald & Janes's, 1977

Cavendish, A. E. J., *An reisimid chataich: the 93rd Sutherland Highlanders, 1799–1927*, published privately, 1928

Forbes-Leith, William, *The Scots Men-at-Arms and Life-Guards in France from their formation until their final dissolution, A.D. 1418–1830* (2 volumes), Edinburgh: William Paterson, 1882

Francisque-Michel, *Les Écossais en France et français en Écosse* (2 volumes), London: Trubner, 1862

Gardyne, C. Greenhill, *The life of a regiment: the history of the Gordon Highlanders from 1816 to 1881*, London: Medici Society, 1903

Higgins, R. T., *The records of the King's Own Borderers or Old Edinburgh Regiment*, London: Chapman & Hall, 1873

Historical records of the 42nd Royal Highlanders (The Black Watch) from 1725 to 1887, Edinburgh: Thomas C. Jack, 1887

Historical records of the Queen's Own Cameron Highlanders (2 volumes), Edinburgh: Blackwood, 1909

Johnston, S. H. F., *The history of the Cameronians (Scottish Rifles), 26th and 90th, 1689–1910*, Aldershot: Gale & Polden, 1957

Leask, J. C. and McCance, H. M., *The regimental records of The Royal Scots*, Dublin: Alexander Thom, 1915

Linklater, Eric and Andro, *The Black Watch: the history of the Royal Highland Regiment*, London: Barrie & Jenkins, 1977

Maurice, Sir F., *The history of the Scots Guards from the creation of the Regiment to the eve of the Great War*, London: Chatto & Windus, 1934

Sym, John (editor), *Seaforth Highlanders*, Aldershot: Gale & Polden, 1962

Chapter One   The Middle Ages

Allmand, Christopher, *The Hundred Years War: England and France at war, c.1300–c.1450*, Cambridge: Cambridge University Press, 1988
Duncan, A. A. M., *Scotland: the making of the kingdom*, Edinburgh: Oliver & Boyd, 1975
Fawtier, Robert, *The Capetian Kings of France: monarchy and nation, 987–1328*, London: Macmillan, 1960
Fowler, Kenneth (editor), *The Hundred Years War*, London: Macmillan, 1971
Froissart, *Chronicles: selected, translated and edited by Geoffrey Brereton*, Harmondsworth: Penguin, 1968
Gillingham, John, *The Angevin Empire*, London: Edward Arnold, 1984
Keen, Maurice, *Pelican history of medieval Europe*, Harmondsworth: Penguin, 1968
Susane, Louis Auguste Victor Vincent, *Histoire de la cavalerie française* (3 volumes), Paris: St Germain, 1874

Chapter Two   The Stuart Connection

Briggs, Robin *Early modern France, 1560–1715* Oxford: Oxford University Press, 1977
Dalton, Charles *English Army lists and commission registers, 1661–1714* (6 volumes) London: Eyre & Spottiswoode, 1892–1904
Elton, G. R. *Reformation Europe, 1517–1559* London: Collins, 1963
Hale, J. R. *Renaissance Europe, 1480–1520* London: Collins, 1971
    War and society in Renaissance Europe, 1450–1620 London: Fontana Press, 1985
Dugué MacCarthy, Marcel *Soldats du roi: les armées de l'ancien régime, 1610–1789* Arcueil: P.R.E.A.L., 1984
Nicholson, Ranald *Scotland: the later middle ages* Edinburgh: Oliver & Boyd, 1974
Robertson, Alexander *The life of Sir Robert Moray, 1608–1673* London: 1922
Susane, Louis Auguste Victor Vincent *Histoire de l'infantérie française* (5 volumes) Paris, 1876

Chapter Three   1688–1746

Baynes, John, *The Jacobite Rising of 1715*, London: Cassell, 1970
Childs, John, *The British army of William III, 1689–1702*, Manchester: Manchester University Press, 1987
Cobban, Alfred, *A history of modern France: Volume 1: Old Regime and revolution, 1715–1799*, Harmondsworth: Penguin, 1957
D'Alton, John, *Illustrations, historical and genealogical, of King James's Irish Army list, 1689*, Dublin: the author, 1855
Donaldson, Gordon, *Scotland: James V–James VII*, Edinburgh: Oliver & Boyd, 1978
Ferguson, William, *Scotland: 1689 to the present*, Edinburgh: Oliver & Boyd, 1968
Gibson, John S., *Playing the Scottish card: the Franco-Jacobite invasion of 1708*, Edinburgh: Edinburgh University Press, 1988
Gibson, John S., *Ships of the '45: the rescue of the Young Pretender*, London: Hutchinson, 1967
Gwynn, Robin D., *Huguenot heritage: the history and contribution of the Huguenots in Britain*, London: Routledge & Kegan Paul, 1985
Leach, Douglas Edward, *Roots of conflict: British armed forces and colonial Americans, 1677–1763*, London: University of North Carolina Press, 1986
Lenman, Bruce, *The Jacobite clans of the Great Glen, 1650–1784*, London: Methuen, 1984
Lenman, Bruce, *The Jacobite risings in Britain, 1689–1746*, London: Methuen, 1980

Maclean, Alasdair, *A Macdonald for the Prince: the story of Neil MacEachen*, Stornoway: Acair, 1982

Mackintosh, Alexander, *The muster roll of the Forfarshire or Lord Ogilvy's Regiment*, Inverness: the author, 1914

MacLynn, F. J., *The Jacobite army in England, 1745: the final campaign*, Edinburgh: John Donald, 1983

Muster roll of Prince Charles Edward Stuart's army, 1745–46, Aberdeen: Aberdeen University Press, 1984

Petrie, Sir Charles, *The Jacobite movement: the first phase, 1688–1716*, London: Eyre & Spottiswoode, 1948

Petrie, Sir Charles, *The Jacobite movement: the last phase, 1716–1807*, London: Eyre & Spottiswoode, 1950

Petrie, Sir Charles, *The Marshal Duke of Berwick: the picture of an age*, London: Eyre & Spottiswoode, 1953

Prebble, John, *Culloden*, London: Secker & Warburg, 1961

Rousset, Camille (editor), *Recollections of Marshal Macdonald, Duke of Tarentum*, London: Richard Bentley, 1893

Scouller, R. E., *The armies of Queen Anne*, Oxford: Clarendon Press, 1966

Skrine, Francis Henry, *Fontenoy and Great Britain's share in the War of the Austrian Succession, 1741–1748*, Edinburgh: Blackwood, 1906

Tomasson, Katherine and Buist, Francis, *Battles of the '45*, London: Batsford, 1962

Chapter Four 1746–1815

Cobban, Alfred, *A history of modern France: Volume 2: From the First Empire to the Second Empire, 1799–1871*, Harmondsworth: Penguin, 1961

Cockburn, Sir George, *Extracts from a diary . . . with particular reference to General Napoleon Buonaparte*, London: Simpkin, Marshall, 1888

Drake, Samuel G., *A particular history of the Five Years French and Indian War*, Freeport, New York: Books for Libraries Press, 1970

Frey, Sylvia R., *The British soldier in North America: a social history of military life in the revolutionary period*, Austin, Texas: University of Texas Press, 1987

Gates, David, *The Spanish ulcer: a history of the Peninsular War*, London: Allen & Unwin, 1986

Glover, Michael, *The Peninsular War, 1807–1814: a concise military history*, Newton Abbot: David & Charles, 1974

Hibbert, Christopher, *Wolfe at Quebec*, London: Longmans, Green, 1959

Maitland, Sir Frederick Lewis, *The surrender of Napoleon*, Edinburgh: Blackwood, 1904

National Maritime Museum, *1776: the British story of the American Revolution*, London: National Maritime Museum, 1976

Pack, James, *The man who burned the White House: Admiral Sir George Cockburn, 1772–1853*, Emsworth, Hants: Kenneth Mason, 1987

Rudé, George, *Revolutionary Europe, 1783–1815*, London: Collins, 1964

Weller, Jac, *Wellington at Waterloo*, London: Longmans, 1967

Willing, Paul, *Napoleon et ses soldats de Wagram à Waterloo, 1809–1815*, Arcueil: P.R.E.A.L., 1987

Chapter Five 1815–1914

Chabert, Philippe, *Alphonse de Neuville: l'épopée de la defaite*, Paris: Copernic, 1979

Cobban, Alfred, *A history of modern France: volume three: France of the Republics, 1871–1962*, Harmondsworth: Penguin, 1965

Gibbs, Peter, *The battle of the Alma*, London: Weidenfeld & Nicolson, 1963

Hamley, Sir Edward, *The war in the Crimea*, London: Sedley, 1892

Hichberger, J. W. M., *Images of the Army: the military in British art, 1815–1914*, Manchester: Manchester University Press, 1988

The Highland Brigade in the Crimea, Edinburgh: Aikman, n.d.

Holt, Edgar, *The Opium Wars in China*, London: Puttnam, 1964

Humbert, Jean, *Edouard Detaille: L'héroisme d'un siècle*, Paris: Copernic, 1979

Miller, A. E. Haswell and Dawnay N. P., *Military drawings and paintings in the collection of Her Majesty The Queen* (2 volumes), London: Phaidon, 1970

Pemberton, W. Baring, *Battles of the Crimean War*, London: Batsford, 1962

Russell, William Howard, *The British expedition to the Crimea*, London: Routledge, 1877

Usherwood, Paul and Spencer-Smith, Jenny, *Lady Butler, battle artist, 1846–1933*, London: Alan Sutton/National Army Museum, 1987

Willing, Paul, *L'armée de Napoleon III, 1852–1870*, Arcueil: P.R.E.A.L., 1983

Wood, Christopher, *Life and work of Jacques Joseph Tissot, 1836–1902*, London: Weidenfeld & Nicolson, 1986

Chapter Six   1914–1918

Aston, Sir George, *Biography of the late Marshal Foch*, London: Hutchinson, 1929

Balfour, Lady Frances, *Dr Elsie Inglis*, London: Hodder & Stoughton, 1919

Barker, A. J., *The neglected war: Mesopotamia, 1914–1918*, London: Faber, 1967

Bewsher, F. W., *The history of the 51st (Highland) Division, 1914–1918*, Edinburgh: Blackwood, 1921

Coombs, Rose E. B., *Before endeavours fade: a guide to the battlefields of the First World War*, London: Battle of Britain Prints International, 1976

De Groot, Gerard, *Douglas Haig, 1861–1928*, London: Unwin Hyman, 1988

Ewing, John, *The history of the 9th (Scottish) Division, 1914–1918*, London: John Murray, 1921

Hamilton, Ian B. M., *The happy warrior: a life of General Sir Ian Hamilton, G.C.B., G.C.M.G., D.S.O.*, London: Cassell, 1966

Hay, Ian, *Their name liveth: the book of the Scottish National War Memorial*, Edinburgh: Trustees of the Scottish National War Memorial, 1985

Junior, Allan (editor), *Humorous Scottish war stories*, Dundee: Valentine, 1930

Mackintosh, E. A., *A Highland regiment*, London: John Lane, 1918

McLaren, Eva Shaw (editor), *A history of the Scottish Women's Hospitals*, London: Hodder & Stoughton, 1919

Moorehead, Alan, *Gallipoli*, London: Hamish Hamilton, 1956

Ross, Isobel, *Little grey partridge: First World War diary of Ishobel Ross, who served with the Scottish Women's Hospitals in Serbia*, Aberdeen: Aberdeen University Press, 1988

Stewart, J. and Buchan, John, *The Fifteenth (Scottish) Division 1914–1919*, Edinburgh: Blackwood, 1926

Tayler, Henrietta, *A Scottish nurse at work*, London: John Lane, 1920

Thompson, R. R., *The Fifty-Second (Lowland) Division, 1914–1918*, Glasgow: Maclehose, Jackson, 1923

Chapter Seven   1939–1945

Blake, George, *Mountain and flood: the history of the 52nd (Lowland) Division, 1939–1946*, Glasgow: Jackson, 1950

Buckley, Christopher, *Norway: the Commandos: Dieppe*, London: H.M.S.O., 1951

Carver, Michael, *El Alamein*, London: Batsford, 1962

de Gaulle, Charles, *War memoirs* (2 volumes), London: Collins, 1955

Draper, Theodore, *The six weeks' war: France, May 10–June 25, 1940*, London: Methuen, 1946

Gilchrist, Donald, *Castle Commando*, Edinburgh: Oliver & Boyd, 1960

Goudeket, Maurice, *Près de Colette*, Paris: Flammarion, 1956

Grant, Roderick, *The 51st Highland Division at war*, London: Ian Allan, 1977

La Sierra, Raymond, *Le commando du 6 juin: No 4 Commando*, Paris: Presses de la Cité, 1983

Lang, Derek, *Return to St Valéry: the story of an escape through wartime France and Syria*, London: Leo Cooper, 1974

Linklater, Eric, *The Highland Division*, London: H.M.S.O., 1942

McDougall, Murdoch C., *Swiftly they struck: the story of No. 4 Commando*, London: Arms & Armour Press, 1986

Martin, H. G., *The history of the Fifteenth Scottish Division, 1939–1945*, Edinburgh: Blackwood, 1948

Messenger, Charles, *The Commandos, 1940–1946*, London: William Kimber, 1985

Moore, William, *The long way round: an escape through occupied France*, London: Leo Cooper with Secker & Warburg, 1986

Richardson, Joanna, *Colette*, London: Methuen, 1983

Salmond, J. B., *The history of the 51st Highland Division, 1939–1945*, Edinburgh: Blackwood, 1953

Seymour, William, *British Special forces*, London: Sidgwick & Jackson, 1985

Shepperd, G. A., *The Italian campaign, 1943–45: a political and military re-assessment*, London: Arthur Barker, 1968

Woods, Rex, *A talent to survive: the wartime exploits of Lt-Col Richard Lowther Broad*, London: William Kimber, 1982

Index